Praise for

Divorce & Beyond

Reading *Divorce and Beyond* is like having an expert team of wounded healers at your disposal. The authors have lived through the mini death of divorce and come out on the other side to renewed heart and flourishing life. The text is both personal and practical, based on the expertise garnered by Bill Koontz, Dan Cox and Paulette Liburd from their experiences, careful research, and over 30 years of conducting Divorce and Beyond seminars and groups for thousands of men and women seeking healing and recovery from the trauma of divorce.

As a pastor who has too often seen the wreckage of divorce, and as a father who has witnessed it within his family, I would say this work is the most helpful guide to healing the wounds of divorce I've yet encountered. *Divorce and Beyond* is not merely a self-help book, though plenty of practical tools are included. At its core it is a "God-help book" as all solid recovery materials must be. If you have experienced divorce and its trauma, get this book. Or if, like me, you know someone who has, get this book! It will prepare you for how best to support them.

—**Barry Long,** retired pastor, *Vineyard Christian Church, Florence, Kentucky,* author of *Swimming in the Ocean* and *Ocean Swimmer's Prayer*

***

Divorce and Beyond shares a wealth of insight and knowledge on the devastation of divorce and provides an understanding of the depth of grief and crisis, creating an introspective look into your former marriage, divorce recovery and reconstruction. Concrete steps and reflection are given to recover and rebuild, while interweaving faith through the teachings of the Bible. For those who are spiritually driven, this book will aid you in healing from your divorce and beyond.

—**Carrie Conlon, BSW, MEd, LPCC,** Divorce & Beyond participant and leader

***

Divorce and Beyond is an invaluable resource for those experiencing the pain of divorce at any level and those who want to help from a biblical perspective. The authors' transparency and vulnerability make the material uniquely powerful, beginning with the opening sentence of Chapter One: "Divorce is painful." Writing not only from their personal experiences of divorce, the authors also offer practical help gleaned from many years of leading support groups and seminars, helping others through traumatic seasons. But more than a "how to" book on managing the emotional and spiritual pain of separation, Koontz, Liburd, and Cox provide solid encouragement and hope for the future. I highly recommend this book to anyone looking for wise and healthy biblical responses to divorce.

—**Dave Workman,** president of *The Elemental Group,* former pastor of *Vineyard Cincinnati Church,* and author of *The Outward Focused Life*

***

There is no shortcut, but there is a path—a road to healing after divorce. The three authors of *Divorce and Beyond* bring their personal journeys and their work with thousands of individuals over three decades to the pages of this book in providing reliable help. And if you've wanted help from God, but felt abandoned or were afraid you'd be judged, *Divorce and Beyond* will help you connect or reconnect. Whether you're at the bottom of the deepest pit of your life or are a person who wants to help others out of that pit, you will find empathy, hope, and trustworthy guidance in *Divorce and Beyond.* This isn't a band-aid—it's deep healing.

—**Dick Alexander,** retired pastor *LifeSpring Christian Church*

***

Divorce and Beyond is an incredible gift to anyone experiencing the loss of the dreams that accompanied their wedding day. I have known Bill since before his divorce and have witnessed his initial brokenness and his recovery journey. God has placed on his, Dan's and Paulette's hearts the passionate desire to help others struggling with the aftermath of divorce. They transparently share their own journeys through the valley to recovery. This book contains the wisdom and insight gained from over three decades of effective ministry to thousands of others. I'm delighted to have it as a resource to give to others.

—**Dr. Dick Towner, EdD,** founder of *Good Sense, and The Springs Retreat Center*

***

Growing up, my parents were divorced, as were every one of my aunts and uncles and almost all of their kids. I wish *Divorce and Beyond* had been there for them. The gracious and truthful work I've seen for years from the Divorce and Beyond team is delivered so gently and respectfully in these pages. There is much to gain from their understanding and experiences of dealing with the trauma of divorce, as well as the experiences of many others. I believe you and/or someone you love will benefit richly from it.

—**Dr. Douglas Howe,** founding director, *The Insignia Foundation*, co-author, *Living the Lord's Prayer*

***

You've heard the saying, "Keep it real". Well, that's what the authors of *Divorce and Beyond* have done. You will find real stories of people who have experienced the pain of divorce but found hope and healing on the other side. Their total transparency will engage your heart at the most intimate levels. Find out for yourself what multitudes of people have already come to know; *Divorce and Beyond* will provide the insights and perspectives needed when you come face to face with the "D" word.

—**Doug Pollock,** speaker and author of *God Space*

***

As a marriage and family counselor, I have helped many people negotiate the difficult years of marriage, divorce and remarriage. What you are about to read is more than a book. It covers so many topics and biblical lessons that it is more like a compendium of great advice for each stage of the recovery journey. It combines psychology, theology, self-disclosure, and practical guidance. I have attended their seminar and often volunteer to teach a workshop about recovering from guilt and shame. From firsthand observation, I can assure you this book is written from the trenches of recovery. It is anchored in wisdom and truth. If you are dealing with divorce or know someone who is, I couldn't recommend a book more than *Divorce and Beyond.*

—**Dr. Gary Sweeten, EdD,** founder, *Sweeten Life Systems,* author *Communicate for a Change*

***

Death of a marriage, abandonment, betrayal, unrequited love, loss of a family—what we call divorce. I have assisted hundreds of people in finding a path out of the fragmented and splintered remains of this experience. For those of you who are lost and punch drunk from this trauma, this book is a compass, an instrument which can help you find your way out from the rubble that was once the place where you lived. Each chapter is insightful, practical, and vulnerable, a true guide from woundedness to greater wholeness. In order to define a new you and realize a new direction, you need to consume *Divorce and Beyond* for it is the compass which can help you discover a new world.

—**Jeffrey Baker, PhD,** clinical & forensic psychologist

***

Divorce and Beyond: Finding hope, healing and growth provides a biblically based roadmap for navigating emotions and healing the wounds of divorce. It is thoughtfully authored by three distinct individuals who each have lived through their own failed marriages and subsequently used their healing to help countless others. Utilizing their own personal stories and the stories of others they have served, this book is engaging, heartfelt, practical, and informative. It is a must-read for anyone navigating their own divorce journey, especially those who aim to keep their Christian faith at the center of their healing.

—Lorene Walter, MD, psychiatrist, former Divorce & Beyond participant and leader

***

I value authors who have personally experienced their topics. Bill Koontz, Paulette Liburd, and Dan Cox are precisely this kind of communicators! My friendship with Bill spans over 40 years, and I have witnessed the excruciating pain and suffering that Bill experienced through his divorce. I have also witnessed his moving beyond divorce by the fruit of his second marriage and the biblical 'joy in the midst of various trials' and 'a peace that passes all human understanding!'

Most of all, these three authors clearly illustrate both aspects of *Divorce and Beyond.* I have never seen a book like this that paints an emerging and hopeful future in the colors of recovery, revival, and radical renaissance with such a brush of realism!

Bill, Paulette and Dan have given all who are facing divorce, in the process of it, or who have experienced it, a great blessing in sharing their research, study, and life journeys! *Divorce and Beyond* will leave an indelible impression on its readers. As one who has experienced divorce, it certainly has on me!

—Dr. Ron Rand, former pastor, College Hill Presbyterian Church, founder *UpBuilding Ministries* and author of *Fathers who Aren't in Heaven*

***

Divorce and Beyond is more than just a book; it's a heartfelt gift born from a powerful collaboration. Bill, Dan, and Paulette have poured their souls into creating a beautiful and uplifting guide that offers genuine support for anyone navigating the challenging waters of divorce. Whether you're contemplating the journey, or already walking through it, this resource will be a beacon of hope. Don't face it alone—let their wisdom guide you toward a brighter future.

—Rosalind R. Smith, LPCC-S, Christian trauma therapist

***

Chock full of hard-won wisdom, the authors of *Divorce and Beyond* deftly unpack the heartbreak and resulting struggles of divorce. You will find here equal parts scriptural encouragement, connection of like-story, and practical tips and tools that can only be born from personal experience and walking thousands of others through similar challenges. It is a must-read for anyone who has gone through divorce, is going through divorce, or has someone they love who has been impacted by the same.

I found the deep-dive into divorce-related trauma to be "eye-opening" and feel better equipped to empathetically come alongside those who are struggling with such. Find hope and encouragement here as you navigate this deeply impactful life event. You are not alone! And be prepared to love Jesus even more as His heart for the hurting is masterfully revealed in these pages.

—**Wade Daniel,** CEO, *Wealthquest Corporation*

DIVORCE

&

BEYOND

FINDING HOPE, HEALING, AND GROWTH

Bill Koontz, Paulette Liburd, & Dan Cox

Published by KHARIS PUBLISHING, an imprint of KHARIS MEDIA LLC.

Copyright © 2025 Bill Koontz, Paulette Liburd, & Dan Cox

ISBN-13: 978-1-63746-328-4

ISBN-10: 1-63746-328-6

Library of Congress Control Number: 2025936136

All KHARIS PUBLISHING products are available at special quantity discounts for bulk purchases for sales promotions, premiums, fund-raising, and educational needs. For details, contact:

Kharis Media LLC

Tel: 1-630-909-3405

support@kharispublishing.com

www.kharispublishing.com

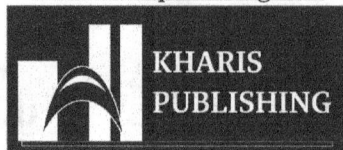

KHARIS
PUBLISHING

Acknowledgments

So very many people have contributed in some way to what is now *Divorce & Beyond: Finding hope, healing, and growth*—in fact, there are too many to specifically identify.

In light of that, though, our appreciation begins where this ministry began, retired pastor Barry Long who, as mentioned in Bill's introduction, was a catalyst of its creation. Also, thanks to Roger Flessing, a VP at Convoy of Hope, without whose persuasion this book might not have been written.

Then to the thousands of people who came to Divorce & Beyond seminars and support groups, who risked trusting us with the pain lodged in their hearts from divorce and then became the ambassadors to others to do the same.

In addition, we extend our appreciation to all the partner churches who have supported D&B, promoted its invitation to those divorced, and hosted support groups in their buildings. Foremost in this group is Vineyard Community Church in Springdale, Ohio, whose support and encouragement were critical to our ministry's formation and the initial decades of its ministry.

Dozens have served on D&B's leadership team through the years, devoting countless hours in shaping it into what it is today, especially those who served as "captains" of the team. Special mention to Devra Rochelle and Laura Koontz for their many years and ongoing faithfulness on this team.

Hundreds have served as volunteers with a "salty" kindness that opens participants' hearts to the message of hope, healing, and growth; most noteworthy are those who have served as seminar table leaders, follow-up support group leaders, and workshop presenters.

Beyond those whose reviews you can read, many have contributed to the content of this book, adding valuable stories and expert advice. But one who has to be mentioned is Jonathan Kopke, who invested countless hours helping us to edit and hone our message.

Finally, thanks to Kharis Publishing who took a risk on these "rookie" writers, believing our story needed to reach a broader audience.

Table of Contents

Introduction

The word "divorce" depicts something tragic, heart wrenching, a devastating loss, and an emotional trauma. On the other hand, the word "beyond" points to the next chapter of life, one of hope, discovery, healing, and promise. That's what this book is about: Divorce & Beyond.

Let's face it: Divorce hurts. A lot! Of course, if you're dealing with a divorce, that's not news to you. You're living the pain; the hurricane force of divorce may overwhelm you to the point of wondering if recovery is even possible. On the other hand, to the people around you, the pain of divorce may seem less consequential, and it may be something they can never understand unless they've experienced it themselves. Even if there are people who have empathy for you, they probably can't commit enough time to help you through a healing process. So where do you go for help? Is your only option to set off by yourself through all kinds of changes that nobody should ever have to face alone? That's a risky proposition, given that the decisions you make in the divorce journey will inevitably have a long-lasting effect on your life.

That's why we three—Bill, Paulette, and Dan—are volunteering to be your companions as you process your divorce. We're not therapists or attorneys. We don't claim to have all the answers. We're three people who've known firsthand the pain of divorce, and we've all come through it with a healing that has transformed our lives from seasons of tragedy, devastating loss, and emotional trauma into seasons of hope, discovery, healing, and promise.

We think there's a real advantage to having all three of us joining hands with you as you maneuver through your divorce. There are certain commonalities that relate to almost everybody who experiences a divorce, but at the same time, each individual's divorce experience is unique. For example, our family of origin, our faith, our social status, and our gender are just some of the factors that shape our experiences when we have to deal with a divorce. To take some of that uniqueness into account, this book promises to give you our three varied (but consistent) perspectives for dealing with the trauma of divorce, understanding yourself, and maybe even expanding your understanding of your ex.

We'll tell you more about ourselves as we go along, but at this point, we want you to know that one of the three of us, Paulette, is an African American woman. Paulette grew up in a Baptist church in the Caribbean, where she was taught that divorce was practically an unforgiveable sin. So even when she was trapped in an abusive marriage, Paulette struggled with a quandary: "Is divorce even an option for me? Will God forgive me for such a decision?" On top of that fear, Paulette was also very concerned about her two primary-school-aged children. As a minority woman with no family or close friends in the area to help her, she wondered how she would care for her children on a single income. Would her single-parent household end up as just another "statistic"? Paulette had dreamed of giving her kids a life of promise. Was that dream over? On her meager salary, would her children ever be able to attend college? How much of the lifestyle she and her children were accustomed to would have to change? These questions haunted her.

The other two of us, Dan and Bill, are white males who had to wrestle with somewhat different questions. Bill was a pastor at the time of his divorce, and he wondered if the end of his marriage would also be the end of his career. On the other hand, when his marriage failed, the corporation Dan worked for had just announced restructuring, which usually means layoffs. What's more, when both Dan and Bill became non-custodial parents, they wondered how their relationships with their children would change. How much of their ability to guide, influence, and even "be with" their children would be lost? Would the mothers of their children try to undermine their relationships with their kids? How much "blame and shame" would be heaped on them in the eyes of their children? You too may be wrestling with some of these questions.

In the middle of all this turmoil, your emotions can be easily triggered, and you may feel like you're on an emotional roller coaster. We know what that's like: One minute you can feel hopeful, but the very next minute you can feel hopeless, maybe even suicidal. What's more, you may be harboring feelings of shame and rejection. Your self-esteem and your confidence may be shattered. We know how rough that is because all three of us have been there too.

We understand the loneliness, grief, and the feelings of anger, fear, isolation, betrayal, guilt, and helplessness that can result from divorce. We know from our own experiences that when we're down, our emotions have a way of convincing us that things will never change or get better. But here's the good news: All three of us have been in that abyss, and we've found a way to bounce back.

We don't have any quick or easy solutions to offer, but we believe that you can bounce back too. We've been able to document what works and what doesn't work, and we can help you gain a healthy perspective so you can take the necessary steps to move forward with your own life.

The following pages will further introduce you to each of us and then to the journeys we took to find hope and healing. Because we're all involved in leading a ministry for people dealing with divorce, in this book you'll also read the stories of many others who've dealt with divorce. Their stories will help you understand why divorce is so hard, what the journey of recovery looks like, what critical steps you'll need to take, and what pitfalls you'll want to avoid. The names of all the storytellers have been changed, as well as any names used in the stories.

How to Use this Book for Your Best Advantage

We designed the chapters of this book for you to read them in succession. If you read just a couple of chapters, you'll miss the context of the preceding chapter(s). That would be like using just some pieces of a jigsaw puzzle; you'd fail to see the whole picture. And if you skip around from chapter to chapter, you'll miss the flow of the topics and how they're intended to build on each other.

For additional insights, we've also developed a video-driven online course, and we believe you'll find it valuable to use it with this book. The online course can help you *experience* what you read. Since the book and the course follow a similar flow, we recommend that you read a chapter of the book and then watch the corresponding section of the online course. You can find the complete course, and apply the passcode **(dbjouney50)** for a 50% discount at:

https://www.relationalpeace.org/collections?category=divorceandbeyond, or scan here:

About the Authors

When you're reading any non-fiction book, but especially one that deals with very personal, sensitive topics like divorce, we believe it's very important for you to know the authors' backgrounds. In the Introduction to this book, we provided a thumbnail sketch of each of us, but what follows will fill in those outlines a little more so you can have a fuller picture of who we are and the experience base that we bring to the subject of divorce—and beyond.

Meet Bill Koontz
Founder, Director, Divorce & Beyond

Every year, I have an anniversary that I have no interest in celebrating: my divorce date. Other sad anniversaries (like the dates when family members passed away) are times when I pause and reflect, but when my divorce anniversary arrives, I don't reminisce or look at pictures. At first, that anniversary would bring sadness and even tears back to the surface. Later, I stopped even paying attention to it. But make no mistake, my divorce was the most traumatic, challenging experience of my life. In fact, it was devastating, even life threatening. In a period of several months, I lost my marriage, my career as a pastor, and for some years, my relationships with my two children. Their own lives were forever affected too. Nonetheless, out of the ashes of my own failed marriage, I started an organization called Divorce & Beyond. It began for me as a "phoenix" of sorts, rising from the wreckage of my marriage.

At the time of my divorce, I'd been in full-time ministry for 13 years, but in the trauma of the breakup, I resigned. Later, I was playing racquetball with Barry Long, a friend and pastor of a church called the Florence Vineyard. He mentioned to me that there were some people in his church who were going through a divorce, and he asked if I would be willing to design something that could aid them in their journey—and I quickly replied, "Hell no!"

A year later, though, Barry and I were playing racquetball again, and this time he said, "Hey, I know you soundly rejected my idea last year, but there are still people getting divorces in my church, and they could really use some help. Are you open to it yet?" Before I could repeat my reply from a year earlier, I felt a check in my spirit, so this time I said, "Let me pray about that."

Several months later, I gathered with about eight people from that Vineyard who were then, or had recently been, going through a divorce. I'd prepared an outline that reflected on the paths of recovery I'd taken, the potholes I'd encountered, and the experiences of other divorced people I'd met along the way. We shared and opened our hearts to one another—and God showed up. By the end of our time together, it was obvious that it had been a valuable experience for all of us. So, in each of the next two years, I continued to offer divorce-recovery seminars for Barry's church, learning more about how my sessions could be improved from the feedback of those who were a part of them.

From the dry bones of my divorce, a new form of life sprang up. I became a living testimony that out of the ashes of a dead marriage can come new life. That new growth wasn't quick or easy, it took time. Frankly, it required hard work, heart searching, reflection, and support.

Later I remarried and began a new career. My wife Laura and I began attending the Vineyard Cincinnati Church. And two years later, this time I approached one of the Vineyard pastors, telling him about what we'd developed and how God had used it.

Over the course of more than 30 years, more than 60 seminars, and more than 250 small groups, the vision of providing hope and healing to those scarred by divorce has resulted in a pathway to healthy recovery for over 5,000 adults and children. They're no longer shackled by divorce's wounds, anxieties, and fears. They've moved forward from pain to peace, and from hurt to healing.

Over the years, much of our Divorce & Beyond material has been refined and improved, all by dedicated volunteers who themselves have traveled through the quagmire of divorce. Their experience of God's healing and hope spawned this vision in them also. In recent years, our leadership team has extended this vision to other churches in the Southwest Ohio area, has created an online Divorce & Beyond course, and has now written this book. But it all began out of the brokenness and sorrow of my own first marriage and the persistent urging of someone who saw a glimpse of the vision and believed before I did that God wanted to give birth to it.

On the evidence of my own transformed life, I can say this to anyone suffering through a divorce: Use this disruptive, difficult experience to learn, heal, grow, and become more the person God created you to be. There is hope. The dark tunnel will end.

"God heals the brokenhearted and bandages their wounds"

(Psalm 147:3 CEB).

Meet Paulette Liburd
Associate Director, Divorce & Beyond

As a participant in the Divorce & Beyond ministry, I've experienced the healing of a broken heart, and although I've remained single, I am "whole."

I was the one who initiated my divorce. I was tired of the lies, broken promises, infidelity, and abuse of my children. To try to avoid a divorce, my ex and I tried counseling several times, but to no avail. We even separated for a while to work on our individual issues, but that didn't help. Even so, filing for divorce was not an easy decision for me. In fact, the decision to seek an attorney was devastating, shameful, and worrisome. Not only did I not have the ready funds to pursue a divorce, but I also had no social or moral support.

Financially, before I could do anything, I had to wait for the next round of open enrollment at work to apply for legal insurance, which then provided the additional funds I needed to pursue my divorce. And emotionally, for me, the devastation of a failed marriage was like a banner of shame. The dead weight of anger, despair, and helplessness hung on me day after day. I felt like I had failed my entire family, and I was so ashamed; it took me three months to gather the courage to tell them of the pending divorce.

You see, I grew up in a church and community where divorce was considered a particularly deplorable sin. Additionally, I didn't want my little family—myself and two children—to become a statistic, another African American single woman with children and no father in the house. But despite the dreadful stigma, I finally got the gumption to say, "Enough is enough," and for the safety of my children, I headed out to find an attorney.

During this turbulent time, my trust in God became stronger, as I had to depend on Him for strength in rearing two children alone while I was also holding down a full-time job. My focus began to shift to giving praise and adoration to God for each day that I was able to safely get up and do my usual routine of household and parental duties: heading up and down the highways, dropping off one child to one school, zipping across town to another school, and getting my last speeding ticket.

Looking back, it was no easy task to continue in a corporate career while caring for two children and navigating the many layers of divorce. There were many fears that confronted me daily. I came to realize that I had to make an intentional shift toward taking care of myself or, "wholeness." I started to invest in me! I gravitated to books, magazine articles, and anything that would help me thrive. One Saturday, while I was "moonlighting" from my own church, I became aware of the Divorce & Beyond seminar and support groups sponsored by the Vineyard Cincinnati Church. At first, I felt anxious and uncertain about attending the group, but it gradually became a place of encouragement and safety, and it pumped new life into me.

I gained meaningful relationships with others who were on the same path. I related to the biblical nuggets of grace and mercy. They enabled me to face the fact that my heart had hardened toward my ex, and they helped me extend the desperately needed forgiveness to him and to myself. These life-saving acts of forgiveness freed me from holding onto the past. I began taking steps toward the abundant life that awaited me.

If you are currently experiencing the travails of a divorce and/or separation, or if you've been through that in the past, my prayer is that you too will come to know the power of God's unconditional love for you on this journey of divorce and beyond. God isn't finished with our stories!

Meet Dan Cox
Associate Director, Divorce & Beyond

"We need to talk."

I'll never forget hearing those four words and the devastating shock the explanation of them brought. My life as I knew it then was about to change in every way. In short, my *second* wife wanted a divorce. One divorce is tragic, but two?

To start at the beginning, my first wife and I dated throughout high school, and we were each other's first real relationship. At the beginning of her senior year, we found out she was pregnant. At that time, we never thought that our behavior had been morally wrong; we were teenagers in the "enlightened" and so called "free" 1960s. Years later I learned from my faith that we had in fact behaved immorally. Despite our foolhardy attitudes, though, when the pregnancy happened, I didn't feel like I had a choice; getting married was "the right thing to do." All the same, I did love my wife, and she loved me, so in our minds, we tried to think of her unplanned pregnancy as just a fast-tracking of our future—although as we found out, it certainly wasn't a solid basis for a stable one.

Getting married, having a baby, and buying a house kept our hopes high for a great future. But soon, problems that were always there, and ignored, began to surface. My wife felt stuck at home while I worked, and if I wanted to do anything afterward with my friends, like play softball, it turned into a huge fight.

I also began to inwardly keep a running record of everything my wife did or said that I didn't like. By the time we went to a marriage counselor, my real hope was that the counselor would just agree we shouldn't be together and give me "permission" to divorce my wife. Obviously, that didn't happen. So, our dysfunctional marriage continued for a while, and even though my wife had her faults, I later realized I was the one who was more the cause of us divorcing.

Although I wasn't a follower of Jesus at the time, I knew there was a verse in the Bible that said God hated divorce. So, between knowing God hated divorce, and knowing that I couldn't point to any specific ways my wife had failed me in our marriage, I was overwhelmed with guilt. When I was asked why I wanted a divorce, I didn't have a good answer.

Then, almost as soon as we separated, I began dating again. That was a terrible decision, and as anyone could have predicted, my new dating life was a disaster. I should have had a bumper sticker that said, "If you're codependent, I'm single!"

After listening to me complain about my marriage and then my dating life, a friend at work told me he knew what I was really searching for. Yep, he was one of *those* Christians. To summarize about three months of conversations and a lot of my questions, I finally realized that I needed God in my life, and I started visiting my friend's church. One night after a service, I committed my life to Christ. I began going to church regularly and reading the Bible. My newfound faith led me to make some radical changes, and I began to feel the peace I hadn't even known I was missing.

Fast forward to several years later. My pastor introduced me to my second wife. While I put too much weight on his tacit approval, it did seem like a match made in heaven.

My newfound love began singing in the Christian band I was in. The two of us taught Sunday School, and we did biweekly Bible studies at our local jail. All of this confirmed to *us* that God specifically wanted *us* together. After dating for three years, we got married.

But four years later, one Wednesday night in March, I heard those four horrible words, "We need to talk."

I couldn't sleep that night. I found a counselor the very next day, but my wife moved back to her parents' house on Friday while I was at work. She told me *not* to call her; we would talk in the counselor's office instead.

The next week, when we had our first appointment with the counselor, my wife explained what a terrible husband and person I was, and she had decided a year before that if things didn't change, she was going to divorce me. What's more, she was not about to come back to the counselor's office again.

So, in eight days, I went from thinking I was in a happy marriage to struggling with the reality that I was getting divorced again. I didn't even see my wife again until the day of our divorce. I was embarrassed and ashamed, and I felt like I had taken something God had given me and destroyed it. I had never been at a lower point in my life.

I could paint a picture of my second marriage that would make you believe the entire breakdown was my wife's fault. How she remarried just seven months after our divorce, and how, without telling me, she kept a list of things I did wrong, just like I had done in my first marriage. But looking back, I now know I was clueless when it came to relationships. I worked too much. Sometimes that was necessary, but not always. I remember one time after dinner my ex wanted to go for a walk, and I told her I was just too tired. About 30 seconds later, my neighbor called and asked if I would help him fix something in his house, and I jumped right up, and out the door I went. You know, "Love your neighbor" and all that? But somehow, I forgot the stuff about "Lay down your life for your wife." After she left me, that guilt-ridden scene played over and over in my head.

Thankfully, my church offered a Divorce & Beyond seminar. I went to it, and then I joined a follow-up support group. There I developed a plan and a path forward that was filled with self-discovery and practical ways of dealing with my emotions. Being around so many people who were experiencing a lot of the same things was very encouraging. It felt safe, and I developed some lifelong friendships.

I married again in 2012 for the third and *last* time. My son Jason is now a happily married adult with two children. When I divorced his mother, he was six; when my second wife and I divorced he was eighteen. I did my best in both cases to mitigate the pain he was unfairly forced to bear. If there was any way to go back and lift the sadness and anxiety he experienced, I would do it in a heartbeat, but there isn't, so I can't. He tells me today he is fine, and the two of us are as close as a father and son can be.

I'm also "Grandpa" to four girls and a boy. I love being a grandpa and I love my new life. There was a time during my divorce when I couldn't even imagine being happy again.

I felt very hopeless. I thought I had reached my end then, but I see now that that end was really the beginning.

Sitting here right this minute, if I could go back, relive that period in my life, and erase all the pain I went through, but lose the life I have now, I wouldn't. I hope this book helps you realize that this can be the beginning for you as well, I just wish I could see the new person you will become.

Our Hope for You

Whether you're in the middle of a divorce, or already divorced, our hope is that this book helps you develop a path forward through the emotions swirling in your head. Remember, you're not alone. You can find others facing similar struggles. And more important—much more important—no matter the circumstances, God is with you. God, the creator of the universe, the Almighty, the everlasting God. He sees you; He loves you, and He has plans for a brighter future. Our prayer, adapted from Saint Francis of Assisi is, Lord make this book an instrument of Your peace. Where there is hatred, let it sow love; where there is injury, pardon; where there is doubt, faith; where there is despair, hope; where there is darkness, light; and where there is sadness, joy.

As the Bible says, "Those who hope in the Lord will renew their strength. They will soar on wings like eagles; they will run and not grow weary; they will walk and not be faint" (Isaiah 40:31).

Chapter 1

Why is Divorce so Hard?

by Bill Koontz

Let's start with the obvious: Divorce is painful, but to understand why, it's instructive to ask: What is a marriage?

Typically, a lot of time, money, and pomp are invested in The Day. I hope your marriage didn't start off like "Penny's," whose time bomb started ticking even before The Day.

When my ex and I decided to get married, we were a young couple trying to pay for a wedding we clearly couldn't afford. The stress of planning our wedding was very intense, but we got through it and the wedding date was set. All I had to do was show up and enjoy the day that I'd dreamed of. Right?

Not so fast. Leading up to the wedding, my prospective mother-in-law told me that I was "too good for her child," causing a huge fight with her son. She chose not to show up for our wedding. My own mother told me that my fiancé was too self-absorbed and wouldn't make a good husband. So, neither my mother nor my soon-to-be mother-in-law supported our marriage. I was totally bewildered. This wasn't going to be the wedding day I'd imagined.

Then leading up to the big day, everything that could go wrong did go wrong, even my shoes weren't delivered until that morning!

With my family and friends waiting, I arrived for my big event totally stressed out, almost an hour late, and in tears. I'd never been so sad and embarrassed. Nonetheless, we said our vows. Adding insult to injury, the photographer—who we'd paid in advance—didn't produce any pictures of the wedding.

Years later, I encountered the consequences of the many damaging choices we made that ultimately resulted in divorce. And unfortunately, I discovered why divorce is so hard, so very hard.

Of course, marriage is much more than a wedding ceremony, and marriage bonds are much more than an exchange of vows. In fact, marriage bonds are the strongest and most precious human connection in our lives. As a result, it's not surprising that breaking those bonds is dreadfully painful. So, to comprehend why divorce is so hard, it's critical to understand the powerful connections that are severed in a divorce. We can think of them in terms of three Cs: a spiritual Covenant, an intimate Companionship, and an exclusive Consummation.

The Bible's book of beginnings, Genesis, records the world's first love story and perhaps its greatest. Think about it: Adam and Eve had no baggage—no family history, no parent issues, nothing to hide, no inhibitions, no pretending, and no emotional wounds. They didn't even have a thermostat or a remote control to squabble over. How thrilling their first gazes must have been! How they must have treasured their companionship and love! An acronym to describe their relationship would be HOT— Honest, Open, and Transparent. In fact, Genesis unabashedly states, "Adam and his wife were both naked, and they felt no shame" (Genesis 2:25). As Paris Hilton used to say, "That's hot!" And Adam and Eve's HOT relationship was without any of the emotional baggage that the rest of us often unwittingly carry. As a result, they were also gentle, kind, and thoughtful, and they had no hidden motives for anything they did. Can you imagine how wonderful, wholesome, and fulfilling their relationship must have been?

Marriage as originally designed by God.

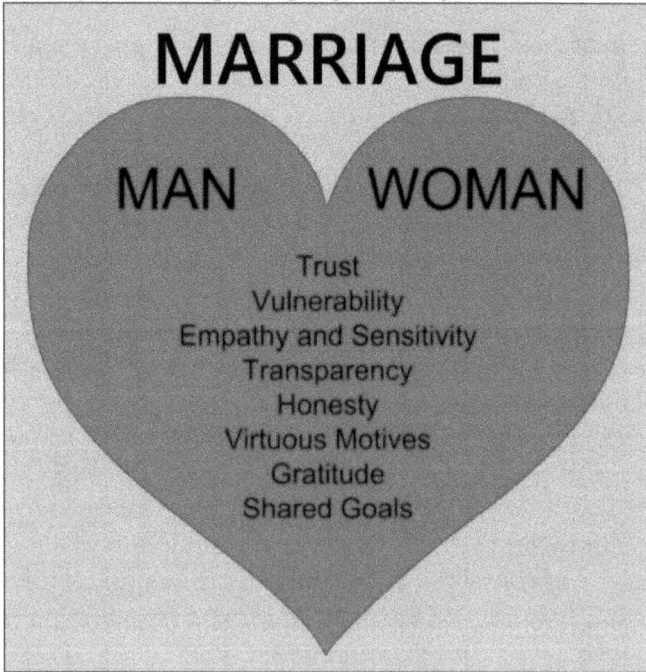

MARRIAGE

MAN ♥ WOMAN

Trust
Vulnerability
Empathy and Sensitivity
Transparency
Honesty
Virtuous Motives
Gratitude
Shared Goals

The Three C's

Covenant

According to Genesis, one very monumental decision must serve as the basis of a HOT marriage: "Therefore shall a man leave his father and his mother and shall cleave unto his wife: and they shall be one flesh" (Genesis 2:24 ASV). In other words, marriage is first of all a *covenant*, a promise or vow to God and to our spouse to "leave and cleave"—to "leave" our parents and "cleave" (cling to) our spouse. We certify this "leaving and cleaving" through the exchange of wedding vows, as you likely did. Those vows were the immensely powerful words that created a spiritual covenant between you, your spouse, and God. And when this covenant becomes broken, we can feel like our life is in shambles.

The disintegration of a marriage begins privately but ends quite publicly. Divorce is hard.

Whether you or your ex initiated your divorce proceedings, after having declared your mutual love in public, you've also had to declare your mutual *failure* in public. You may feel like trust has been irrevocably scarred, and perhaps you feel terribly embarrassed. Maybe your loyalty was thrown out the window, as if it was meaningless. You might feel that your ex, by breaking your covenant, has emotionally trampled on, spit on, and mutilated your very being.

Companionship

The marriage covenant and its vows create a safe environment for an unparalleled depth of *companionship*. As we've seen, Genesis describes this covenant as "leaving and cleaving." In principle, it's fair to say that "leaving" requires the subordination of every other relationship to the marriage. Ideally, subordinating every other relationship eliminates any exits from the highway of marriage. It's this complete leaving that opens the way to genuine cleaving. Essentially, the wedding vows say, "I'm forsaking all others because I realize God's design is for this relationship to be preeminent, and when it is, we'll experience God's greatest blessings for each of us."

What's more, "cleaving" could be described as a mutual interdependence, a healthy co-reliance. The companionship between spouses is intended to be unmatched by any other relationship. I suspect that at one point you would have described your marriage as such. The companionship of marriage is unparalleled in its vulnerability, its emotional nakedness, and its intimacy. One person becomes your confidante—the one who knows your secrets, innermost thoughts, desires, fears, vulnerabilities, ambitions, and hopes. A spouse is the one and only person in the world who knows you better than anyone else, and believes you were worth marrying and staying married to.

I remember the first time my second wife, Laura, and I had an engaging conversation. It wasn't even on a date. In fact, it was after I came home from a date. What? you ask. Yes, I had been on a date with someone else, along with my mom and stepdad, celebrating their anniversary. Laura had kindly consented to watch my two children. When I came home, the kids were already snuggled in bed. Laura told me about the frisky mouse she encountered in my kitchen pantry, and from there we just began to talk. The conversation moved into the living room by the fireplace and proceeded for the next hour and a half. It flowed. It was comfortable and inviting, and when Laura left, I thought, "I'd like to get to know her better." Two weeks later, we talked again, and then again a week after that. Finally, I asked Laura to join me on an actual date. As our relationship developed, we became soulmates. Deep disclosure and understanding emerged, which led to our marriage.

We all have a longing to intimately know another person and to be intimately known. Marriage is intended to be the protected, reliable, lifelong relationship in which we can safely become emotionally naked. This emotional nakedness is a huge component of true intimacy.

On the other hand, when you're the recipient of divorce papers, your soulmate no longer thinks you're worth the effort it would take to stay married. At that point, you've already experienced emotional nakedness, at least to some degree, so your privacy, secrets, longings, and hopes have already been compromised—perhaps even exploited. That hurt is unlike anything you've ever experienced before. It's as if you've been sliced open, and you're bleeding profusely. You need a relational emergency room, but none exists. There's no 911 for marital emergencies—no life-support treatment for marriages on the brink. In those circumstances, your treasured companionship becomes nothing but a colossal regret. Divorce is hard.

To make things worse, when you realize your marriage has failed, you imagine your friends and maybe even some of your family members are thinking things like, "I couldn't have put up with you either." Or they're thinking, "I'm shocked. You always seemed so nice, but there must be a side of you that we don't know." Beyond that, if you have children, they too may be exposed to ugly things people actually say about you. And all of this—the things you're told were said about you, and the things you've imagined being said—are just the beginning of the torments that go on and on.

Consummation

Marriage is, of course, *consummated* in sexual union. Think about it: God could have had us procreate in far less personal and less exhilarating ways. Instead, He's designed an experience that's intimate, binding, and fun. Sex is a physical unmasking, a complete abandonment to another person, a thrilling culmination of energy, an explosion of hormones. Beyond all that, though, sex is a physical vulnerability that creates such a soul tie that God intends it to be experienced only within the sanctuary of a lifelong covenant.

What's more, coupled with emotional intimacy in both partners, sexual consummation breeds a breathtaking confidence and completeness. We become more whole than ever before. And of course, sex is the gateway to creating new life; two become one to create one more.

Unsurprisingly, any violations of that exclusive consummation are devastating and humiliating. Humiliation is probably why the following "urban legend" circulated broadly shortly after the destruction of the Twin Towers in New York.[1]

The first divorce directly related to the September 11th terrorist attacks has been filed in New York. It appears that a guy with an office on the 103rd floor of the World Trade Centre spent the morning at his girlfriend's apartment with his phone turned off. He wasn't watching TV either. When he turned his phone back on at about 11am, it rang immediately. It was his hysterical wife wailing, "Are you OK? Where are you?" He said, "What do you mean? I'm in my office of course!"

Divorce is hard. This kind of sexual infidelity is a disastrous betrayal—a serious violation of a sacred bond. A common reaction to this depth of betrayal is to feel totally stripped of your dignity. It's a raping of the soul. Sexual betrayal leads to questioning your own sexuality and desirability, and even questioning whether your whole marriage was a lie.

In summary, these three C's—Covenant, Companionship, and Consummation—are intended to be the glue that bonds a marriage, enabling it to last forever. More than 2,000 years ago, a very wise man said, "A cord of three strands is not easily broken" (Ecclesiastes 4:12). In other words, the three strands of a rope, and the three C's of marriage, are stronger than the individual strength of each. Their strength is multiplied when they're bonded together.

But the three Cs aren't only for endurance: they're also for healing. Every person brings wounds to a marriage: rejection, fear, guilt, abandonment, shame, and perhaps even abuse. The deepening, consistent experience of love in marriage has the capacity to bring a level of healing to all these old wounds. But when the three Cs – Covenant, Companionship, and Consummation – are broken, great is the fall, *multiplying* the wounds rather than healing them. That's why divorce is so hard.

How the Three Cs Get Broken

Men and women are different – not just in appearance, but physiologically as well. For example, the male hormone testosterone and the female hormone estrogen play a huge role in the function of our brains. These hormones affect the way we process everything from stress, sadness, anger, and happiness to concrete facts and random minutia. God created the two sexes to complete and complement each other.

Some male-female differences we find attractive, enjoyable, and welcoming, but other gender differences can be more challenging, even conflictual and stressful. Nevertheless, God's intentions are for those differences to be leveraged for our growth. In marriage, the differences become even more noticeable, but God can use all of them to help us become more whole and to become "one flesh." His design is to take our differences and use them to challenge us and to heal us. Depending on how we deal with these challenges, married

---

[1] https://www.snopes.com/fact-check/911-adultery/

couples will either draw closer together or drift further apart. Tragically, when our differences are turned against each other, hearts can become cold and brittle.

Complicating this situation is the fact that every one of us not only brings into marriage our gender differences, but also our brokenness. An analogy that helps in picturing this dynamic is that of a bag of rocks. Regardless of how healthy a family system may be, at some level every family has a degree of brokenness. From birth on, we all accumulate "rocks" of woundedness. As we age, those rocks may shrink or enlarge, depending on the health of our relationships with parents, siblings, extended family members, peers, other significant people, and especially God. But in this life, the rocks never completely go away. That's part of the human quandary.

God designed marriage to enhance wholeness and completeness—for love to shrink the rocks each partner brought into the marriage. Too many times, though, rather than being reduced by the power of love, the rocks enlarge by the lack of love.

These growing rocks aggravate our natural differences. When those differences are turned against each other, and when rocks are hurled, the Covenant, the Companionship, and the Consummation of marriage begin to be compromised in our hearts and eventually in our behavior. Marriage can even become weaponized, and it can devolve into broken promises, emotional outbursts, exploitation, and sexual betrayal. Consequently, in divorce, when we're forced to recognize that the oneness of marriage has been destroyed, there is grieving, sorrow, and loneliness. You can feel like a piece of you, perhaps a large piece of you, is gone, often leaving a gaping wound. There is nothing uglier.

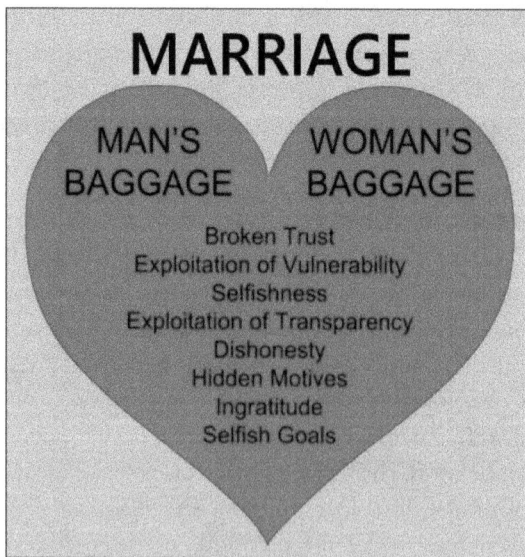

MARRIAGE

MAN'S BAGGAGE

WOMAN'S BAGGAGE

Broken Trust
Exploitation of Vulnerability
Selfishness
Exploitation of Transparency
Dishonesty
Hidden Motives
Ingratitude
Selfish Goals

All marriages come with baggage that each person brings from past wounds and patterns of thinking and behavior. As time goes on, if this baggage isn't addressed, it can contaminate a marriage, creating stress, revealing unhealthy coping mechanisms, and undermining the relationship.

When a marriage fails, our impulse is to bombard ourselves with questions: "How did this happen? How *could* it happen? How did this collapse occur?" None of us went into marriage anticipating that this kind of conflict and pain could ever happen. And yet, your ex, who knew better than anyone the most hurtful thing that could ever be said to you, may have said that very thing. We never could have imagined the brutal thoughts, words, and actions that could materialize in a relationship that began with such promise and anticipation.

Speculate with me: What if you were just as loving, accepting, and understanding as Jesus? Would your marriage still have failed? Maybe, maybe not. You would, of course, have been faultless, but your spouse would still have brought some rocks into your marriage, and their rocks could have still undermined your covenant. And looking at the situation from the opposite side, what if you had been married to a person who was every bit as loving, accepting, and understanding as Jesus? Would that marriage have failed? Again, your divine spouse wouldn't have brought any rocks into your marriage, but you surely would have, and your rocks alone could have been enough to destroy your relationship. In fact, we see that Jesus Himself couldn't unilaterally preserve every relationship He was in. At least one of His closest friends brought enough rocks into the friendship that he ultimately deserted, even betrayed Jesus. My point is this: No matter how good of a spouse you were, that's no guarantee that the rocks you and your ex brought into your marriage wouldn't have caused it to unravel.

And here's another sobering thought: In the Bible, we have the story of Lazurus who, along with his two sisters, was a very good friend of Jesus, in fact it says that He loved Lazarus. Lazarus later died before Jesus responded to the message that Lazarus was very sick. For whatever reasons, Jesus delayed coming, and Lazarus died before Jesus came on the scene four days later. Mary and Martha, Lazarus' two sisters, were troubled by why Jesus hadn't come sooner, both saying to Jesus, "If you had been here, he wouldn't have died." Jesus' delay allowed the natural forces of death to prevail.

Perhaps you, like I, have voiced groaning objections as to why Jesus didn't intervene in our marriages as they rambled down a dead-end runway toward death. Certainly, it seems He could have miraculously saved my marriage and your marriage, and He could have prevented the suffering of all the people who were affected by the destructive forces of our divorces. I wondered for years why He didn't intervene in the downhill spiral of our relationship that ended in such a tragic travesty. It undermined the very foundations of my trust in Him. A three-letter word took up residence in my heart during those years: "Why?"—"Why?" with an attitude. Perhaps you're all too familiar with that word as well, or its close companion, "If only." Jesus allowed Lazarus to die, and in the midst of their bewilderment, both Mary and Martha voiced those words, "If only." But this is followed by the shortest verse in the Bible, "Jesus wept," shortest perhaps for effect. It powerfully conveys His personal grief and His compassion for the grieving of Mary and Martha. In so doing, Jesus entered the chasm of their disappointment.

Disappointment is one of the prevailing feelings that divorced people contend with: disappointment in themselves, their ex, and even God. Disappointment with God? When you actually look at those words in print and focus on them, it doesn't take long to rationally realize that those three words are an oxymoron, that there's a contradiction inherent in them. Can a perfect God disappoint? No, but that doesn't mean we can't feel disappointed—extremely disappointed—with Him, especially in the midst of great loss. However, it really wasn't God who disappointed us; it was ourselves and our exes. We do have some control over us, but our exes, we have no control over. So, we cry out to God to supernaturally intervene, and if He doesn't, we tend to place our disappointment on Him.

Divorce is like any great loss. Anyone who's lost a child, family member, close friend, or too young of a parent wants to know "Why?" So, when we can't make sense of a great loss, and we can't understand "why" God doesn't choose to fix it, disappointment follows. That three-letter word "why" often lies at the heart of it. While it's natural to grapple with that universal question, its answer is many times elusive.

In my own case, when I did finally figure out some answers, it seemed they were related to another word: "brokenness." As you'll read in the chapter about "Compass Scriptures," Jesus declared that divorce happens because our hearts are hard or broken. While Lazarus died because of physical decay, our marriages die because of the decaying effect of each of our choices—choices that are usually rooted in the hardness of our hearts. The more honestly we face the realities of our brokenness, the brokenness of our ex-spouses, and perhaps the brokenness of anyone else who contributed to our divorce, the more honestly and readily we can resolve our disappointments and the questions of "why." Then we can also let go of those reasons that lie beyond our understanding. After years of turmoil, as I struggled with that three-letter word "why" and the disappointments that accompanied it, I finally accepted the reality that due to my brokenness and the brokenness of others, I'll never fully know the answer to the question "Why?"

God in His vast, unequaled wisdom determined thousands of years ago that the human beings He created would have the freedom to choose. That included even the choice to reject Him as well as one another. Ultimately, that freedom to choose allowed Judas to betray Jesus. And the power of each of us to choose lies at the root of why my marriage and yours disintegrated. Some, maybe much, of the hardness or brokenness we discover within ourselves can be softened or healed. However, we certainly can't control the steps someone else is willing to take or not take toward healing.

We are flawed beyond our understanding. As I grappled with my own contributions to the blowup of my marriage, I also wrestled with the sorrow of my own failures. That wrestling match eventually led me to humbly surrender my demands to know why, and to begin trusting the God who created both me and my ex, and to begin believing that out of the ashes of the death of our marriage, the choice to pursue a resurrection of life awaited. Of course, I'm not referring to eternal life, but rather to the newness of life that Paul refers to in his letter to the Romans when he writes that we "walk in newness of life"

(Romans 6:4, NKJV). In that newness, we can discover how God can, yet again, breathe life into a soul buried beneath grief and despair. Yes, divorce is hard. The questions it raises are hard, and many of them will be further explored in subsequent chapters of this book.

The collapse of a marriage is explosive and expensive. A grand marriage can become a fifty-grand divorce!

So, What Is Divorce?

While Wikipedia is often not a good source of information, its description of divorce is helpful vernacular. It says, "Divorce (also known as dissolution of marriage) is the process of terminating a marriage or marital union. Divorce usually entails the canceling or reorganizing of the legal duties and responsibilities of marriage, thus dissolving the bonds of matrimony between a married couple under the rule of law of the particular country or state."[2]

Here are a few statistics from *Forbes Advisor*, updated November 20, 2024,[3] and NCHstats,[4]

- 43% of marriages are dissolved. Second and third marriages actually fail at a far higher rate, though, with 60% of second marriages and 73% of third marriages ending in divorce.
- As Baby Boomers enter retirement, their divorce rate is creeping up. Adults aged 55 to 64 have a divorce rate of 46%.
- Age: Couples who marry before 18 are 48% more likely to divorce within 10 years, while those who wait until after 25 reduce their likelihood by 24% according to studies.
- Cohabitation: Couples who cohabit before marriage have up to a 40% higher chance of divorce.
- Religion: Strong religious beliefs reduce divorce risk by 14%, while lack of affiliation increases it by the same percentage.
- Education: College attendance reduces the risk of divorce by 13%, while high school dropouts are 13% more likely to divorce.
- The average length of a marriage prior to divorce is eight years.
- In 2019, there were about 750,000 divorces in the U.S.
- If you live in Nevada, perhaps you'll want to move to Louisiana or Illinois. Nevada has the highest divorce rate, and Louisiana and Illinois have the lowest.
- Occupations affect divorce rates.

---

[2] Divorce - *Wikipedia*

[3] Revealing Divorce Statistics In 2024 – *Forbes Advisor*

[4] Robert McAllister, "Divorce Rates in US 2024 – Current Trends and Analysis," *NCHstats*, December 11, 2024.

- Money is a leading cause of marital stress and conflict, so unsurprisingly, couples with lower incomes face a higher likelihood of divorce.
- An interesting phenomenon is that more women are filing for divorce than men, even though they have the higher potential of financially losing out at the end of the process. Women initiated 69% of all divorces, compared to 31% for men.

Beyond these statistics, though, we all know that divorce is much more than just numbers and legal processes. In fact, it's somewhat remarkable that definitions of divorce are so devoid of its human toll. In each of our Divorce & Beyond seminars, I've asked the group, "What is Divorce? Give me one or two words that would describe yours." There's always a large variety of responses, demonstrating that no two divorces are alike. As people verbalize their answers somewhat cathartically, I record them on a large sheet of newsprint, using assorted colors to try to capture the mood and thrust of each: Broken Promises. Relief. Second chance. Explosion. Devastating. Destructive. Hard. Gut-wrenching. Finally, over. Horrendous. Heart-blowing. I could fill page after page, but you get the gist.

In fact, as you've been reading this, some metaphors for your own divorce have probably bubbled up in your mind. What are they?

While there's certainly no perfect answer to that question, I think the metaphor that best captures the anguish of divorce is "car wreck." In a car wreck, there can be varying degrees of damage. Some cars are totaled; some are not. Some people walk away with minor injuries; some end up in an ICU. Some injuries and damage you can see; some you cannot. The same is true in divorce. There are as many unique levels of injury and types of damage as there are divorces. Some are earth-shattering; others are less consequential.

Now, before we move on, let me add a concluding thought to this chapter: Marriages generally end either by death or by divorce. People often mistakenly think that those two endings are similar, but they're dramatically different emotionally and spiritually, and therefore, they call for very different grieving processes. The pain of being left behind by divorce can actually be worse than the pain of being left behind by death. (I mean no disrespect for those grieving the death of a spouse. Indeed, that can be devastating, especially if the death is not from natural causes. This comparison is only made to help people better understand the immense loss that many feel as a result of the rejection of a former mate. The gnawing sadness of what a marriage could've been as opposed to what it was, is very different.)

In one of our Divorce & Beyond groups, we had a man, a medical doctor, who had lived through both the death of his first wife, and a divorce from his second. He always insisted that, for him, the divorce was much, much worse. He explained that he and his deceased wife had loved each other very much, and if it hadn't been for the cancer that took her, they would still be together. What's more, when the man's first wife died, she left behind many fond memories, and throughout his grief, he was assured by friends, relatives, and his pastor that they weren't going to leave him to sort things out on his own. He told us that it seemed like he didn't have to cook a meal for six months! For the longest time, people sincerely asked him if he was okay, and they let him know that if he wasn't, they were there for him day or night.

In contrast, however, when the man's second wife had an affair and left him, she accused him of horrible things he hadn't done, embarrassed him in front of friends, and violated his trust. She didn't seem to care how much she hurt him. What's worse, when this ex-spouse left, there was nothing but silence, and the man suffered by himself with very little support from friends, family, or church. I've heard divorce described as the death of a spouse where the coffin stays open and the dead person continues to influence the living, especially if there are children involved.

The following anonymous story captures the similarities of two marriages and extent of the differences between the loss of a spouse to death and the loss of a spouse to divorce.

There Were No Flowers

The following is a fictional story. On the other hand, fiction is often "truer" than reality.

Once upon a time, not so long ago, there lived two women, Mary and Jane. Mary and Jane were the best of friends, sharing a similar, seemingly idyllic lifestyle. Both were fine Christians and were extremely active in their church. Each had been married for over 10 years, and each was blessed with two beautiful children.

Life appeared wonderful for them, but Mary and Jane shared a secret that, if made known, could have shattered their dream worlds. Their husbands abused them physically and emotionally, and both husbands were also involved in extramarital affairs. Mary and Jane instinctively concealed their torment and humiliation from everyone. Only when the two of them met privately could they permit their suffering to show. Little did they know that within a week, these best friends would never again share their similarities.

Mary's husband died suddenly of a heart attack. At about the same time, Jane's husband announced that he wanted a divorce, and she and the children would have to leave "his" house.

Mary's secret died with her husband. No one needed to ever know that his heart attack was brought on by one of his "little indiscretions." As far as everyone was concerned, he was the loving father and faithful husband that Mary had always pretended he was. On her mantle, the family portraits that once distressed Mary became "hallowed shrines." Her dusty wedding album with yellowing pages now held a permanent place on her coffee table near the Bible. Deceptive thoughts and stories replaced the agonizing memories of abuse and heartache.

On the other hand, Jane's secret instantly became public gossip. Everyone now knew that her husband was not the devoted man she had consistently alleged. Her family portraits were now loathsome reminders of what had never really existed. Her dusty wedding album was now blackened ashes. The years of abuse, heartache, and agonizing memories crashed together.

Contrast of Concern

The funeral of Mary's husband was elaborate, and the church was filled with heaps of flowers and throngs of sorrowful friends. The pastor praised the loving and faithful husband and father.

The church family rallied to Mary's side, laden with food and sympathy. For several weeks following the funeral, hardly a day passed without someone from the church either calling or coming by to see if Mary and the children were alright. "If there's anything we can do, just let us know," echoed throughout the weeks. Everyone said how good it would be for a fine Christian like Mary to get married again, find a good father for her children, and fill the void that her late husband had left.

Meanwhile, the concern for Jane was not so exuberant or sincere. Although it was her husband who dishonored the marriage, some people were sure that it must have been her fault.

There was no elaborate church service to help bring closure—only a desolate hour in a somber lawyer's office. No friends called or came by. People who had known Jane almost her entire life avoided her. No one said, "If there's anything we can do, just let us know." There were no flowers.

Unlike Mary, Jane's potential for remarriage was greatly marred by the adverse opinions of some: "If she gets married again, it'll just be for money and for someone to take care of those kids of hers." Jane's troubles—past, present, and future—were now on public display.

For a Christian woman under the conviction that divorce is a deplorable sin, dealing with its actuality can be traumatic. Fears of failure, hopelessness, and uncertainty become everyday occurrences. She cries until tears are exhausted. The need to lash out at someone is overwhelming, but instead she takes it out on herself. She feels she can never again be of value. Family members can't fully understand her feelings of despair. They sympathize with her, but they think she was foolish for having lived all those years in a terrible situation.

Without cause, people Jane had known all her life were seemingly passing judgment on her. She was the victim, but she had now become the accused. People didn't consider the circumstances of the divorce—only the fact that Jane was now a "divorced woman." Those two words sounded ugly to her, but just then, she felt ugly.

Reader, can you identify with Jane? Thankfully, a story like Jane's does not have to end there, and neither does yours. If, like Jane, you feel ugly inside, over time that feeling will dissipate as you learn to trust that God's love isn't based on how you feel or how others feel about you. As you become more whole, your judgement of others will slowly turn into forgiveness, and your pain will turn into peace.

With just a little initiative, you can find support. Visit our video-driven, online course, and take advantage of our 50% discount at, relationalpeace.org/collections/divorceandbeyond. (There is a QR code at the end of the book to link you to this website.) In addition, other resources can be found that also deal with the multitude of attitudes and emotions that tragically accompany divorce. You can find divorce-recovery groups in churches. As you share your story in bits and pieces and listen to others do the same, your trauma and disappointment will slowly begin to heal. A counselor can also be instrumental on your path to recovery. Helping you understand your brokenness as well as your ex-spouse's is key to your healing. You will never forget the role your ex played in your divorce, but by taking healthy steps towards recovery through understanding, those memories will lose more and more of their power.

In conclusion, each divorce is unique, and therefore its suffering is unique as well. That suffering and what to do with it will be explored in the next chapter called "The Crisis Cycle of Divorce."

Questions to Ponder:

1. After reading this chapter, name the factors that have made your divorce hard and painful for you.

2. From the "Baggage Heart Chart," what words describe the baggage you brought into your marriage? Have your pieces of baggage grown in size or number? Describe how.

3. Which, if any, of the statistics from Arthur Zuckerman pertain to your divorce?

4. How would you describe your "car wreck"?

5. What feelings did you have after reading "There Were No Flowers"? Were there any ways you identified with that story? If so, what were they?

Chapter 2

The Crisis Cycle

Part 1: The Timeline

by Paulette Liburd

What do you do when the "wholeness" of your marriage unravels? What do you do when the relationship becomes stressful and destructive, and the "covenant of oneness" begins to crack? You've tried sticking it out, and the only result has been that you and your spouse have grown further and further apart. The easy intimacy that you once enjoyed has evaporated. The diagram below is a way of illustrating the course that a marriage relationship takes as it unravels, culminating in divorce. But the chart also shows the possibility of rebuilding a life after divorce.

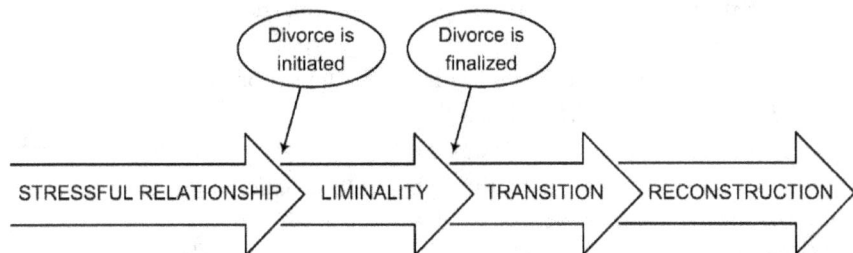

Let's explore the four sections of this timeline, each with its own unique characteristics.

The first period is, of course, the Stressful Relationship Phase. During this period, your marriage is disintegrating. Small annoyances have become full-blown sources of frustration.

The story of my own hapless marriage started when I met my ex (I'll call him "Anthony") at the college we both attended in the Caribbean. I was the only female in our quantitative analysis class, and I've never been sure if that was a blessing or a curse. Not only was I the only female, but I also happened to come from the same small island where "Anthony" grew up. So, when he first approached me with his adorable smile, I was excited to find a fellow British native who was so smart and interesting. We talked for days on end about cricket, our families back home and abroad, as well as our future goals and plans. It was refreshing to have such deep conversations with someone who seemingly had very similar plans. However, unlike "Anthony," I was a Christian, and I was quick to let him know that I wouldn't date him because of this.

In our sophomore year, "Anthony" and I both migrated to the mainland to complete our studies. He went to Texas, and I went to Alabama. While I was there, he let me know that he had accepted Christ and was baptized. He sent me a copy of his baptismal certificate and asked, "Could we date now?"

Looking back at that time, I laugh. Those long-ago years were such an innocent time! With God's help, our long-distance relationship survived. We were married in Texas after I graduated. I started working a full-time job while "Anthony" continued his studies. Upon his graduation and the six-month birthday of our firstborn, we relocated from Texas to Ohio in December. To put it mildly, this move was indeed an adjustment. We were a young family from the Caribbean, spending the Christmas and New Year season in sub–zero temperatures for the first time, and in a hotel! Did I mention that I was nursing a six-month-old? To make matters worse, the hotel must have given their main cooks time off during those holidays! Needless to say, that wasn't a happy time in our marriage. But spring finally arrived, and we were still an intact family that had survived the difficulties of a very stressful time.

Nineteen months later, now in our own home, we welcomed our second child, and the stress began to return. Although "Anthony" and I had decided that I wouldn't work until our children were in school, he began to make comments about me not working and how he was the only one responsible for the bills. Now, I must let you know that I was nurtured by strong, independent, Black women—some married and some not. Therefore, "Anthony's" comments really stung when he insinuated that I was less than sufficient to be a provider and actually dependent upon him. I had no problem letting him know that I was poorer as his wife than when I had lived with my mother, a single woman. I was not going to idly stand by; I went to work, the night shift, at a hospital. As illustrated in the chart above, this was the start of our *Stressful Relationship Phase.*

Before proceeding, both marriage partners contribute to the demise of the marital relationship. On later pages I detail the contributions I made.

Soon "Anthony" began to complain that I was more of a mother than a wife. Remember, we had moved to a new location where we had no family and hadn't made any new friends. He wondered why I couldn't just get some random person to come in to sit with the kids so I could spend "quality" time with him. I thought this was so selfish of him! My mind went back to every selfish thing he had done since we met, and of course I pointed out every one of them. According to "Anthony," there was nothing that I was doing right. We constantly bickered back and forth about the best way to raise our impressionable children. What's worse, since I was now working, it appeared that my husband was jealous that I spent so much time with our children, and he concluded that I was choosing to neglect him. The stress mounted as we continued a downward spiral.

If you've been through a period like this, or you are going through a period like this right now, you know just how stressful it can be. Maybe you've been to counselors, or you've sought advice from trusted friends and pastors, but nothing seems to help. You're probably more on edge, and your skin crawls whenever you're around them—the person you vowed to be with until death. Or maybe in your own home, you feel as if you have to walk on eggshells. You may be contending with broken promises, lies, communication breakdowns, emotional and/or physical abuse, a lack of intimacy, or even addictions.

Personally, when I was in this phase, I felt like pulling my hair out. It seemed like I had all of the above going on at once. Day after day, there were arguments surrounding the discipline of the children. Imagine my disbelief when I got a call from the daycare saying that my daughter showed up with bruises on her face and that they would need to alert children's services. This was one of those "pulling my hair out moments" and I also wanted to take a bat to "Anthony's" head! I rushed to the daycare to see my beautiful daughter with bruises. "Anthony" contended that while he was trying to "discipline" my daughter for not eating correctly, she had moved and got struck in the face. The authorities investigated, and to my surprise, they simply gave us warnings and a sheet on how to appropriately discipline children. To me, it seemed that "Anthony" had merely been given a proverbial slap on the wrist.

Unsurprisingly, "Anthony's" behavior persisted, but the incident I recall most vividly was when I came home to find a trail of blood from the living room to the bathroom. Bewildered, I inquired as to what had happened. "Anthony" told me that our son sneezed on him, and "Anthony" backhanded him because "he was told several times to cover his nose when he sneezed." This was the straw that broke the camel's back for me. I didn't hesitate to get children's services involved, and I filed for a divorce.

Prior to our marriage, people had waved "red flags" in my face. This group of people included my mother, whom I loved and adored, and who had never steered me wrong—ever! The group also included "Anthony's" mother who told me that I was too good for her son! At the time, it seemed to me that she wasn't even interested in her own son's happiness, and I came up with excuses for all of his negative actions.

One example of my excuse-making may seem rather trivial on its own, but it's only one of many. Before "Anthony" and I got married, my mother came to visit me while we were living in an area that was hot and humid, and one particular day was brutal! We were shopping at an outside mall. "Anthony" took off on his own because he said my mom and I were taking too long. When he returned, he was carrying a drink. My mom asked him, "Where are ours?" He said he didn't have enough money to purchase enough for us. Now to be fair, at that time "Anthony" was a student finishing his engineering degree, and he only worked during internships and when school was out. However, my mom viewed his attitude as selfish and a lack of concern for others. Although I felt the same, I defended "Anthony's" action as just a lack of disposable income. My mom pointed out that if "Anthony" didn't have enough money to purchase drinks for all of us, he should have gone without. To sip on a drink in the hot, humid weather and not offer one to your fiancée was a telltale sign of selfishness!

This self-centered behavior continued on many fronts, and there were glaring signs of "Anthony's" abandonment issues resulting from his own parents' divorce, but I ignored it all. Admittedly, before my marriage, I had second thoughts of whether I should go through with it. And in fact, on my wedding day, I actually cried all the way to the hall, praying that I wasn't making a mistake. But I foolishly consoled myself by thinking that if I loved "Anthony" enough, he would change after we got married.

During the early years of our marriage, despite being warned about "Anthony's" selfishness, I was determined to prove all the nay-sayers wrong. However, I was the one who ultimately was proved to be wrong. In addition to the abuse I noted, "Anthony" began to spend more and more time outside our home, which eventually led to more extreme acts of selfishness: affairs and lies. I had no desire to be intimate with a mate who seemed to be just coming home to sleep.

All of this abuse, selfishness, and unfaithfulness culminated in my decision to *initiate a divorce*. In your case, perhaps you too may have been the one to make that decision. Or perhaps you and your spouse decided together that your relationship had become too stressful and destructive to continue. Or perhaps you were the one on the receiving end of your spouse's decision to call it quits. But in any case, it was an extremely painful decision for me, and undoubtedly also for you.

Here is a brief synopsis of a young lady who endured her own stressful relationship. *Carmen writes:*

"I was in an abusive marriage 6 years ago. I experienced many types of abuse—physical, financial, emotional, mental, and spiritual. I spent an entire year planning my escape for me and my two boys. I'd lost myself and lived many years in survival mode and in a panicked state of mind. It was very toxic and unhealthy. After much needed counseling, I took charge and filed for a divorce. My life is now in a very different place. Both of my children successfully graduated high school and are college students. I have found a position in the healthcare field that enables me to be self-sustained until I become a full entrepreneur, one of my lifelong goals."

Isn't this a great comeback?

Once the decision to divorce has been made, the next part of the timeline is what we call the Liminality Phase. The word "liminality" comes from the Latin *limen*, which means "threshold." A period of liminality is one of standing on a threshold—leaving behind one stage of life but not yet arriving at the next. The adjective "liminal" describes the uncertainty—the disorientation—of this phase when the decision has been made to get divorced, but the divorce hasn't yet been finalized. Standing on that precipice can be terrifying, and as in all phases, emotions can sometimes be paralyzing and other times energizing. Often, though, it seems they just create a lot of fog, clouding your judgment.

As I've mentioned, I was the one to initiate my divorce. I was tired of all the lies, broken promises, infidelity, and abuse of my children, both emotional and physical. But making this decision plunged me into deep soul-searching. Divorce was against all that I was taught and all that I had believed from an early age. In fact, I believed that divorce was an unforgivable sin. Doesn't God hate divorce? Beyond my remorse for the sin of divorce itself, I didn't want to bring disgrace to my family. As the firstborn and the first in my immediate family to get married, I wanted my marriage to be an example to my siblings. As such, I believed I carried the burden of doing things right, of being true to my commitments and upholding the standards I had been taught by my immediate family, my church family, and my community. This was paramount to me, and living up to the standards I was taught brought satisfaction to my ego. Therefore, the shame of failure was unbearable, and I detested the thought of becoming a social statistic, especially one related to the decline of yet another African American family.

To make things worse, as I've mentioned, I knew there were close family members and friends who had predicted that my marriage wouldn't last, and confirming their predictions was torturous to me. I actually considered the hypocrisy of staying in my destructive marriage just to avoid all these new forms of misery. I thought I had done everything right: waiting to finish college before marrying and securing a job before having children. My ex and I had even taught Sunday School together for a long time. All of that was the responsible route, wasn't it? So why would God allow this fiasco to happen to me? I wondered if I was being punished.

It took several years for my divorce to become final, and that dragged out my Liminality Period. While the divorce process can be amicable, it can also be manipulated by either party, elongating the court proceedings. If you're the one to file for the divorce, for a multitude of reasons your spouse may try to drag out the proceedings. In my own case, my ex took a job assignment where he traveled internationally, and it seemed like he used this travel as the basis for asking the court for continuance upon continuance. As our case dragged on, there were times I wanted to give up and just stay separated.

All the same, we have to acknowledge that there can be legitimate reasons for continuances in a divorce case. For example, a person's job may legitimately require extensive travel, and it can be to both parties' advantage to work around that travel schedule in order to maintain that person's income. Likewise, there could be health issues that delay the proceedings, or maybe continuances are needed in consideration of the children's school calendar. Hang in there: The process will eventually be completed. Your divorce will one day be finalized, and your period of liminality will come to an end.

Keep your seatbelt buckled though. The next season, which I'll call the Transition Phase, can be even more challenging to your psyche because it cements the reality that the life you once knew is now gone. Over. Done. This is uncharted territory and navigating it can be scary. In each phase, you may face a new low, and this Transition Phase is not likely to be any different. While you were proceeding through the divorce, there was some semblance of working toward a goal: divorce. Making it to the finish line may have been excruciatingly painful, and when you finally get there, it feels like you've completed a big step, and you have. But then, instead of the relief that you might have expected, you may instead feel like you're still on an emotional roller-coaster ride that'll never end.

In my case, after my divorce was finalized, I had two school age children to raise as a single parent. For financial reasons, I had to rent a rather modest townhouse, and I had to change school districts. There were many times when money was tight. I couldn't afford extras. I had to rein in the budget and talk with my kids about why. To make matters worse, my ex was pointing out to the children that he paid child support and that it should cover all the needs they had. He even told them that I should be giving them money to spend on whatever they wanted! During his visitations, he would take them out to eat (something I couldn't afford to do), even when he was on dates with other women.

During this Transition Period, it's important to recognize that your surging emotions can continue to cloud your judgment. As you ponder important decisions, seek the counsel of trusted friends, pastors, or other professionals. I scheduled counseling for me and the children. My son in particular had many rough patches. There were times he would go to counseling only to sit there and say nothing. He would then come home and sit by himself in the basement for hours on end.

Here is a similar story that a woman I'll call "Mary" wrote to me about her struggle with her 43-year marriage and why it ended in divorce.

It was 1974, and I was 23. By then, I had been a bridesmaid for 13 weddings, but I was still waiting for who the Lord had for me. I was determined to choose a man who loved the Lord with all his heart and soul. And then he came along. We met as co-workers in a youth ministry. We shared our faith and values in so many areas. Dating was amazing, but somehow, I had a "check in my spirit" and didn't know why.

Even so, in August of 1975, we got married, but much to my disappointment, our first five years together brought confusion, heavy burdens, and broken promises. I realized that, as a woman, I was being objectified rather than loved as a precious gift from the Lord. Sex addiction was a struggle for my husband, but neither of us, at that time, knew what that addiction entailed. I urged that we should go to a counselor who was a Christian, and we did. In fact, we went to six or eight counselors throughout our marriage. My husband always promised to abstain from his addiction, but these were promises that would not be kept.

The journey of life continued. We thought that entering the ministry full-time would surely help and put us in a safe place. It did not. It just put more pressure on us, and my husband increased in the behaviors and thought patterns that go with this addiction: blame, denial, gaslighting, and broken promises, along with taking less and less responsibility for the family, finances, and parenting. In response, I took on more and more responsibilities, determined to keep our family going.

The years continued. The struggles brought me again and again to the Lord. I have to say that struggles do produce growth if the Lord is part of the process. My faith grew. I developed skills I never thought I would have. The Lord encouraged me to complete my studies and get a higher degree. That brought in the money we needed to stabilize our family situation. I made sure I had a support community in my church. Mental health counselors brought me the wisdom I needed to set healthy boundaries, learning how to communicate without being angry all the time, and learning how to apply my faith in my circumstances.

More years dragged on. Finally, the pain intensified in the 43rd year of our marriage. After consulting God and making myself accountable to friends and family, I finally requested a separation. And after still more months with no change on the part of my husband, I knew I had to choose divorce.

The Lord had gone before me to make the path straight. Even though I thought I was betraying God by choosing divorce, He showed me otherwise. He blessed me again and again with housing, a new job, an anonymous financial gift, and friends who prayed for me, walked with me, and loved me unconditionally. From all of my grieving, I lost my health, but the Lord carried me through many harrowing days. My prayer to him was, "Lord, don't let this experience go to waste. Let me help other women who are struggling with husbands who have this addiction. May they heal as you are helping me to heal." And that is exactly what God is doing as I continue to trust and follow him. I'm moving on with a new life, growing closer to my God and King.

"Mary's" story is a long and winding road that finally led to healing. Like hers, your struggles through a stressful relationship, decision to divorce, liminality, finalization, and transition will eventually lead you to the brink of healing. At that juncture, it's crucial to begin the Rebuilding Phase, the fourth and final part of the divorce timeline. Depending on the circumstances of your divorce, you may have had some previous periods of time that you've begun this phase. But the end of the Transition Phase will mark in earnest the beginning of the Rebuilding Phase. It will be defined more by acts of your will than by a deadline on a calendar. The Rebuilding Phase is when you purposefully decide to work on yourself. For example, you might ask yourself if there are any activities you enjoyed as a single person, and that still appeal to you, but that you haven't done lately. Is there an element of growth that you've always wanted to pursue but you couldn't find time for during your marriage? This is the time to try new and different activities.

The Rebuilding Phase also involves assessing your own shortcomings when it comes to relationships and asking how these contributed to the demise of your marriage. Even if your ex shot the torpedo that ultimately destroyed your marriage, there are ways you can improve your relationship skills. Even though "Anthony's" abuse was the deal breaker in my marriage, I discovered many ways I could improve my relationship skills. These relational shortcomings also contributed to the demise of my marriage. Taking an honest inventory will bring immense insights and pay long-term dividends. The starting place for this inventory is your response to the following probing questions. Read through them slowly, and to enhance the insights they provoke, pause after each one, and write down your responses.

1. What wounds did *you* bring into your marriage from your childhood and from your relationships with your parents, other family members, teachers, dating partners and friends? How did those wounds affect your marriage?
2. Why did you initially choose to marry your ex? What were your reasons and motivations? What factors did you initially overlook or minimize? What

character flaws did you miss? What growth opportunities do your responses suggest for you now?

3. How have you been further wounded during your marriage? What negative thoughts and feelings toward your ex and yourself have taken up residence in your heart? When did those thoughts and feelings begin? Have they been expressed toward your ex or through self-talk in destructive words or actions? In conversations with God, have you begun to repent of and ask forgiveness for any such thoughts or incidents?

4. How have you changed, positively and negatively, because of your marriage and divorce? How would you *like* to change?

These questions and others like them may be too emotionally challenging to dig into immediately, but when you're ready, dig you must. For example, I initially didn't think I had done anything wrong. But slowly I realized that I held a grudge toward my ex for "sowing his wild oats" (as he trivialized his own behavior many times). All the while he was philandering, I had to be there for our children and endure all the emotional heartache that followed. I had become distant and cold to my ex.

When I first went through the Divorce & Beyond program, it gently guided me to recognize that my hardened heart toward my ex was perpetuating some of my problems, and that realization opened me to experience God's forgiveness and grace. I realized that, to some extent, it took *both* my own dysfunction and my ex's dysfunction to end our marriage. For this, the Divorce & Beyond ministry was invaluable!

My answers to the above questions may help you with yours.

I brought into my marriage the wounds of being raised by a single parent. I saw my mother navigate the ups and downs of raising four children by herself while the "baby daddies," in my opinion, got off scot-free. They had never provided any consistent financial or emotional support for us children. In my woundedness, I grew up as a strong independent woman, never wanting that disorder for my own family. But I realize now that this woundedness actually played a part in my choice of a partner and the subsequent demise of our marriage. I chose my ex for his smile. I genuinely loved the way he laughed. We both were from a small island with a tight community, and we both believed that higher education was a must for us and for our children. That's all I considered, and I obviously ignored the selfish tendencies that I should have seen in his character.

I was further wounded by the way my ex related to our children. After our divorce, he did only what the courts demanded, and he tried to re-write our story by giving the kids a false narrative to make me look bad. Because of that, I didn't want anything to do with him. I kept my distance. I wanted my children to learn from the merits of their experiences with each of us. But the way my ex was manipulating them made this very challenging, and I finally realized that encouraging their relationship was detrimental to the children.

I actively sought healing by participating in the Divorce & Beyond seminar and a follow-up small group. I immersed myself in that group of new friends walking the same path as me, and in God's grace and forgiveness. I routinely prayed for God's healing for me and my children. I do believe His grace is sufficient to protect and heal. I take Him at His word that He will be a father to the fatherless. I thank God that my children are now adults with relationships of their own.

The journey through the Reconstruction Phase isn't unique to divorce recovery. It describes most recoveries from grief—loss of a loved one, a pet, a job, or anything that you've valued. However, many people describe their journey through divorce as entailing the most intense grief they've ever encountered. It certainly was for me. I've lost grandparents, other loved ones, and pets, but my divorce was the most soulful grief I've ever dealt with. It was a crisis beyond comparison. I had dreamt of growing old together with my husband. That dream has ended, but others have emerged in its place.

The journey I've described is uniquely personal. The death of some marriages is a sudden surprise, seemingly coming out of nowhere like an emotional heart attack. The death of other marriages is more like a slow-moving emotional cancer. While the pace of the timeline may differ in these dissimilar circumstances, both require a similar path to healing. In the Divorce & Beyond ministry, our observation has been that it takes a *minimum* of one to two years to sufficiently recover—and for some people, more years than that.

For me, it took almost five years to recover. I resisted owning any contribution to the failure of my marriage. Plus, I directed all of my attention to the health and education of my children. I chose to shuttle them every day to different schools that were miles apart. I also held down a very stressful job. I didn't have any energy left over to work on me, so I put my own health and healing on the back burner. Nevertheless, over time, I began to relax, and I realized that God had a purpose for me in my singlehood. I became more active in my church community, and I accepted the grace that God freely gives to all. Give yourself grace but focus honestly on assessing yourself and your own role in the collapse of your marriage.

Finally, I would be remiss if I didn't pass along this straightforward warning: Some divorced people try to shortcut the grief process by remarrying too quickly. They try to bandage the gaping wounds that were left when their earlier marriage dissolved. But that decision will only stunt the recovery process because they won't have given the wounds enough of an opportunity to heal. A marriage entered into too quickly after divorce is called a "rebound marriage," and it often ends in another divorce. Hope and stability will come only as the result of taking the time necessary to journey through the whole healing process. Only then can we truly turn the crisis of divorce into a growth opportunity.

As we've said at the beginning of this book, divorce is hard. An oath to cherish each other has been cast aside. The partnership has disintegrated. What was once a thriving relationship is over. Divorce is the breaking of a covenant, the loss of companionship, and perhaps the betrayal of consummation. The heart is torn apart, and the rip is jagged and painful. It often plunges a person into an abyss of emotional dysfunction. In the next sections of this chapter, Bill will dive into the denial, anger, bargaining, and depression that comprise the valley of grief, and then he'll visit the other side of the valley: perspective, healthy relationships, spiritual renewal, acceptance, activity and humor, and eventually new goals and lifestyle. My hope and challenge for you is to see you on the other side of the valley, experiencing healing and restoration.

Questions to Ponder:

1. Which phase on the timeline best describes your present situation?

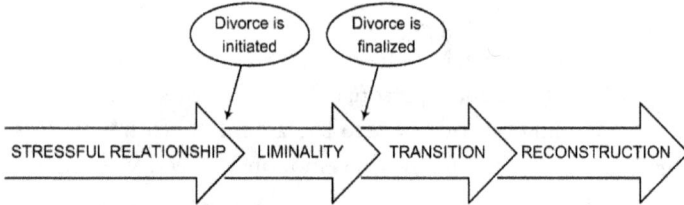

2. What insights have you gained about that phase?

Part 2: The Crisis Cycle, The Valley

by Bill Koontz

In the chapter "Why is Divorce So Hard?" I compared the three Cs of marriage—Covenant, Companionship and Consummation—to a rope of three strands. In divorce, these strands fray and begin to unravel one by one. It's painful. In fact, life itself may seem to be unraveling. Familiarity is gone, intimacy lost, finances depleted. Friendships are confused and may be forever changed or lost. Others' perceptions and yours are damaged, and perhaps there's vocational instability or confusion. Collectively, these events can be overwhelming.

One of the analogies we used in "Why is Divorce So Hard?" was that divorces are like car wrecks. Just as no two car wrecks are alike, no two divorces are alike. What was yours like? Were you totaled? Were you, or are you emotionally hospitalized? What was the extent of the injuries to your self-worth? Was your divorce a shock or something you knew was coming? Were there passengers (children) on board? If so, what's their status? The full impact of the divorce may not even be measurable yet. It's overwhelming. You may not even have any idea about which way to turn—which way to go for help. Again, there's no 911 you can call.

That dilemma makes me think of the summer after I graduated from college, when I decided to take a road trip, courtesy of my thumb, from North Carolina to Florida. At that time, hitchhiking was more common and less risky than it is today (for both the hitchhiker and the driver). Nonetheless, that trip ranks right up there as one of the most absurd things I've ever done. (But if you ask the people closest to me, they can probably come up with a whole list of others.) That trip was absurd because, when you're hitchhiking, although you know where you want to end up, whether or not you get there is dependent on somebody else who may or may not know the way and may or may not want to go there too. And yes, there's some risk in sharing a vehicle with a stranger. What's more, as I stood along the roadsides of North and South Carolina, Georgia and Florida, dozens of vehicles streamed by, ignoring my thumb. Wondering why they wouldn't stop caused me some level of embarrassment. I wondered what kinds of labels I was being assigned.

On one leg of my road trip, when I came to the end of the day, I was still many miles from my destination. My kind truck driver companion dropped me off at about 8 pm in a smaller Florida town, and I decided the safest place to spend the night would be in the local police station. That seemed preferable to sleeping on a park bench and having the police wake me up with a spotlight in my face in the middle of the night. While the police weren't very supportive of what I was doing, they did let me sleep on their couch.

The journey of recovery and healing following a divorce has some similarities to my wayward road trip. After a divorce, you know where you hope to end up, but getting there without some help seems impossible. And in too many cases, the helpers you thought you could count on disappoint you—or worse, they disappear. Unfortunately, as in hitchhiking, you have no assurance that those who see your situation will have any real interest in interrupting their lives and routines to assist. Most people don't want to get involved, so they emotionally and/or physically drive on. On top of all that, those who do stop to listen to the dilemmas you're facing probably don't understand your situation, nor do they want to take the time to try to figure out how to help. So, your search goes on for people who can actually be helpful in getting you from one place to the next. Your antennae are up, seeking the verbals and non-verbals that indicate someone is willing and able to pick you up and join you for at least some part of your journey. Like hitchhiking, that can be rather perilous. Even if you find others who are on the same road of divorce, they're usually so wounded themselves that they may be of questionable value.

What to do? Typically, when we're struck by an avalanche of emotions and unfamiliar circumstances, we try to cope the same way we've always tried to manage challenges. But as Dr. Phil asks, "How's that working for you?" Probably not well. Maybe our coping skills never did work well, but now the consequences are much higher. Divorce reveals our emotional vulnerabilities, and it challenges our coping mechanisms unlike anything else. Even so, when divorce happens, we all tend to resort to our own coping SOP (standard operating procedure). Whether that involves relying on pet peeves, defense mechanisms, insecurities, victimitis, blame-o-rama, excusaria, momentary social anxieties, or just head trash, we all use the only SOPs that we know.

Have you ever thought about how automatically we all revert to doing things "the way we've always done them"? For example, cross your arms. Now try crossing them with the positions of your hands reversed. It's far more challenging than you thought, right? And here's another example of an everyday maneuver that's second nature to us. When you put on your slacks or pants, regardless of which leg you automatically want to put in first, try putting in the other leg first. Stand close to a wall; you might fall over! These simple examples demonstrate that we all have subconscious habits for how we go about physical motions. We do the same thing when we're managing our emotional lives except that our emotional reflexes are a lot more complex. Our reactions to the catastrophic changes divorce confronts us with reveal a great deal about who we are, especially our inadequacies. Developing other ways to react seems "unnatural"—even foreign.

The trauma of divorce can be overwhelming. To make things worse, in divorce recovery, you have to develop new emotional responses while you're right in the middle of what is likely the biggest crisis of your life. It's like being dropped into a Sunday NFL game and being expected to play at the level of the pros surrounding you. You don't know the playbook, and you certainly aren't trained or equipped to take on that professional level of physicality. In addition, you're facing a spiritual opponent who's purposefully seeking to cloud your thinking and undermine any success. In fact, your enemy wants nothing more than for you to get wiped out of the game.

There are no simple ways to develop better emotional responses, but we do have to figure out healthier ways to respond if we're going to move forward. Even though it would be nearly impossible to improve the predictability of hitchhiking or surviving in an NFL game, there *are* learnable skills that can help people find their way through a divorce. We can think of those skills as "maps" to recovery.

On the one hand, I like maps. Using a map to figure out the best route from one place to another has some appeal. But still, there's part of me that prefers to intuitively figure out where I'm going without using a map. However, as you're probably discovering, trying to intuitively navigate divorce recovery doesn't work well. If only there was a recovery GPS! Our intuitions just keep taking us back to the same old dysfunctional coping mechanisms that have failed us before. Perhaps you've heard the axiom, "You're not defined by what happens to you, but by how you respond to what happens to you." But what can you do when the only responses you can come up with are the old familiar ones that aren't working? What can you do when you feel like you've been dropped into a wilderness without a map?

Let me illustrate the value of maps by telling you about one of my favorite places on the planet: the Boundary Waters wilderness that straddles the border of the United States and Canada in northern Minnesota and southern Ontario. The most unique feature of this million-acre region is about 1,200 lakes, most of which are connected by portages or trails. Only a handful of these lakes allow motorboats. The rest are traveled only by natural means—human effort or wind, waves and currents in canoes or kayaks. Many of these lakes are dotted with islands. This remote area is a beautiful, pristine wilderness that boasts crystal-clear star gazing, serene landscapes, and some phenomenal fishing and wildlife viewing.

I've taken over 20 trips into this wonderland, ranging from 7 to 10 days. Those trips involve packing "portage packs" with all the food, clothes, and gear you'll need, and hauling those packs and your canoe over portages from one lake to the next, and eventually to the next night's campsite. While that's certainly physically challenging, there are mental challenges as well—like figuring out how to find the next portage and arriving at the next desired campsite in the boundless wilderness. Of course, there's very valuable help available for that: maps and a compass. If a person has never been over this terrain before, there's no hope of finding portages and campsites without them. And even now that I've paddled over a thousand miles through the Boundary Waters, traversed over a hundred portages, and found dozens of campsites, a map and a compass are still among the most important pieces of gear I carry.

Maybe you're going through your first divorce. Or maybe you've had multiple divorces. In either case, the journey to recovery and healing requires a map. Your emotions are over the top. Sometimes their power may paralyze you from making choices. Other times, the choices you're making are often just desperate attempts to feel better, rather than coherent movements toward real healing. In my own case, immediately after my divorce, I was unaware of any resources to assist me. I ended up emotionally hitchhiking, and I definitely made some unhealthy choices and turns—"Looking for love in all the wrong places," as the song goes. That floundering just constructed additional barriers to my recovery, further delaying my healing. I needed a map!

But listen up. Decades after my own time of floundering, I can tell you that it's not necessary for you to wander an unmarked path. No one needs to chart their own way like the first explorers on a new continent. After thousands of conversations with people who've attended our seminars, and after countless discussions in small groups and conversations over lunch, coffee, or beer, and, frankly, after surviving my own personal struggles, I can share with you a recovery map of sorts. It's divided into ten stages, and it lays out a route that thousands have taken to find healing and wholeness again.

While each stage of this map is unique, the various stages do overlap. They're not always a linear progression; the map portrays a winding trail that can sometimes loop back on itself. You may find yourself dejectedly wondering, "Haven't I been here before?" But it's quite normal for the stages to be repeated. All the same, at any point on your journey through recovery, one stage tends to be at the forefront. Each stage has its lessons to be learned, and if any one of them is cut short, it'll leave behind an unfinished task that'll rear its head again until you come back and address it. What's more, some stages will have a higher level of intensity than others. Like the car wrecks that they originate from, each recovery is unique.

Unsurprisingly, the first stages of the valley are remarkably like the first stages of grief after a significant loss. "Grief" is defined by Webster as deep sorrow. In this grieving process after divorce, this sorrow can lead us to perform an inventory of our lives. And while that inventory may at first be confined to what we're grieving, it can soon become an open season reevaluating all aspects of our lives. That can be helpful, but it can also be brutal. That is, the Spirit can use our inventory to bring "godly sorrow"—correction and health—but the enemy can also use it to accuse and demean. It has been said that this sorrow will either make someone better or bitter. Initially, either path will feel more like dying than growing, and ultimately both result in a change of outlook on life. The goal of the remainder of this section is to point out pitfalls that could lead you to a brutal and bitter destination instead of allowing you to find the insights that would lead you to a healthier and better future.

In the first stages of grief, it feels like there is only night. The darkness within and around you seems bottomless, debilitating, and seemingly impenetrable. At times, the night may seem like it's getting even darker, but recovery is not a "drive-through window" experience. Tears will come, and they need to do their cleansing work. Don't be surprised if the intensity of the darkness unexpectedly becomes greater than you've ever experienced before. That's simply an indicator of the depth of your hurt. While your pain cries out for the morning, there's wisdom in not trying to rush through the night. Rather, let the night do its work.

Dr. Elisabeth Kübler-Ross's research "on death and dying" resulted in a ground-breaking book by that title in which she identifies five stages of grief.[5] I believe that the first four of her stages correspond to the first four of our ten stages of recovery from the "death of a marriage." (See the diagram below.) Of course, we have to keep in mind that while the Kübler-Ross names for these stages are useful to us here, there are significant differences between the grief that follows a physical death and the grief that results from a "marital death."

In the rest of this section of Chapter 2, I'll discuss the dark night that encompasses our first four stages of grief. Then in the final section of this chapter, I'll move on to the other six stages and cast some light on the road to recovery.

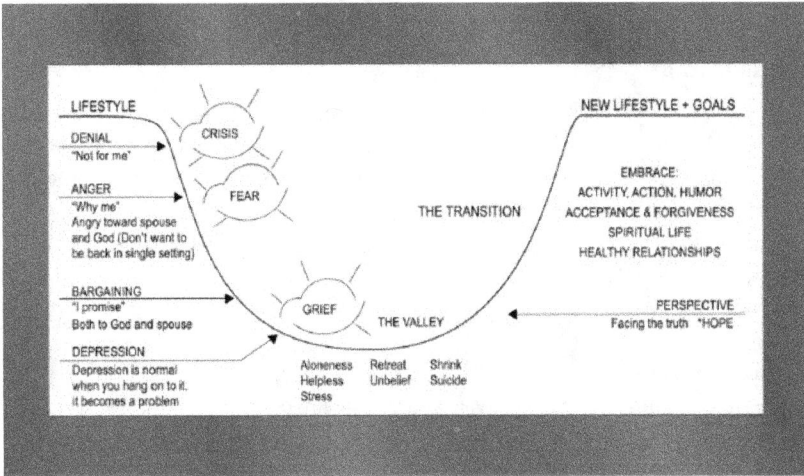

Questions to Ponder:

1. Think of a time when you were lost. What feelings accompanied it? Did you ask for directions? Why or why not?

2. Recall a previous time when you experienced grief. How did you deal with it? As you reflect on that, what was helpful? How would you handle it differently?

---

[5] Elisabeth Kübler-Ross, On Death and Dying (New York: Collier Books/Macmillan Publishing Co., 1970)

The Valley, Stage 1: Denial—Screening out the hurt

Denial is the most common of all coping strategies. It's used to construct an emotional place that seems "safer." It's motivated by the yearning to feel secure. As part of our human nature, we mentally and emotionally try to screen out that which seems overwhelming. We fear the pain we are facing. For most people, divorce is one of the most emotionally charged experiences they've ever encountered. The emotional baggage is heavier than anything they may have ever carried before. And in that extreme situation, when people default to their usual coping mechanisms, they find that those mechanisms are insufficient—which may only increase their denial. I'm going to describe three major forms of denial. You may experience any one or all three.

❖ Rationalization

The first form of denial is rationalization: "This isn't happening. It must be a dream." I remember that when my own marriage first fell apart, I repeatedly woke up in the middle of the night in my still unfamiliar bed wondering, "Where am I? What's going on? Am I dreaming? Is this really happening? It can't be!"

In rationalization, we think that if we can talk and act as if the breakdown isn't actually occurring, it won't, but whatever we refuse to acknowledge has power to influence our future. Effectively suppressing reality isn't the same thing as successfully dealing with it.

❖ Minimization

A second form of denial is minimization. It surfaces during the breakdown of the marriage as attempts to minimize the fractures in the relationship. Then it rears its head during the divorce itself by not taking any (or at least not taking enough) responsibility for one's contributions to the marriage's demise. A third form of minimization involves understating the ways our former spouse contributed to the marital failure and instead placing excessive blame on ourselves.

Here's one example of rationalization from a woman named "Anne."

I gave everything I had in me to save our marriage. I tried to get my husband to go to counseling, both professional and through our church—both of which he refused. Believing that our marriage wasn't irretrievably broken, I asked the divorce court to send us to counseling. My husband refused the court's recommendation. I prayed, and I asked friends and family to try to help. I finally realized that regardless of the help intended and extended, nothing would help unless my husband was willing to receive it.

As our marriage decayed, there was physical and verbal abuse. One time, my husband said, 'When I hear about fatal car accidents in a traffic report, I hope it's you, so I'd be rid of you.' One way I contributed to the breakdown of our marriage was by my denial of how I was allowing myself to be treated. I virtually became a doormat. I stuck my head in the sand for a long time. In addition, I thought I could fix the marriage all by myself. I believed that if I was truly committed to my marriage, regardless of what was happening, everything would work out in the end.

I asked God for help and for the answers to keep my marriage together. I knew it was never God's intention for any marriage to end in divorce. But I believe God's answer to me was, 'I can only help if both of you will let me. You have, but your husband has locked me out.' That's when I finally woke up.

"Anne's" attempts at minimalization only prolonged her pain and delayed her healing.

❖ Withdrawal

Another form of denial is withdrawal from hurt, like recoiling from physical pain. If you burn your hand, you instinctively withdraw it, and when the hurt of divorce surfaces, there's a similar tendency to withdraw from activity and relationships. You just don't feel like doing anything. You may especially avoid relationships with people who are closer and more prone to raising questions that you may not feel like answering. While these questions may actually come from a genuine place of care and concern for you, it just doesn't matter. You don't want to "go there." So, you talk less with family and close friends, or you avoid them altogether.

Do you recognize rationalization, minimization, or withdrawal in your life? At some point in a divorce situation, it's almost inevitable that these destructive forms of denial will surface to some degree. They're instinctive ways of trying to escape from or at least dull the pain you're experiencing. Unfortunately, instead of helping you, these forms of denial can lead to more serious problems that can further isolate you from sources of real help. Some of these problems are:

- Reaction formation – A defense mechanism in which a person expresses the opposite of their true feelings, sometimes to an exaggerated extent. This dynamic can be summarized by Shakespeare's famous line in Hamlet: "The lady doth protest too much, methinks." For instance, a man who feels insecure about his masculinity might tend to be overly aggressive. Or a woman struggling with loneliness may tend to be overly social. For another example of a reaction formation, think of a person who desperately craves love but can never seem to develop a relationship. That person may begin to outwardly criticize or ridicule the opposite sex. In any case, by denying their true feelings, a person can protect their self-esteem. Reaction formation may seem to work as a temporary coping mechanism, but it's unproductive in the long run. It ignores underlying beliefs or feelings that need to be addressed,

- Over-gratification – Seeking to reward oneself in an exaggerated way. Examples could be uncurbed gaming, overspending, overeating, promiscuous sex, excessive drinking, or using recreational drugs. The goal of over-gratification is to use these things to comfort and soothe yourself, even to the point that they become a type of friend—maybe your best friend. You know you're in trouble if you plan for and anticipate this gratification—if it becomes what you look forward to each day.

- Gaining unhealthy attention – Acting out in ways that covertly express one's pain. Here are some common ways that people can act out pain: being rebellious, being stubborn, being late for work more frequently, expressing a general "woe is me" mindset, lashing out with anger, or making sarcastic jokes about the opposite sex.

Do you recognize any of these destructive patterns in yourself? If so, which one(s)?

Another form of denial in divorce is hanging on to false hope. This occurs when one spouse doesn't want the divorce. "Anne's" story had elements of this. She failed to see the difference between having hope in God and hope in a fallen person. People with false hope hang on to symbols as an expression of their belief that their marriage will somehow be restored. Examples would be continuing to wear their wedding ring or having a place setting at the table for their ex after the divorce is finalized.

Jim Smoke, in his book *Growing Through Divorce*, raises several questions that help separate false hope from reality.

- Do both parties want reconciliation?
- Will both parties work toward reconciliation for as long as is necessary?
- Has either party become involved with another partner?
- Has either spouse learned something that could change the dynamics of the marriage?[6]

The answers to these questions can clarify whether it makes sense to continue to invest in a faltering relationship—or if it's time to let it go.

Dealing with denial usually involves time alone for introspection, plus time with a trusted person or group who can help you process what's happened, what you're feeling, and how you're working through those feelings.

Time alone can seem a bit scary, even intimidating. Your feelings are strong, maybe even overwhelming. You resist wrestling with them. But there comes a time when you know you must face them.

To plan a time alone, begin by identifying what has been a safe place for you previously. It's typically a physical place that feels emotionally settling, comfortable. A place where you can push the "pause button" on life. A place where you can reflect and begin to allow your psyche and spirit to catch up with the turmoil swirling around you. It should not be a place where painful memories are easily triggered. It could be a particular chair or room. It could be a special place of retreat. Perhaps it's an outside place where you can walk, jog, or ride, but it also has to have a spot where you can sit quietly and reflect. You may want to bring something to record your thoughts and feelings.

You might play some music that could help open up your feelings. There were several songs that I revisited again and again because they helped me uncover and unpack emotions that I was either unaware of or just needed to re-experience. Select something

---

[6] Jim Smoke, *Growing Through Divorce* (Eugene, OR: Harvest House, 1995), p. 11.

to read that could help you pull back the curtain on what's going on inside. Personally, I discovered that reading some of the Psalms helped me open and explore my inner life. Psalms 6, 13, 25, 30, 42, 86, 130, and 142 prompted me to write notes in the margins as I identified with the experiences, thoughts, and feelings of the writers.

For parents of at-home children, there's another factor to consider in choosing a place to be alone: Make sure the place you select is away from your kids. That may seem backwards at first. Most parents would be inclined to put off self-help efforts in order to spend the time helping their kids deal with the divorce. But think about the instructions you hear on an airplane: "If you're traveling with someone who requires assistance, secure your own oxygen mask first, and then assist the other person." You can't help anybody if you're not getting any oxygen for yourself. Taking steps to care for yourself will ultimately benefit your kids too. Of course, it's never okay to neglect your children in order to focus on your own desires, but at the same time, you don't have to feel guilty about occasionally making loving arrangements for the kids while you set aside some time to focus on your own healing.

In addition to time alone, a trusted person and/or group with whom you can open up your life will be a tremendous resource. Our deepest wounds come from relationships, and deep healing is also facilitated by relationships. If these wounds are left unattended, they will sabotage other relationships. So, find a fishbowl where you can't escape being known, where you lose the fear of being known, where people listen, pray with you and for you, give beneficial feedback, and share good counsel.

The big variable here is, of course, whether you're willing to open the door to your divorce and be vulnerable with what's going on inside you. It may take a little time for you to test whether you think your friend will be able to help bear the weight you're carrying. If they're able and you're willing, you'll likely learn things about yourself that will be invaluable in your quest to not only survive this ordeal but even to grow because of it. Schedule regular intervals to meet so that you can anticipate, look forward to, and even plan what to share. Meeting at regular intervals (as opposed to just when you feel like it) will keep the healing process on track. After support-group meetings, we've heard countless people say that they "didn't feel like coming that night, but they were so glad they did." In fact, not feeling like meeting is probably a really important indicator that meeting would be very helpful.

If you have both a trusted person and group, then you're fortunate. Lean into them both. Trust them. Allow yourself to depend on them. It'll likely feel a bit—if not a lot—uncomfortable. This may be new territory for you and a deeper level of support than you've ever needed before, but don't let the discomfort keep you from taking the risk. And after your first meeting, don't try to immediately decide whether you'll continue this course of action. What's more, be aware that your discomfort may actually rise after the first session as you realize what "emotionally undressing" feels like. But I encourage you to meet at least three times. After that, if you honestly don't sense any value, then maybe you do need to seek help elsewhere.

Now let me give you what may be a startling insight: Some level of denial can be good, when it screens out the hurt, in order to move forward. Using an analogy of the physical body, people in the medical profession tell me that when the body is inflicted with extreme trauma, it begins to restrict oxygen and blood flow to the extremities in order to preserve these life-giving resources for the vital organs. Furthermore, when they're treating such a patient, doctors begin with the most severe injuries to the exclusion of lesser ones until the patient is stabilized. In the same way, it's impossible for a person going through a divorce to address all of their emotions and issues at one time. When your coping patterns are overloaded, it's okay that some wounds are denied temporarily in order to focus on your major traumas. In fact, that's probably what's going to happen whether you plan it that way or not. So, it's important to be patient with the recovery process. That's a major reason why it's wise to avoid any romantic relationships for at least a year or two after a divorce. It'll likely take that long for the denial to conclude and for you to allow sufficient healing to happen.

Some denial can also be good for your children. They can't possibly process all they are feeling in a short time. Depending on their age and emotional maturity, it will take months or years for them to identify and explore all of their feelings. For a number of years during my own boyhood, my parents' marriage was in turmoil. Home was sometimes not a safe place. At those times, emotions were high, even hot. Arguments were loud. I can still remember one incident at about 3am when I woke to the sound of yelling downstairs. After it seemed like it wouldn't stop, I went down the stairs to the stark discovery that my parents were pushing each other. I was really scared, but I ran in between them and pleaded with them to stop. Fortunately for all of us, they did. But as a child, I desperately needed a place where I could put all this turmoil out of my mind.

During several summers in my childhood, my younger brother and I spent weeks at my grandparents' house. They lived in a very small community where my grandfather owned a gas station, a large tractor with a backhoe for digging, and a truck which he used to haul dirt, gravel, and water in a large storage tank. He was a big, strong man who loomed even larger in my boyhood eyes. He and my grandmother were well respected in this tiny town and served as leaders in the local Methodist church.

I introduce my grandparents because, during the turmoil of my parents' marriage, their home and presence were the safest place on earth to me—an oasis of sorts. Their gas station was a short walk from their house, but on the other side of the main highway that ran through their town which didn't have a single traffic light or even a stop sign. I looked forward to going to the gas station early in the morning with my grandfather. When we crossed the highway, he always held out his pinkie for me to grab and hold onto. It was so large that the palm of my hand wrapped neatly around it. Grandpa would say, "Hold on tight," and I would. But my security didn't depend on the strength of my grip, rather it was the strength of his grasp as he folded his palm around my wrist. There was no safer place for me on the planet. In the same way, rest assured that as you cross over the highways of the crisis cycle, it's not your grip on God that keeps you safe, but the power of His grasp on you.

I don't recall ever talking with my grandparents about my parents' messy marriage. Rather, their lives were simply a refuge, an escape from the mess, a good place to experience denial. If you have children, look for such a place for them.

At the same time, it *is* possible for children to learn how to process some of the trauma they're experiencing. Schools, churches, and children's agencies can be a good resource. In addition to the day-long adult seminar that Divorce & Beyond hosts, we also offer a "Kidcare" seminar that runs concurrently. It's staffed by people who are skilled at helping children identify and process their feelings with age-appropriate exercises. Children often leave Kidcare with a sense of understanding and relief. It equips them to have some appropriate discussions with their parent(s)—discussions that'll expand both the adult's and the children's awareness of what each is going through.

Questions to Ponder:

1. What forms of denial are you most susceptible to?

2. In addressing denial, which setting seems easier: While you're alone, when you're with a trusted person, or when you're in a group? Why? Which seems the most challenging? Why?

The Valley, Stage 2: Anger—Responding to the tearing of the marital bond

After an argument, one divorcing couple drove for miles in silence to a son's ballgame at a rural school. Along the way, the husband pointed to a mule in a pasture and sneeringly asked, "Relative of yours?" And just as pointedly, the wife jeered, "Yes, by marriage!"[7]

As denial surfaces, or perhaps even before it does, anger usually begins to emerge, often at an intensity that you've never experienced before. As my own anger began to surface, I was verbal and loud, frightfully intense, but also very tearful. No, not just tearful; I was sobbing, weeping. It was the beginning of a prolonged journey that, at the time, seemed to distance me from God. To some degree, I was withdrawing from Him, but I was also entering a new dimension of relating to Him—one of expressing raw emotions to God, even shaking my fist at Him, and spewing my angry disappointment. Worship became very difficult. For me, focusing on the goodness and faithfulness of God had always evoked intimacy, open-heartedness, vulnerability. But at that point in my life, I struggled deeply with worshipping God amid such discontent with Him. I felt forgotten, shattered, alone. The writer of Psalm 31:12 expressed my misery well: "I am forgotten as though I were dead; I have become like broken pottery."

Anger emerges from five sources: fear of the unknown, frustration with life being out of control, shame, having our values transgressed, and the hurt of rejection.

When we're angry, we haunt ourselves with internal diatribes. The "if onlys" become way too common:

- If only we'd moved to another city
- If only I'd taken that other job
- If only we'd joined a different church
- If only we'd moved to another neighborhood
- If only I'd listened to my friends
- If only we'd made more time for each other
- If only we'd controlled our tempers better

The list is bottomless.

While some parts of anger are intensely internal, anger also blames outside circumstances and other people. Many times, anger is directed toward the ex-spouse: "It's all your fault. You're such a self-centered jerk. You're ruining my life. How many times do I have to flush before you go away?"

After my own divorce, I was angry for months. During the worst of it, a friend, who was also going through a divorce, invited me to his condo in Florida. He was flying, and I was driving so I could also visit my grandmother who had retired down there—the same grandmother I referenced earlier. But during the divorce settlement, my ex had received

---

[7] Story, Source unknown

the minivan we owned, and since that was our only vehicle, I had needed to buy another one. So why not a Trans Am equipped with glass T-tops, black racing stripes and hood scoop? It certainly suited my disposition! Oh, and guess what color I chose: RED. Fire engine red! Think of the one Burt Reynolds drove in the movie *Smokey and the Bandit*©. (If you don't remember it or you're too young to have seen it, it's worth googling.)

Wouldn't you know it, the day I was supposed to begin my drive to Florida, a court hearing was scheduled. It was supposed to start at 10, but as court hearings go, it was delayed. There's nothing like wanting to be on the highway to Florida in March, but instead being stuck in a waiting area with my soon-to-be ex for an extra hour. I was getting irked. Finally, the court proceedings concluded at noon. I literally hustled out to my packed car, jumped in, and headed south on I-75. I fumed and simmered, and I was determined to get to Florida even if it meant setting a new land speed record. The highway patrols in Kentucky, Tennessee, and Georgia must have been at an afternoon and evening seminar, because I never saw a single one. Lucky for me, because I reached the Florida state line about 9pm, a drive that's normally 10½ hours.

The drive through Kentucky is scenic and picturesque, traversing mountains and bridges that are hundreds of feet above the rivers below. But uncharacteristically, I had little interest in the natural beauty. In fact, I found myself wondering, "What the hell— why don't I just drive off the side of this bridge and get this life over with?" Yes, you could say I was a bit angry. (Later in this chapter, there are additional comments addressing suicidal tendencies.)

Several months later, I joined this friend and several others on his 48-foot motor sailer for a four-day trip to the Dry Tortugas, a small group of islands west of the southern tip of Florida in the Gulf of America. One evening we encountered strong, gusty winds creating six-foot swells. The fuming seas mirrored the fuming anger inside me. As the boat crashed up and down the waves, I ventured onto the pulpit area, the narrow walkway that extends out over the water at the front tip of the boat. Gripping onto the handrails on each side, I rode the rocking waves like I was on a wild bull in an arena. Defiantly, I shook my fist, daring the waves to knock me off. My anger had encountered an experience that matched its intensity. It was both terrifying and satisfying.

Now that I've confessed that I could have been the poster child for expressions of anger, let's try to understand a little about the emotions that grip all of us.

- First, emotions, including anger, are neither right nor wrong; they're amoral. How we deal with them is a moral choice.
- Feelings come from thoughts. Therefore, if we're angry, it's important that we get to the thoughts that are the source of the anger. Usually they're thoughts like, "This isn't fair." Or "My life, this whole situation, is totally out of control." Note that though feelings are neither right nor wrong, thoughts can be accurate or inaccurate. Anger driven by inaccurate beliefs can be problematic. Anger is an umbrella emotion. That is, there are other feelings that lie beneath it, feelings like fear, frustration, and shame.

- Then there's the obvious: When powerful emotions arise, our capacity to think clearly diminishes, leading us to act irrationally.

Most people process anger in one of three ways: they repress it, they let it explode, or they deal with it in a healthy way. While no single process describes how any particular person always deals with anger, most people do have a default approach.

❖ **Repressing anger**

First, some people repress anger. They bury it. This is sometimes referred to as "stuffing" the anger. Repressing anger can be a way of denying the reality of a situation. It can also be a way of trying to appear as the "innocent" victim who "doesn't get angry." But like unseen mold growing in a basement, repressed anger can eventually make you sick—sick as in oversleeping, underachieving, becoming accident-prone, developing phobias, or obsessively eating, dieting, or cleaning. Another possible outcome is that repressed anger can slowly fester into passive-aggressive behaviors such as the "silent treatment" or "flight," succumbing to the urge to run away from the pain. What's worse, repressed anger can eventually propel a person into "fight," the next, more malevolent way of dealing with rage.

❖ **Exploding anger**

The second way of dealing with anger is by exploding: making targets of people or things. Why? To try to exert control, or to project superiority, or to broadcast hurt. While exploding may feel like a cathartic release, its short-term gratification often comes with a high price tag to be paid later.

One form of exploding is cutting down another person with words. And one variety of cutting down is blaming: "You always" or "You never." Another variety is gossiping. "Can you believe what she said?"

Some angry people put their fists through walls, throw things, succumb to road rage, kick the dog, or worse yet, hit someone. Fortunately, there are ways to vent explosive anger before it erupts in physical and verbal outbursts. In fact, anger can actually be healthy if it's dealt with properly. The problem is that most of us have had few (if any) examples of how to work out anger in a healthy way, and therefore may consciously or subconsciously doubt that that's even a possibility.

That was true for me. Although I wasn't consciously aware of it, at some level I believed that anger was always "bad," and that was how I treated it. When my ex got angry, I began to shut down and withdraw. I didn't trust her anger, and I didn't trust mine. So rather than try to engage and learn from our anger, I disengaged. This usually served only to fuel my ex's anger. My disengagement was essentially rejection. I was wrongly insisting that, "Anger is not okay, so when you're angry, *you* are not okay."

Since those days, I've learned how anger can be dealt with in more constructive ways.

- Take responsibility for your anger; own it. It's your anger, no one else's. Know what triggers it. Avoid or plan for times that have historically ignited it. Devise strategies for how to best manage those times. This is especially important during and after a divorce. Estranged spouses know each other's triggers and can use that "military intelligence" to their own advantage. Anger can be a powerful tool for manipulation. But you can be the one who breaks this tit-for-tat cycle, so it doesn't fuel vicious debates and adversely affect any children.

- Get in touch with the source of your anger. What are the deeper emotions and beliefs that your anger stems from? Present anger can be tapping into unresolved past injustices, amplifying the present reaction. This leaves those around you wondering why you're "overreacting" when your expression of anger isn't commensurate to the present circumstance. Resolving old injustices can make anger management around current events much more doable. So, examine the sources of your anger and talk about them with a trusted person or perhaps with a counselor who's skilled with anger management.

- Channel your anger's energy. Anger stimulates adrenalin, and adrenalin needs to be physically worked out of your body. Counselors call this "emotional flooding"—a good word picture. For some, anger can ignite so quickly and with such intensity that taking a break and seeking physical expression for it needs to happen quickly. What are constructive physical outlets that can use up unwanted adrenalin? Some examples would be exercise, gardening, yardwork, walking, biking, hiking, and swimming.

Because I'd worked for a tree company while I was in college, I started a tree cutting/trimming service during my divorce to earn some extra money. (Divorce is hard on the wallet, right?) What I didn't realize was how much of a stress-relieving endeavor this work would be. I actually found it satisfying to burn pent-up energy by cutting down trees. Is there something you can begin doing to relieve stress and maybe even make some extra cash?

Explosions of anger take on different forms for different temperaments. In contrast to the physicality of my chainsaw approach, here's one example of how a leader in the Divorce & Beyond ministry vented her anger in a letter to a metropolitan newspaper.

Faulting No-Fault

Thank you for the article titled, When the Ex-Spouse Is a Real Louse: Former Spouse Find Courts Guilty.

It's sad when your spouse deserts and abandons you, but now the legal system deserts you also. The courts don't care if your spouse cheated, abused, or destroyed your life, because states now have a statute for "no fault divorce."

In layman's terms, your spouse can leave you, and all the court says is the magical words, "This marriage is irretrievably broken." No witnesses, testimony, or proof required to validate that statement.

Two people must mutually agree to marry. No one can make someone marry against his or her will. So why should someone be forced into a divorce?

This country has taken away your right and dignity to remain in a marriage if you choose. They've taken a valued institution and made it a farce. We wonder why over 50% of marriages end in divorce. A more appropriate vow in marriage should be, "Until death do you part, or until the grass looks greener on the other side." And don't worry, the court will support you with that.

Note that the writer of this opinion piece was criticizing the court system – and only subtly attacking her ex. As I'll say in the Forgiveness chapter, attacking your ex is never a good idea.

❖ **Expressing anger in a healthy way**

There's a third option for dealing with anger rather than repressing it or letting it explode: You can express your anger in healthy ways. What are those ways?

- To God
  Primarily through Job and the Psalms (such as Job 10, Psalms 42, 88), I discovered that the biblical writers had no qualms about letting God know their anger and disappointment. I realized that God is "okay" with our anger, and that, in fact, God welcomes genuineness. God didn't reject the psalmists, and He wouldn't reject me. But as illustrated by the psalmists, anger with God needs to be a dialogue, not a one-way rant. Express your anger, but then pause and listen. You may not always sense a response. That's okay. Over time you will.

  Although my anger has diminished now, it's fair to say that I was angry with God for a number of years. I had a very difficult time letting go of my disappointment with Him. I thought He should have intervened differently, not only on my behalf, but also on behalf of my children and other people who were bearing the consequences of the demise of my marriage. However, even though it took years, I learned that God was patient with me. He understood me. He understood my anger and responded mostly with a graceful, listening ear—but also with truth.

- To Yourself (Changing the story I tell myself))
  We all have inner dialogues: "stories we tell ourselves" that are usually silent but can sometimes be voiced out loud. Anger usually magnifies and fuels negative mental expressions. Rehearsing and believing this negative self-talk takes you on a downward path that, over time, can become a well-worn path, even a rut. It requires decisive action to halt this spiral and speak truth to yourself, about yourself, others, and the situation. Review the "constructive ways" of dealing with your anger that are listed above and apply them to these inner dialogues.

  Below in stage four, Depression, I'll discuss what's called "the S Method" of dealing with negative thoughts. Utilizing that S Method will be critical to healing your anger.

- Through physical activity
Our emotions trigger a hormonal response. Even after we rationally speak truth to ourselves, our body can continue to process the emotions physically. Therefore, it's vital to address the impact anger has on our physiology.

    I mentioned this previously, but its value can't be overstated: Plan regular outlets for your pent-up hormonal responses. For example, I played racquetball, and I scheduled matches with several partners every week. Sometimes I cared very little about who won; I just wanted to hit that small round ball as hard as I could. At times, my partners suffered the consequences with welts on their backs or legs—evidence of me just whacking the ball rather than placing it.

- With significant friends
It can be helpful to verbalize your anger to a very few trustworthy, emotionally mature people with whom your conversations make you healthier. These need to be people who can balance grace and truth—people who know when and how to effectively listen, and also when to "speak the truth in love." Meet with them regularly. Schedule your talks in advance so they're not jeopardized by the whims of whether or not you "feel like talking."

    During my own divorce recovery, I met regularly with two good friends, Barry Long, and Mark Snyder, both of whom had excellent emotional IQs. We'd meet for lunch, play sports, and hang out with their families. It was cathartic and healing. They would empathize, challenge, encourage, provide feedback, and pray with me. Friendships that accompany you through this scarring ordeal will likely be forged in stone. The bonds that are formed in these emotional trenches are life-changing and life-long. I'll be forever grateful for these two friends. "The soothing tongue is a tree of life" (Prov. 15:4).

- With the person involved
Sometimes, an opportunity arises when both you and your ex are ready to listen to each other and learn. If that happens spontaneously, it's usually because it's related to children. Less often, it may be related to actually wanting to understand one another. In any case, if that opportunity does arise, determine some ground rules that you both agree to uphold. Your informal rules should insist on the use of "I statements" rather than "you statements." For example, "I felt ignored" would be a lot less combative than "You ignored me." Your rules should also call for "reflective listening"–a commitment to understand before trying, or more likely demanding, to be understood. You can demonstrate that you're really listening if each of you objectively rephrases what the other has said and then asks if your restatement is correct. Major in asking questions and then listening without interrupting. Above all, agree to respect each other even if there is disagreement.

It would also be wise to agree upon a specific length of time for your conversation. Keep the first (and maybe only) conversation short, like 15 minutes. Even if it seems to be going well, end it at the designated time. You can then agree to have a follow-up conversation, perhaps for 30 minutes.

Finally, it may be advisable to invite a mutually agreed-upon third party—a mature, trusted friend, pastor, or counselor—to sit in on your conversation. If you decide to do that, you and your ex should specify the exact role of this third party. It would definitely not be an appropriate role of any third party to take sides. Perhaps the most important role of the third party would be to help both of you adhere to the ground rules you've agreed on and refrain from blowing up. In addition, you may mutually decide that a role of the third party is to help both of you clarify your thoughts, or to help both of you understand what the other is saying.

Frankly, even when you're sincerely looking for a chance to mutually express hurt and disappointment in a healthy way, that may not seem possible. Perhaps it will at another time. But if it doesn't, that's okay. Let it go. We'll address this whole issue more fully in this book's chapter on forgiveness.

Questions to Ponder:

1. Are you more likely to repress anger or explode with anger?

2. Which of the healthy ways of expressing anger is strongest for you? Which one do you want to improve upon?

The Valley, Stage 3: Bargaining—Trying to force changes

Bargaining is a defense against the feelings of helplessness experienced after a loss. It happens when people struggle to accept the reality of the loss and the limits of their control over the situation.

Bargaining results in a spoken or unspoken negotiation between parties to settle what each gives or receives in a relationship. In the contentious context of divorce, I call it "Let's Make a Deal... in which I win." The bargaining stage of a divorce is most often a mixture of anger (blaming others and/or the circumstances and wanting them changed) and depression (blaming yourself and wanting yourself to change). Most commonly, bargaining in a divorce is based on "measuring cup love"—a conditional love that always measures what I get against what I give. People going through a divorce try to bargain in a variety of ways, but their basic attitude can usually be described as, "Take what I can; give only what I must." And once bargaining is tolerated, it usually begets more bargaining. This transactional style of relating, especially if it feels successful, can quickly become a pattern with negative consequences. It can seem like a way to control and even get back at an ex-spouse. But it will prove to be unproductive.

Basically, bargaining tries to maintain as much control of our lives and circumstances as possible. We attempt to manipulate the other side and force changes—which in reality will only cause more problems. Typically, bargaining is combined with the use of guilt.

- "If you cared about the kids, you would agree to let me keep the house."
- "If you want a civil relationship, then you need to do this my way."
- "If you want extra time with the kids, then you need to increase your child support."

We can also try to bargain with God.

- "If you work this out (the way I want it), I'll start going back to church."
- "I'll end the affair if you get me my job back."

Bargaining with God will be a very frustrating experience. Think about it: Do you really have any bargaining chips with the all-knowing God? Yet in our desire to blame, even God is usually not spared.

The healthier alternative to all these forms of bargaining is to recognize that it's simply ineffective to try to leverage another person into changing, or to leverage the circumstances to your advantage. Trying to do so usually makes the other person aggravated and makes us emotionally sick. It's more productive to simply accept them as they are and do everything you can to work toward a mutually beneficial solution.

Despite all that, though, there may be a few narrowly defined circumstances in which bargaining can be healthy. Those circumstances involve applying leverage in the best interests of everyone concerned.

- "If you'll go with me to a counselor to help both of us learn better parenting skills, then I'll consider an amended visitation schedule."

- "Can we trade weekends? I'd like to take the kids to see their grandpa on his birthday."
- "If you want to pursue reconciliation, then would you agree to being guided by our pastor?"

Questions to Ponder:

1. What unhealthy bargains or "deals" do you try to make?

2. What healthy ones have you tried, or would you like to try?

The Valley, Stage 4: Depression—Turning anger inward

The Bible speaks of depression as the "soul cast down," a descriptive word picture (Psalm 42:5 NRSV). There are many forms of depression. In the context of divorce, I'll be referencing depression as a form of anger turned in toward ourselves.

The loss of someone we once loved is crushing, even suffocating. Often there's also a loss of relationships with family and friends. When you're walking in numbness, it's a struggle to make it through each day. How do you go on after such a great loss? Does the aching ever stop? Will grieving and mourning continue forever? Like George Bailey in *It's A Wonderful Life©*, you may feel that you're "at the end of your rope." It wasn't part of the movie script, but when Jimmy Stewart said Bailey's prayer, which was simply, "Help me," his eyes filled with tears. Stewart said that as he muttered Bailey's prayer, it broke him as he "felt the hopelessness of people who had nowhere to turn." Likewise, David in Psalm 109 was at the end of his rope: "poor and needy," his "heart ... wounded," (v.22), and his body "thin and gaunt" (v. 24). He was fading "like an evening shadow" (v. 23) and sensed himself to be an "object of scorn" in the eyes of his accusers (v. 25). A good friend once advised me, "When you reach the end of your rope, tie a knot and hang on to God."
As this verse illustrates, at this point in your journey, it's critical to be aware of your self-talk. For example, there are four types of phrases that are prevalent in the stories people tell themselves while going through divorce.

❖ **I am not okay.**
The first form of destructive self-talk is saying, in effect, "I am not okay." When we do that, we devalue ourselves: "I'm a failure. What's the use? My ex is right, I'm a jerk." Rejection and heartbreak from the person with whom you made lifetime promises will often result in all-time record lows of your self-image. Those promises you made and received opened you up to deep vulnerability, and when they're broken, the resulting pain can feel nearly unbearable. Sometimes in our darkest moments we give in and judge ourselves as worthless.

Become adept at spotting your negative thoughts, choosing to stop them, standing against them, substituting thoughts that are true and seeking others to help you. This is called the *S Method*, named after five key "S" words: *spotting, stopping, standing, substituting* and *seeking*. It is explained in more detail on pgs. 183-184. (I didn't invent it, and I'm not sure whom to credit for it.). Grow into an expert at speaking the truth to yourself, such as that expressed by the Apostle John when he wrote, "See what kind of love the Father has given to us [you] in that we [you] should be called God's children, and that is what we [you] are!" And then as if anticipating the frailty of our hearts, he adds, "This is how we will know that we belong to the truth and reassure our hearts in God's presence. Even if our hearts condemn us, God is greater than our hearts and knows all things" (1 John 3:1, 19-20 CEB).

Even though you may feel like a failure, it's imperative that you spot the moment you speak that to yourself, choose to stop it, stand against it, and substitute truth about yourself. If you have difficulty thinking of additional truths, then ask family and friends to help you.

The woman named "Anne" (whom I mentioned earlier) described her battle like this:

I went into a depression that seemed inescapable. At the end of every work week, as I pulled away from the office, I could feel myself sinking. I had a few days before I had to motivate myself to care again. How sad. The weekends were sooo long. I tried to stay busy with grocery shopping, paying bills, and sometimes having coffee with a friend. Still, mustering the energy I needed to pull off the covers and step out of bed was exhausting. On more than one occasion, I ignored my to-do list, cancelled coffee plans, and stayed in my pajamas all day with covers pulled up to my chin.

One day I texted my supervisor, 'I'm sorry I need to take the day off. I'm not feeling well.' My supervisor sent back a sympathetic text. Then I decided to be honest: 'The pain is simply too hard to hide.' That's what I'd been doing: hiding my sorrow, my depression.

One morning, curled up in my blankets, I said a prayer: 'Lord, I don't want to be depressed.' I sensed a reply: 'Start by walking.' I used to have some good exercise habits, including walking. By this point, I'd reached an unhealthy weight again, but walking seemed doable. Those words, 'Start by walking' spoke to me right where I was. Depressed. Unable to move. Overweight. The words penetrated deeply.

That day, I renewed my membership in a gym that had a walking track, and I walked— more slowly than in previous years, but I walked. I felt a change. I felt a lift, which was exactly what I needed. It began with three little words: 'Start by walking.'

Depression has its physical symptoms such as a loss of appetite or a craving for unhealthy foods, tiredness or no energy at all, excessive sleep or lack of sleep, trouble concentrating or focusing, loss of interest in fun activities, or compulsions for alcohol, work, drugs, sex, and the like.

Physical health can be a pathway to mental health. That's why "Anne" could state that she "felt a change, a lift" after she started walking. So, ask yourself, "What can I do physically to fortify my mental health?" The list of possibilities is as long as people's varied interests. The key is to find those that fit who you are, and it's even better if you can sometimes do them with a friend. Here are some suggestions to consider. What are two or three that fit you?

- Biking
- Hiking
- Running
- Lifting weights
- Paddle boarding
- Kayaking/canoeing
- Rock climbing
- Skiing – water or snow
- Swimming

- Tennis
- Racquetball or squash
- Basketball
- Pickleball

Any other fitness activities that get your heart pumping can help. Or choose less intense activities such as:

- Gardening
- Washing your car
- Walking
- Yoga
- Fishing
- Painting
- Pottery
- Playing a musical instrument

Any physical activity that gets you off the couch and moving can help improve your mood. If you think you're not doing enough, circle the activities that you could begin.

In a Mayo Clinic article dated September 27, 2017,[8] researchers wrote that regular exercise may help ease depression and anxiety by:

- Releasing feel-good endorphins, natural cannabis-like brain chemicals (endogenous cannabinoids) and other natural brain chemicals that can enhance your sense of well-being.
- Taking your mind off worries so you can get away from the cycle of negative thoughts that can feed depression and anxiety.

Regular exercise has many other psychological and emotional benefits too.

- Exercise can help you gain confidence. Meeting exercise goals or challenges, even small ones, can boost your self-confidence. Getting in shape can also make you feel better about your appearance.
- Exercise can help you get more social interaction. Exercise and physical activity may give you the chance to meet or socialize with others. Just exchanging a friendly smile or greeting as you walk around your neighborhood can help your mood.
- Exercise can help you cope in a healthy way. Doing something positive to manage depression or anxiety is a healthy coping strategy. Trying to feel better by drinking

[8] Mayo Clinic Staff, "Depression and Exercise," *Mayo Clinic*, accessed June 18, 2025, https://www.mayoclinic.org/diseases-conditions/depression/in-depth/depression-and-exercise/art-20046495

alcohol, dwelling on how you feel, or hoping depression or anxiety will go away on its own can lead to worsening symptoms.

❖ **My situation is not okay.**

A second phrase that's common in unhelpful self-talk is some variation on, "My circumstances are not okay." By saying such things, we devalue our situation. Of course, in divorce there will always be circumstances that are not okay. They require focus to figure out if they are solvable or not, and if they are, how. But when the tragedy of divorce overwhelms and its grief glares you in the face, life can loom before you like a bottomless pit. Then we tend to get stuck, and that throws our negative self-talk about our situation into overdrive.

- "My ex is unbearable."
- "Life is just miserable. It's been unfairly stolen from me."
- "My job is demeaning. It's a dead end, leading to nowhere. My boss is clueless and uncaring."
- "The kids blame me. My ex blames me. My family blames me. Even my friends blame me."

Mark Lutz, former growth and healing pastor at Vineyard Cincinnati, has sometimes referred to this behavior as "awfulizing." True, a situation may be painful—but painful can still be manageable. When I describe my situation in the extreme, my language implies that the situation is impossible, and I lose my motivation to work on it.

A man named "Ted" who attended one of our seminars described the trap this way:
I remember waking up with the heaviness of my divorce. As the tears fell, I would iron them into my dress shirt. I thought to myself, 'I'm wearing my grief everywhere I go.' I spent many days in my office feeling hopeless, lonely, and in shock. One day it was too much for me, and I had to get up and go for a walk. I told God, 'I don't think I can do this. You have to help me.' I walked and prayed for about 30 minutes. When I returned to my office, I noticed that someone had left a card on my desk that contained the verse from Isaiah 41:10: 'Do not fear, for I am with you; be not dismayed for I am your God. I will strengthen you and help you; I will uphold you with my righteous right hand'. I got a strong sense that God was listening to me.

When I introduced myself at the beginning of this book, I mentioned that I was a pastor when my wife filed for divorce. For more than six years, I'd been the youth and young adult pastor at a large church. A few weeks after she filed the divorce papers, my ex leveled some accusations defaming my character. As my credibility was questioned, my ministry was too. My senior pastor asked me to resign. I was hurt and incensed. When I refused, he responded that he would recommend my termination. It was a bold gamble for me, but I believed it would be wrong for me to resign and, in effect, plead guilty to the unfounded assertions against me, so I still refused to resign. Surprisingly, the leaders of the church voted against my termination. But three months later, I resigned anyway, realizing that, emotionally and spiritually, I was struggling too deeply and unable to adequately lead. I could see no light at the end of this tunnel. My situation did indeed seem bleak. And by constantly saying to myself, "My circumstances are not okay," I devalued the positives that I still had.

❖ **My forever is not okay.**
When our self-talk includes laments along the lines of "My forever is not okay," we devalue not only the positives that we still have, but also our prospects for the future. Part of this sentiment is a fear of the unknown, the oldest and strongest emotion of mankind. It feeds hopelessness. For example, we might think:

- "My whole life sucks, and it'll never change. It's going down the toilet fast, and it'll never get better."
- "I'll always be unwanted and alone."

This particular form of self-talk can culminate in suicidal thoughts. Often, depression feels like a huge sense of hopelessness, a sense of desperation, unlike anything you've encountered before. I recall months of feeling like I was in a dark tunnel with no visible rays of light in sight, and there was a specific occasion that starkly portrayed how I felt. On that same four-day boating trip that I described earlier, as we were returning, I was in charge of monitoring the autopilot steering during the 3-6am shift. Beyond any sight of the mainland in the Gulf of America, the wind was gusty, and the night was pitch black. The scene eerily matched my life. The lyrics of a song came to mind: "The darkest hour is just before dawn." And as dawn did break over the horizon, I wondered, "Will that ever occur in my life?" Those same types of haunting thoughts are what had made me race my red Trans Am through the hills and ravines of Kentucky thinking, "What the hell! Why don't I just drive off this bridge!" The fears, loneliness, and desperation of my heart were crying out for help, no, really for a rescue.

So, yes, along with being angry, I was depressed for about six months. It affected my sleep, which then affected my awake time. My energy for anything was depleted. Finally, desperate, I went to my doctor who prescribed medication to help me sleep. I started going to counseling, and I formed a small group, meeting every other week. Both provided invaluable support. Both helped me see through the dense thicket of lies I was believing. Some fresh air began to circulate through my mind and heart. Slowly I began to climb out of the pit of depression.

Perhaps you are out of ideas, strength, or hope. If depression has intensified to the point of suicidal thoughts, it's essential to address it immediately. These steps are a vital beginning.

- Call the suicide hotline: 988. Someone should always be available to answer, listen, and talk.
- Go to the nearest emergency room where a trained professional can assist you.

- Schedule an appointment with your doctor and be straightforward that it's regarding suicidal thoughts so the scheduler doesn't respond with something like, "The doctor's next available time slot is in three weeks."
- Then schedule an appointment with a counselor, and if you don't know one, ask a trusted professional (like the doctor you just scheduled, a pastor, or the attorney you're working with) for a referral.
- Beyond that, share your suicidal thoughts with your most trusted friend(s), and at the same time, look for a support group that focuses on divorce, grief, or trauma recovery.

❖ **God is not okay.**

The fourth common type of "not okay" self-talk is any variation on "God is not okay." When we start thinking like this, God becomes another "person" from whom we want to withdraw or blame. Depending on the baggage you carry in life, this can manifest itself in many ways. One way is feeling like God has abandoned you, so why should you care about Him? Another evidence of this kind of thinking is the feeling that God is blaming you. Of course, that sense introduces an immense amount of guilt, so you just try to escape and hide from God. Or perhaps you start feeling like God is saying, "It's payback time," and He doesn't understand what your ordeal is doing to you. A final possibility is to conclude that God just doesn't exist. Note that this "conclusion" is not actually a mental, rational conclusion, but rather a reaction to emotional pain. In my experience, most atheists are wounded theists.

In my own case, I was not okay with what God was allowing. Some people told me my life reminded them of Job's. While Job's losses were far greater than mine and I had better friends, in some respects I did feel a bit Job-like. My marriage was in ruins, my relationship with my children was very wounded, and my career was in ashes. I felt neglected by God and extremely disappointed by how He'd allowed my life, my ministry, and particularly my children to suffer like this. All the same, at least most of the time, I continued going to the church I'd resigned from, and I knew there were people there who still cared about me and prayed for me. I longed to experience some kind of reconnection with God, something that could break through my disappointment with Him. But worship felt hollow. Sermons seemed unsatisfactory. Most of the time, as soon as the church service ended, I hurried to return to my lonely apartment. In actuality, though, the worship and sermons and fellowship were still the same high quality they'd always been, and I had to admit that it was me who had changed.

The next Easter weekend, I was out of town visiting my grandmother. By that time, my grandfather had "graduated", so Grandma and I were both lonely, and we valued each other's company. On Good Friday, I was yearning for spiritual refreshment. I picked out a local church service and sat by myself in the back with no real expectations. Perhaps it was being at an unfamiliar church. Perhaps the timing of that service happened to meet an open crack in my heart. Perhaps the fact that it was Good Friday made a difference. Perhaps the pastor spoke with unusual insight. Perhaps. But in any case, the service and the message resonated with me. The theme was rejection and how Jesus experienced it many times in the final 24 hours of His life.

- The rejection by His twelve closest friends – one who outright betrayed Him, another who outright denied Him (not once but three times), and the other ten who for the most part abandoned Him.

- The rejection by the crowds who, just five days earlier, had welcomed Him into Jerusalem, praising Him, waving palm branches, and placing them on the road before Him.

- The rejection by those He loved and would love through His dying breath.

- And finally, in the greatest rejection of all, His Abba Father turned away from Him until it was "finished."

Here the rejection reaches a peak as Jesus, in the midst of unimaginable suffering, quotes Psalm 22:1, "My God, my God, why have you forsaken me?" He cries out on behalf of all who have wondered about the caring presence of God, all who have felt forsaken, even abandoned in soul clenching darkness. Jesus could only choke out these nine words, but the verse continues, "Why are you so far from saving me, so far from my cries of anguish? My God, I cry out by day, but you do not answer, by night, but I find no rest" (Psalm 22:1-2).

Hundreds of years earlier, the prophet Isaiah had predicted the whole scene precisely: "He was despised, and rejected of men; a man of sorrows, and acquainted with grief: and as one from whom men hide their face he was despised; and we esteemed him not.... and with his stripes we are healed" (Isaiah 53:3,5, ASV). Slowly it began to sink in. God, in Jesus, experienced immeasurably more rejection than I did or ever could. I realized afresh that I could identify with a God who was willing to suffer and be rejected. He fully understood my heartache and, in fact, embraced it with His. In addition, He chose to be rejected, humiliated, shamed because of His love for those who rejected Him, including me. And in the midst of it, Jesus, with nails in His wrists and feet, trusted the Father. The continuation of Psalm 22 captures it explicitly, "Yet you are enthroned as the Holy One." The message penetrated my wounded soul. The amazement and wonder of it all massaged my being. I chose to begin the journey "to be at home with my Father." I began to sense the assurance that David sensed when he faced great uncertainty: "When my spirit grows faint within me, it is you who watch over my way" (Psalm 142:3).

Now, before we leave this discussion of the depression phase of divorce, I need to point out that when it's properly harnessed, depression can actually be helpful.[9] Whether depression is helpful or harmful depends on how we deal with it. It's unhealthy when we turn it on ourselves and begin to tear down our self-image. But it can be helpful when it shows us the destructive things we've done so we can correct them. *Heartbreak has a way of exposing pretenses.* It can open an opportunity for us to examine the baggage we're

---

[9] "10 Ways Depression Can Be Good for You," *Psych Central,* November 9, 2021.

carrying—to chip away at past wounds and hardness of heart. So, if you're experiencing some level of depression, why not allow it to speak to you, to force hard questions. Let it reveal how you've allowed your former spouse to define your worth—how you've allowed someone (or something) to be the hinge upon which your self-image has been swinging, intensifying your heartbreak. Let depression bring it to the surface where you can deal with it. If you find this overwhelmingly challenging, then again, a licensed therapist can provide valuable assistance.

Strategies that can help with depression have been sprinkled throughout this section. On the following pages, there are some fun ideas to supplement what you've already read. My favorite is No. 37! Once you've read through the list, circle the ones you're going to start, and post those on your fridge. Don't wait until you feel motivated enough to try these ideas; try them until you start feeling motivated.

60 WAYS TO CLIMB OUT OF YOUR RUT...

1) Seek out a new friend or friend group.
2) Visit a local place you've never been to before.
3) Cultivate a new hobby.
4) Take a class.
5) Wear something different.
6) Read a different magazine.
7) Try a food you've never tried before.
8) Go to bed an hour earlier and wake up an hour earlier.
9) Take a new route home.
10) Use green or turquoise ink pens for informal correspondence.
11) Take a walk instead of watching TV.
12) Give a "difficult person" in your life a sincere compliment.
13) Look through a mail-order or online catalogue and send someone a present.
14) Leave for work 10 minutes early and let people cut in front of you in traffic.
15) Drop a social activity you don't particularly like anymore.
16) Get a double-dip ice cream cone.
17) Change toothpaste.
18) Send a silly card to someone.
19) Browse in a bookstore.
20) Go to a junk shop.
21) Buy a new wallet.
22) Don't follow the news for seven days.
23) Attend services at a different church/synagogue/temple.
24) Change parking spaces.
25) Sleep on the other side of the bed.
26) Write a letter.
27) Get a therapeutic massage.
28) Do something you've always wanted to do but have postponed.
29) Join a health club
30) Enroll in a weight-loss program.

31) Stop smoking for seven days.

32) Put a funny cartoon at someone's desk.

33) Redecorate.

34) Rearrange the furniture.

35) Volunteer at a church, a shelter, a soup kitchen, school, or whatever.

36) Laugh. Watch a comedy or a TV series that you've previously enjoyed.

37) Switch the toilet paper so it unrolls the other way.

38) Try a new kind of cereal.

39) Take a 15-minute walk, or climb a few flights of stairs on your coffee break.

40) Drop a "lucky" $10 bill on the street and make someone's day.

41) Walk or jog on a new route.

42) Don't watch TV for a week.

43) Get your hair cut differently.

44) Begin a foreign language course.

45) Pick up some vacation travel brochures.

46) Give a coworker a pat on the back or verbal affirmation.

47) Visit a pet store or shelter.

48) Tell a joke. (A clean one!)

49) Buy a box of crayons and a coloring book to use to relieve stress, or to delay a refrigerator binge.

50) Try an exotic brand of coffee.

51) Ride to the end of a city bus line and back.

52) Play "tourist" for a day in your own town.

53) Buy a toy you've always wanted (but never got).

54) Buy a blank book and write down your thoughts.

55) Take a bath or shower by candlelight.

56) Turn off your music and enjoy the silence.

57) Take some flowers to nursing home residents.

58) Wash your car inside and out.

59) Buy your pet a new collar.

60) Keep adding to this list.[10]

---

[10] "60 Ways to Climb Out of Your Rut," Various sources.

Questions to Ponder:

1. How prevalent are each of the following in your mind?
   a) I am not okay.

   b) My circumstances are not okay.

   c) My forever is not okay.

   d) God is not okay.

2. What steps can you take to address the one that is the most prevalent?

3. If you have wrestled with suicidal thoughts, what steps would be helpful to take?

4. How could depression actually be helpful for you?

Part 3: The Crisis Cycle, Recovery
by Bill Koontz

Recovery, Stage 5: Perspective—Beginning to accept the changes

"Often when you think you're at the end of something,
you're at the beginning of something else."
— Fred Rogers[11]

This fifth stage of the divorce-recovery process is the beginning of accepting the changes that the divorce has triggered. In this Perspective Stage, you're no longer dominated by denial, anger, bargaining, or depression. Grappling with negative emotions continues, but they have less power. You're getting better at understanding the cyclical nature of grieving. While you'll probably still be surprised at times by your own mental and emotional swings, those swings will no longer hijack you. Rather, in this stage, you begin to see problems inherent to the divorce in their proper perspective. While the sense of loss may still be significant, a person in this stage no longer feels that all is lost.

Most likely, your divorce has resulted in some doors closing halfway or entirely. Dealing with that disappointment and hurt is part of the grieving. However, during the Perspective Stage, there's a dawning recognition of how the stress of divorce has shrunk your vision of life. And because of that realization, the tunnel vision that has narrowed your perspective begins to broaden. The protective shell that you forged to shield yourself from pain is cracking, and light is seeping through. There's a sense that a springtime of sorts is unfolding.

In fact, spring is a good metaphor for the Perspective Stage. Those of us who have four seasons in a year can appreciate that. As I write this, here in southwestern Ohio, it's currently spring. Some days are still cold, but even those are definitely warmer than most of the winter days have been. There's still the occasional surprise of snow, sleet, or freezing rain, but again less often than in the winter. There are new beginnings emerging: flowers blooming, trees budding, grass greening, birds chirping. Walks are becoming more frequent. There's fresh air blowing. Bikes, boats and lawnmowers are getting prepared.

That's the way of the Perspective Stage. There's still work to be done. There are still cold, dreary days ahead, but the tide is turning, albeit slower than desired. Someone once said that "treasures are always buried." Perspective recognizes the truth of that statement and commences to search for the underground seeds that are about to sprout. From the ashes of previous dreams, possibilities begin to materialize in the heart. Serena Williams

---

[11] Fred Rogers, The World According to Mister Rogers: Important Things to Remember (London: Hachette UK, 2003), p. 39.

once said, "I really think a champion is defined, not by their wins, but by how they can recover when they fall."[12]

Glimpses of the five phases ahead (Healthy Relationships, Spiritual Awakening, Acceptance, Activity and Humor, and New Goals) are coming into view. Hope is no longer a foreign word. It may still be unfamiliar, but it's no longer foreign. The mind generates thoughts like, "I'm going to make it." The willingness to trust is resurfacing, and will lay the foundation for the next phase, Healthy Relationships.

The amount of time it takes to get to the Perspective Stage will vary and the timetable is never the same for any two people, but it's vital not to short-circuit the recovery and healing. It will come when the season is ready. Be patient. Give grace. In the meantime, continue to lean on the support of others.

Be aware that the phases that follow don't occur in a linear fashion. Numbering them is descriptive, not prescriptive. They're typically interwoven, each impacting the other. The health of one will positively affect the others, and vice versa. In that sense, they're never really completed. The tentacles of divorce stretch out for many years, and some will never completely dissolve, but that's not necessarily bad. Memories of divorce can begin to serve rather than haunt. For example, the memory of the hardship and heartache of divorce can strongly reinforce your commitment to healthier relational patterns. Likewise, memories of divorce can continue to provide motivation for counseling, and they can appropriately slow down the desire for a second marriage.

Questions to Ponder:

1. Does the Perspective Stage still seem like a long way off, or are there perhaps occasional glimpses of it? If so, what choices can you make to move closer to it?

2. Do you tend to compare your recovery progress with others? Who are they? Why do you make the comparison? Is that helping you?

---

[12] Fearless Motivation, "Push Yourself, Because No One Else Is Going to Do It for You," *FearlessMotivation.com*, October 5, 2016.

Recovery, Stage 6: Healthy Relationships

During my own divorce recovery, I was reluctant to join the singles groups that existed around our metropolitan area. For many months, I wouldn't accept my new "single" identity. I refused to attend singles events or groups because, for me, to go to a singles venue was to once again confront the failure of my marriage and be forced to accept my place in what I viewed as the second-rate category of "single again." So, at first, I refused to embrace the opportunities that awaited me, or to see the possibilities of new beginnings. But eventually, as I came out of the withdrawal and isolation that's inherent in the previous stages, a desire emerged to reconnect and relate to family, friends, and colleagues, and along with that desire came the hope of new relationships.

Most likely, as you've employed strategies to find support, one of those has been to accept the significant support of close friends (maybe new ones) and a group of others who are also traveling through the trauma of divorce. If so, you've had opportunities to tell your story. A man who I'll call "Tim" wrote this next story about his own experiences.

God is close to the broken hearts of those struggling through divorce. But when they go to places like church, they may feel unseen, unloved, and unsupported. I know I did. There I was—lonely and in pain—in the midst of thousands of people. A friend approached me numerous times and told me about Divorce & Beyond: 'I'm not pressuring you, but I think the seminar and a support group would really help you.' My response was pretty much the same each time. I lied, 'Thanks man, but I'm doing okay.' But over time, his kindness and persistence wore down my resolve and punctured the "safe" distance that I'd placed between myself and others. I finally broke down and went to the seminar. As it turned out, my friend was right. The seminar was helpful.

Next, I joined a support group. People in the group took turns sharing their divorce stories. Most of them cried. Others were in a state of shock. Some expressed anger. When it got around to me, I always passed. I thought, 'There's no way I'm sharing all of this with strangers. That's too much transparency for me.' Underneath that attitude was my fear that I'd be rejected—validating my belief that I was indeed unseen, unloved, and uncared for. This scenario repeated every time the group met until one night, I decided to tell these strangers (my new friends by this time) my story. I must have talked for a long time. When I looked up, many people were crying, others sat with their mouths wide open, and others looked like they were proud of me for sharing something so deep and painful. They came up one by one and hugged me. I realized in that moment that I was seen, loved, and cared for. In the years that followed, I served in various capacities in the Divorce & Beyond ministry, and God used that experience to continue to heal my heart while I helped others find healing for theirs.

Often, when new friendships spring from these support groups, they last for many years. Somewhat like the comradery among military veterans, friendships that are formed "in the trenches" develop deep bonds. It's a bond that's rooted in shared struggle—a bond among people who've survived the worst period of their lives and learned together, not only how to manage it, but how to thrive after it.

During this period of growth, relationships typically get healthier in other aspects of life as well. Wrestling with the ways you've contributed to the breakdown of your marriage can yield insights that will influence the health of other relationships. For example, codependency in a marriage is rarely isolated to just the marriage. Dealing with it in one space can help you deal with it in other relationships as well. Similarly, when people recognize that they've been using manipulation to control outcomes and to protect themselves in marriage, they often discover that the same behavior patterns have been woven into the fabric of their other relationships with children, family members, and friends. It's beneficial to capitalize on these discoveries by applying new insights to all relationships.

In my own case, I'm quite capable of painting a picture that makes it sound like my divorce was entirely the fault of my ex. She could do the same, and so could you. But through uncomfortable introspection and reflection, I discovered how I too had contributed to the breakdown of our marriage. I realized that, from the turmoil and hurt that I'd experienced in my parents' marriage and divorce, I'd developed a fear of emotional intimacy. I instinctively avoided negative emotions and withdrew from conflict. How big of an impact do you think that had on my marriage? Hmm. How about Huge! I didn't even realize it, but at some level I had a deep fear of getting too close and exposing my own hurts. Consequently, I let unresolved conflicts pile up, and I didn't allow honest feedback and negative emotions to do their work in clearing out the obstructions that came between me and my wife. And these behavior patterns were obviously no recipe for success.

As I grappled with and repented of these patterns, I realized that they also affected my other relationships with family, friends, and colleagues. While I must admit that these tendencies still have some impact on me, their influence has diminished over the years. For example, in my workplaces, I've often supervised employees and volunteers. I've realized that I was seldom willing to give honest feedback to my coworkers because I believed it could harm my relationships with them and have negative repercussions on how they viewed me. But as I ventured into giving honest feedback (with grace and truth), I discovered that doing so actually brings health to these relationships, and it results in a freer mutual exchange of creative ideas.

Questions to Ponder:

1. Are you reluctant to engage in new relationships with other singles? Why?

2. How do you feel about being "single again"? Why do you feel that way? What do you think are the origins of those feelings?

3. Do you see any healthier relational patterns emerging with others? If so, what are they?

4. Is the depth of your relationships improving? If not, why not? If so, in what ways?

Recovery, Stage 7: Spiritual Renewal—Seeing God work things out for good

Romans 8:28 says, "We know that in all things God works for the good of those who love him, who have been called according to his purpose." Even though that was once a primary verse in my life, for a time, it was whited out in my spirit. For several years after my divorce, it was a verse that I refused to read because I would no longer acknowledge its truth. I was simply too angry and disappointed with God. Even to this day, in some situations I wonder how God is going to fulfill that promise, but I no longer hold it in disdain. On the contrary, that promise again holds a prominent place in my faith.

But coming to this place was a long journey—far longer than it needed to be—and it's not hard to understand why. My emotions created a barrier to honest dialogue with God. As I described earlier, I was angry and disgruntled with Him. I took greater control of my life because my trust in God was compromised and had diminished. My level of dependency on God shrank.

Previously, I've mentioned that grief narrows one's vision and perspective. That's not only true regarding the present and future, but also in how one views the past. For some time, my narrowed vision effectively blocked me from seeing the ways that God had intervened and demonstrated His character in my life. It retroactively clouded my previous experiences with Him.

Re-characterizing God is an ineffective way to cope with pain and disillusionment, but unfortunately, in varying degrees, this is a common way to react to overwhelming circumstances. In varying depths, seeds of doubt about the character of God are planted. He isn't good, trustworthy, faithful, just, or maybe even real. Eventually, these doubts can grow into lies because they seem more comfortable than the reality of who God is.

Proverbs 18:14 observes, "The human spirit can endure a sick body, but who can bear a crushed spirit?" (NLT). That described me. The circumstances of my divorce had crushed my spirit, and I wasn't able to bear it on my own. An untended crushed spirit will extract a payment. My crushed spirit resulted in an uncertain, fearful outlook toward my present and future. It was many months before I would open the dungeon of my crushed spirit to God and experience the promise of Psalm 34:18: "The Lord is close to the brokenhearted and saves those who are crushed in spirit."

Sadly, it wasn't just my own emotions that were hiding God's goodness from me. Other people joined in, some unknowingly, others willfully. Their words, tone of voice, body language, and actions formed a current that was difficult to swim against. That's why it's critical to surround yourself with friends and groups that exhibit a godly balance of grace and truth. Both of those elements are essential. A wise king once penned, "The soothing tongue is a tree of life, but a deceitful tongue crushes the spirit" (Proverbs 15:4). And what's more, "A word aptly spoken is like apples of gold in settings of silver" (Proverbs 25:11).

In addition to avoiding unhelpful relationships, be aware that you also have an unseen enemy working against you. In fact, his aim is to destroy you. Take it from Peter, who traveled with Jesus, became a leading spokesperson, and heard Jesus say to him, "Satan has asked to sift you as wheat" (Luke 22:31). Peter knew firsthand the schemes of the devil, and consequently he warns, "Be self-controlled and of sober mind. Your enemy the devil, prowls around like a roaring lion looking for someone to devour. Resist him, standing firm in the faith" (1 Peter 5:8-9a). Don't make things easier for him. Be alert to your vulnerabilities and his tactics to take advantage of them. Be aware that when you've been hammered by a divorce, you're not at your strongest. Ask others to pray for you and with you. Be vigilant, stand strong, be courageous. But don't fret about this. One verse after Peter warns us about the devil, he assures us, "The God of all grace, who called you to his eternal glory in Christ, after you have suffered a little while, will himself restore you and make you strong, firm, and steadfast" (1 Peter 5:10).

In my own case, the emotional journey of recovery eventually opened the vista of relating to the Father in a fuller way. Because of the depth of my disappointment in Him, I'd developed a tight hold on control, and the willingness to relinquish that control came slowly. In fact, the greater the feelings of disappointment, the more unnerving the letting go of control can be. It's common for people who've experienced the trauma of chaos to vow to themselves that they'll always keep their world under control in order to guarantee that they'll never suffer like that again. However, constantly trying to maintain control actually results in a *higher* level of anxiety, and ultimately, it just forces people to recognize that they've demanded the impossible of themselves. In order to experience recovery, it's imperative to renounce vows of control. The only question is when. Personally, I slowly realized that trying to maintain control brought dysfunctional results. It didn't make me into a better version of myself; it just made things worse. But God was patient with me. Rather than being angry and rejecting me, I think He was mostly just sad. And yet, His invitation to me was steadfast. He beckoned me to take steps of rebuilding trust in His goodness, provision, and love.

Slowly over the course of some months, and usually with a bit of reluctance, I began to acknowledge in worship and prayer that God could be trusted. I had to admit that He was and is "f, fa, faith, faithful." This change of heart wasn't easy. It was a choice—a choice that was rooted in the pages of a Book whose writers, spanning more than a millennium, had made the same choice in soul-searing, dramatic ways. As I made that choice over and over again, my feelings of disappointment began to subside, and my feelings toward God began to realign with the truth of who He really is. This in turn broadened the parameters of my experience with Him. It impacted my worship, the lens I viewed Scripture through, and the way I recalled God's faithfulness in the past. I realized that God had *never* abandoned me. Indeed, God was meeting me in the depths of my brokenness.

A woman whom I'll call "Jackie" describes her own spiritual awakening.

God began a renewal in my life by showing me how I contributed to my divorce. My expectations of my husband were so high he could never have met them.

Also, I thought a 'good wife' was an agreeable wife, not questioning my husband's thoughts, plans, or ideas. But now I know that attitude was a disservice to both of us. I should have had a voice. I should have come alongside my husband as a partner. I should have challenged and encouraged him to grow. I was a peacemaker and avoided all confrontations. God has shown me that that wasn't a healthy way to operate in a relationship.

My life had revolved around my husband. Now it revolves around God. The Lord has reminded me that I'm his daughter, and my identity isn't in my job, or in being a wife and mother, but in being God's child.

Now I wear a pendant around my neck with the inscription 'El Roi,' one of the names of the Lord that means, 'The God who sees me.' After my divorce, I needed that constant reminder. I know now: He sees me!

Psalm 147:3 is the theme scripture of Divorce & Beyond: "[God] heals the brokenhearted and binds up their wounds." When have you been "brokenhearted" in the past? Did God "bind up your wounds?" God still fixes broken hearts today.

About *twelve* years after my divorce, I had a particularly significant experience of God's healing. I was invited to a retreat by my very good friend, Dick Towner. In the evening, we watched a potter make and shape a pottery jar. It was very moving as we were invited to interpret what we were observing as a metaphor for how God had shaped and was still shaping our lives. The potter was in no hurry. Rather, as the wheel rotated, she patiently smoothed the clay, casting aside any unwanted excess. When cracks and defects inevitably appeared in the vessel that the potter was forming, she placed her hands over them to restore its shape. As we watched this process, worship music played softly in the background. Scriptures were read. Gazing at the spectacle, I reminisced back through my life, abruptly stopping when memories of my divorce flooded my mind. Hitting the pause button, I stayed there, slowly replaying the events and feelings of that period, experiencing what's been called "lingering with what provokes/rankles/piques you." Even after years and years of countless tears, I wept again. But this time, the tears were a mixture of sadness and thankfulness. The Holy Spirit massaged my spirit, and I took yet another step of healing.

At the conclusion of that retreat, someone read the Bible passage where God instructs Jeremiah, "Go down to the potter's house, and there I will give you my message" (Jeremiah 18:2). This thought came to me, "You, Lord, are the potter, and we are the clay. We're all the work of your hands." But this verse, verse 4, washed over me: "But the pot he was shaping from the clay was marred in his hands; so, the potter formed it into another pot, shaping it as seemed best to him." God can reshape us even when we're marred or broken. He, the Master Potter, can and is willing to create new and precious pottery from our shattered pieces. God doesn't look at our broken lives, mistakes, and past sins as unusable material. Instead, He smooths out our fragmented pieces and reshapes them as He sees best. Even in our brokenness, we have immense value to our Master Potter. In

His hands, the broken pieces of our lives can be reshaped into beautiful vessels that He can use. Loss and pain don't have the final word. In fact, our relationship with God can actually deepen as a result of having lived, survived, and even thrived through the experience of divorce. God desires to redeem what has been broken.

Reflect on your divorce experience. Then read the last two paragraphs again. And then again. Soak them in. Let the Spirit wash over you. Shed some tears. Heal some more.

Finally, here are some Psalms that were helpful to me as I meandered through the trials and travails of divorce. My prayer is that you'll also find solace, wisdom, encouragement, and strength in Psalms 13, 23, 25, 27, 30, 31, 32, 34, 42, 51, 57, 86, 130, 139, 141, 142, and 143—not all at once, of course.

As you explore these psalms, here's a helpful approach that comes from the American Bible Society.[13]

- Pray, "God, I desire to connect with you, as I seek you in your Word."
- Read the selected section of Scripture slowly. Take note of intriguing words and phrases and read them a second time.
- Reflect on what strikes you as you read. Think through what God is communicating to you at this point in your life.
- Respond to the passage. Speak to God directly about what's on your mind and heart. Look for ways to live out what you've uncovered.

Questions to Ponder:

1. Did your relationship with God deteriorate leading up to and during your divorce or did it get closer? Why was that?

2. As you think of yourself as a "potter's vessel," how would you describe the current state of your pot?

3. How do you think God is shaping you?

4. Which of these psalms stand out most to you? Why?

[13] American Bible Society, *Uncover the Word* (Philadelphia, PA: American Bible Society)
Philadelphia, PA 19106-2155
Phone: 215.309.0900

Recovery, Stage 8: Acceptance—Coming to terms with reality

At times, we can mistake denial for acceptance, but they're actually quite different. Denial masks pain and hurt, while acceptance begins to embrace them for the value they can have in helping us grow. I've mentioned that denial is camouflaged by words of rationalization, patterns of sin, escapes, hunger for approval, and the like. But when we reach the Acceptance Stage of recovery, we're freer from these symptoms, and instead, we experience growth from hurt, compassion for others, and fresh freedom to feel all our emotions.

In the Acceptance Stage, forgiveness and healing continue their work, creating a growing relationship with God. They can also open doors with our children and our friends. In the Acceptance Stage, we even soften our hearts toward our ex-spouse and in-laws, while also gaining a new perspective on our circumstances. We begin to see our situation as a heartbreak that God is healing, rather than as a horror we want to forget. What's more, we begin to see our ex-spouse as God does—as a person He loves. We realize that while our own contributions to the breakdown of our marriage are undeniable, they're nonetheless misdeeds that God has forgiven. This perspective helps us to forgive and accept ourselves and our ex-spouse more fully.

In the Acceptance Stage, the day seems brighter. We again enjoy living. We're more whole. A story from a man I'll call "Dick" describes this experience well.

I now see that my broken marriage reflected the broken people that were in it. Since brokenness is really broken thinking, I've realized that my broken thinking led to many small choices that led to bigger problems. Those problems really contributed to the failed relationship. But I also understand that my ex contributed to our problems too.

The recovery process has led to many victories. Understanding codependency and how it governed my choices and actions has led me to self-acceptance. That has led to better relationships with my sons and other family members, and it's ushered me into other more authentic and godly relationships.

My mindset has been transformed by renewing my mind in God's Word. I've found so much freedom, it's become my 'high and strong tower'—a place I can run to and be safe. I've found that I no longer have to hide from God's love! It's unconditional and readily available.

The Divorce & Beyond seminar and support group helped me heal my broken heart. I now serve as a table leader in the seminar, and I co-facilitate a support group.

Questions to Ponder:

1. Do you sense your heart softening toward yourself, your ex-spouse and any other relationships that have been challenging (in-laws, former friends)? In what ways do you sense that?

2. What steps can continue your heart softening?

3. Have you thought about beginning a new serving role? What options would you consider?

Recovery, Stage 9: Activity and Humor—Establishing a new normal

In the early days of divorce, we felt disabled or even immobilized by all the upheaval, but the ninth stage of recovery is when we return to improved productivity. Travel and group activities become more inviting and interesting. Smiles, laughter, and a sense of humor return and help in the healing process. There's a renewed sense of joy in life, and the work you've done begins to pay off.

Previously I referred to my deep appreciation for a national park called the Boundary Waters. The Canadian side of this park is called the Quetico. In the ninth stage of my own recovery, the most significant activity I undertook was to accept an invitation to return there with three other men. That entailed packing all our food, equipment, and clothing, driving 15 hours each way, carrying canoes and supplies from one lake to another, paddling our canoes for eight days in this pristine wilderness—and the biggest carrot— unmatched fishing. It had been seven years since my first trip to the Boundary Waters, and while I eagerly anticipated the challenges and thrills inherent in such a trip, I knew I was still a bit raw and tender from the divorce. Even though I knew each of the three men with whom I was traveling, I was anxious about how they viewed me, this former pastor whose life had been shipwrecked. What questions would they ask? What conversations would arise? Furthermore, this kind of wilderness experience would foster solitude. Was I ready and willing to encounter the wilderness of my own soul more deeply?

It's natural to wrestle with these kinds of questions and feelings when you're beginning this phase, but don't let them deter you. Press on as you have through the more nightmarish phases of this journey. Like most of your worries during the crisis cycle, many of your forebodings will actually turn out to be unfounded. They were in my case.

Our drive up to the Boundary Waters was filled with chatter—some funny, some trivial, and some purposeful. But there were also times of silence. The other three men in the car seemed to be sensitive to my unspoken misgivings.

On this backwoods adventure, the peak experience for me happened on an evening when a very slow-moving thunderstorm approached us from the northwest. I climbed to a high rocky area just beyond our campsite, and I gazed at the lightning and listened to the rumblings that were threatening our peaceful place. Alone, I pondered yet another metaphor: a life disrupted by a severe storm. Once again, my feelings were strong, and I had another opportunity to "linger with what had provoked/rankled/piqued me." Before long, as I watched the storm and pondered this metaphor, I got drenched. The wind brought pellets of rain, soaking my clothes through to my skin underneath until I was cold and shivering. Finally, the storm stopped, but the metaphor didn't. It was time to retreat back to the camp, build a fire, change clothes, and voluntarily share with the other three men why I'd stayed out in such a storm.

There's something about a campfire that invites vulnerability. As we sat around ours, drops were running down my face again—not from the rain, but from my tears. I shared how cathartic it had been for me to see the rising thunderclouds, brace for them, endure them, and then bounce back in their aftermath. I shared how standing in the raging storm had mirrored the trauma of my divorce—feeling its fury, persevering through the raging winds and driving rain, and finally moving on to a safer, healthier place. The greatest gust I had faced in the storm of my divorce was the impact it had on my children and my relationship with them. I recounted to my three friends how I'd vowed to never put my own children through the trauma I'd gone through during and after my parents' divorce, and yet, to my great disappointment, that was exactly what had happened. I'd wept many times over the pain and trauma my children had endured as a result, and there at the campfire, I realized again that they too had had to stand "outside" in a raging storm.

My friends sensed that this was a critical moment for me. They responded with empathy and prayers. It was a powerful time. As a result, this cloudburst of rain and tears became yet another step forward in my recovery. That's the kind of breakthrough that re-engaging with life's activities can yield.

Questions to Ponder:

1. What new group activities have you begun or could you begin?

2. Describe what a "new normal" looks like to you?

Recovery, Stage 10: New Goals—Fashioning your future

Stage 10 of divorce recovery brings an ability to focus on the positive aspects and potential of what you've learned, and to plan for the future. New possibilities emerge, options like going back to school for further education, pursuing a new job, or regaining your physical fitness and health.

For me, this final stage of recovery involved a new career, which also required further education. Initially, this wasn't a decision I made willingly. Following the resolution of my divorce, I thought I could return to the work that was most familiar to me, namely ministry. I'd had a measure of success as a minister. I was an innovator, having started a campus ministry, a youth ministry, an outreach ministry, and a youth worker network, locally and state-wide. But I was in for an awakening. A year after my divorce, I applied for three ministry positions, but I wasn't accepted for any of them. These were the first times I'd ever been rejected in applying for a ministry position. It was a bitter pill to swallow, and I bemoaned my situation. What was I to do now? In the year leading up to my divorce and the year following it, I'd started a makeshift painting, tree-trimming, and landscaping service. It paid the bills, mostly thanks to the kindness that people I knew showed in hiring me, but I realized that work wasn't my future.

A friend, also going through a divorce, happened to be the regional manager for a national insurance company. He was in the process of restructuring the local office into what he believed was the future of financial services: financial advising rather than financial selling. He insisted that I had the aptitude to do well in this venture. At first, I resisted, stubbornly believing that my future remained in ministry. But as the dead ends continued, I acquiesced and took an inventory to measure my potential in the financial services field. To my amazement, I scored remarkably high. So, I said I'd try it for two years.

Those two years were not only successful, but also very meaningful. I discovered that as people developed the level of trust needed to reveal their financial lives to me, that trust also opened the doors for them to reveal other areas in their lives that they wouldn't ordinarily reveal to others: family struggles, job struggles, heart wounds, even marriage and sex struggles. It was gratifying to not only be a part of their financial successes, but also their family successes. That two-year experiment began what became a 30-year career. At the same time, the financial rewards of my day job made it possible for me to serve in ministry in significant ways in the church that my new wife and I joined.

During the darkest days of my divorce, I never could have imagined the future that awaited me: over 30 years of a successful married and working life, two more children whom I dearly love, new ministry opportunities (including Divorce & Beyond), and hundreds of new relationships and acquaintances. If you are in a place of uncertainty, whether in your career, family, residence, or whatever else, don't give in to despair. It's impossible to see what lies around the corner. The key to success is to keep pursuing recovery and health. As those develop, new possibilities will too. In chapter 7, Paulette further addresses the challenges of beginning a new lifestyle and the new goals inherent to it.

Questions to Ponder:

1. Where do you think you are in the Crisis Cycle?

2. Do you feel stuck?

3. What's one step you could take today to move forward?

4. How would you describe your support system?

5. What possibilities of new goals could be ahead?

The following steps highlight much of what I've written in this chapter. Feel free to copy them and hang them in a place that you frequent.

Steps in Discovering the Opportunities in Your Crisis[14]

1. Your crisis is a time to take care of yourself and find out what your needs are.

2. Going over your "story"—telling it again and again—is necessary. You need to do that to get past it. Tell it until you get tired of hearing it.

3. Look for support from others. Ask for help. Really. Build your own team (family, friends, groups, pastors, counselors). Make agreements with people about how they're willing to be helpful and use those helpers as you need them. If you work outside your home, decide if your work environment can be another source of support, or at least a helpful distraction. But remember that when people agree to help you, that doesn't transfer the responsibility for your problems from you to them. You (and God) are still responsible for your life. If the help other people give isn't completely adequate, it's inappropriate to fault them. Rather, thank them for whatever help they've been able to give, and go forward looking for the next person who may be able to further help. You are responsible for seeking as many people as you need, and you are responsible for figuring out how to apply what those people give you. This is the life God has entrusted to you. None of us can solve all of our problems alone, but at the same time, we can't expect other people to solve our problems for us.

4. Learn to treat yourself well. Deal with your feelings. Punch pillows, talk, exercise, use relaxation techniques. What have you always wanted to do, but didn't do because of your marriage? What do you like to do? Do it!

5. Remember that even though the recovery process takes at least one to two years, it *does* have an end. You *will* get better. There *will* be an end to the tunnel.

6. Be patient with yourself. Give yourself time to heal. Don't expect too much too fast from yourself during this stressful time.

7. Acknowledge your loss. It's real, but you'll survive. Let yourself feel the pain. Pain is proof that you're alive. You will get through the pain faster if you accept it, and ultimately, you *will* feel better.

8. Remember that you are okay.

9. Progress is not linear. Sometimes it's two steps forward and one step back.

10. Rest. Your body needs energy in order to repair itself. Listen to your physical needs. When you feel rested, then be active.

11. Keep decision-making to just the essentials. Judgment is clouded when people are under stress.

12. Surround yourself with things that are alive—plants, fish, flowers, pets.

13. Reaffirm your beliefs.

---

[14] "Steps in Discovering the Opportunity in Your Crisis," Various sources.

14. Schedule activities in advance for weekends and holidays. These are difficult times during a divorce. By preparing for them ahead of time, you'll be better able to handle them when they come.

15. If you're painfully bound to the past by mementos (a picture in a frame, a familiar cologne in a dresser drawer, or a wedding dress in a dry-cleaner bag, for example), hide them or get rid of them.

16. Plan for a positive outcome.

17. Eat well. A healthy diet helps fuel recovery.

18. Forgive others and forgive yourself. (There's more about that in Chapter 6).

19. Start anew!

Before I close this chapter, let me give you one more form of reassurance that can accompany you through this whole ten-step process of recovery. Perhaps you, like me, have questioned, "What is God doing while I'm flying through all this turbulence, and what's with His timing?" Jesus often responded to such questions with a story. I'll offer up the following simple but profound story.

God and the Spider

During World War II, a US marine became separated from his unit on a Pacific Island. The fighting had been intense, and in the smoke and crossfire, he'd lost touch with his comrades. Alone in the jungle, he could hear enemy soldiers coming in his direction. Scrambling for cover, he found his way up a high ridge to several small caves in the rock. Quickly, he crawled inside one of the caves. Although he was safe for the moment, he realized that when the enemy soldiers who were looking for him swept up the ridge, they would quickly search all the caves, and he would be killed.

As he waited, he prayed, "Lord, if it be your will, please protect me. Whatever you allow, though, I will love you and trust you. Amen."

After praying, he lay quietly listening to the enemy soldiers drawing close. He thought, "Well, I guess the Lord isn't going to help me out of this one." Then he noticed that a spider was beginning to build a web over the small entrance to his cave.

As he watched, listening to the enemy searching for him all the while, the spider layered strand after strand of web across the opening of the cave.

"Ha!" the GI thought. "What I need is a brick wall, and what the Lord has sent me is a spider web. God does have a sense of humor."

Then, as the enemy soldiers drew closer, he watched from the darkness of his hideout, and he could see them searching one cave after another. As they came to his cave, he got ready to make his last stand. To his amazement, though, after the enemy soldiers glanced in the direction of his cave, they moved on. Suddenly, he realized that with the spider web over its entrance, his cave looked as if no one had entered it for quite a while.

"Lord, forgive me," prayed the young man. "I had forgotten that in you a spider's web is stronger than a brick wall."[15]

Amid the seemingly overwhelming challenges of divorce recovery, it can be hard to recognize the webs that God is weaving in our lives, sometimes in the most surprising and unanticipated ways. But remember that with God, a mere spider's web becomes a brick wall of protection. Perhaps your webs will become recognizable within hours or days. Be aware, however, that unlike the situation in the story, it may take months, or even years to see the webs that God has woven for you.

Now a closing thought: A huge benefit of learning how to walk through and heal from the crisis of divorce is that the next time (and there likely will be a next time) you face a crisis of sorts, you'll be able to sidestep some of the pitfalls and resist some of the unhealthy tendencies that tripped you up. Instead, you'll be able to draw from this well of

---

[15] "God & the Spider," source unknown

recovery and apply the processes and the skills to deal with it. As Shakespeare penned, "What was past was prologue."[16]

Ten years after my divorce, seven years after my remarriage, and only a couple of years after the birth of my two children from my second marriage, I was diagnosed with a slow-moving potentially terminal disease. The prognosis was that I had five, at the most ten years to live. In the aftermath, I wrestled with the grief, and many of its feelings, questions, bewilderment, and agony, but it was very condensed. Instead of this process stretching out over years, it was literally weeks, about three. I was amazed that a month after this diagnosis, I was ready to move forward into a challenging treatment regimen, ready to face uncertainty with faith instead of fear, ready to face the prospect of a shorter life, ready to invest in my wife and children with whatever time I had left, and ready to prepare a succession plan for the business I had started. During the following ten years, I went through four different experimental drug trials that extracted my strength, and cumulatively totaled nearly 700 days, almost two years of life. Many, many people prayed both for me and with me.

I am convinced that it was because of the emotional, mental, and spiritual health and practices I had learned, that I survived well beyond the prognosis I had been given. Although none of the above medical treatments were effective, I not only continued to survive, but also to function fairly well for *fifteen* years, at which time a cure was discovered, and my treatment was successful. So, invest in your recovery with excellence. It will strengthen your resolve, increase your perseverance, and pay huge dividends as you face an unknown future and its challenges.

Previously, I listed "60 ways to get out of your rut." Below are another 46 ideas for incorporating something new into your life. Your first impulse may be to avoid all of them, but I assure you that, as you overcome your reluctance and embrace any of them, you'll likely notice a positive boost. They're all ways of doing something to invest in yourself that will produce dividends!

---

[16] William Shakespeare, *The Tempest*, Act I, Scene II.

46 Ideas to do Something New[17]

1. Find a box, fill it with stuff you don't need, and donate it.
2. Write about a favorite memory, maybe your favorite vacation you took as a kid.
3. Make a scrapbook.
4. Pick up trash that isn't yours.
5. Send a handwritten note to someone.
6. Sign up for an online course and finish the first lesson.
7. Go to bed earlier than usual and wake up earlier than usual.
8. Sleep in a different room in your house.
9. Try a new exercise or exercise routine like yoga or Pilates®.
10. Begin volunteering for a nonprofit organization.
11. Read a good book before going to bed.
12. Print out some favorite digital photos and make an album.
13. Go antiquing.
14. Call someone you appreciate and tell them why.
15. Take some new photographs.
16. Meditate, sit still, ignore the mind's chatter, and listen to your soul speak.
17. Do an indoor activity: go-cart racing, swimming, racquetball playing, roller skating.
18. Volunteer for the day at a local dog shelter, home for the elderly, or a soup kitchen.
19. Give up a bad habit.
20. Try a new recipe you've had your eye on.
21. Play an outdoor game like golf or Frisbee golf, pickleball, tennis, or maybe even try skydiving.
22. Drop off non-perishable food items to a food pantry, or clothing at a local church or organization.
23. Write up a bucket list if you don't already have one.
24. Go for a drive in the country and enjoy the scenery.
25. Tell a police officer, fireman, teacher, nurse, military person that you appreciate what they do.
26. Listen to an interesting podcast.
27. Plant seeds and grow something in a window box or garden.
28. Repaint a room in your home.
29. Fix something for someone else.
30. Bake cookies and share them at work, with friends, or with a neighbor who may be on their own.
31. Walk around your neighborhood after eating dinner.

---

[17] "46 Ideas to Do Something New," Various sources.

32. Watch a sunset, sunrise.
33. Go for a bike ride, hike, or run.
34. Leave some shelled peanuts out for the birds and squirrels.
35. Research your genealogy.
36. Camp out in a local campground or even in the backyard.
37. Set up a bird feeder outside your window and watch the birds eat.
38. Write an "I'm grateful for …" list.
39. Invite a friend over to see a fun movie.
40. Play a board game with friends or family.
41. Make plans to visit an out-of-town friend.
42. Pack a picnic and take a blanket.
43. Go to a museum or cinema.
44. Read an old classic.
45. Sign up for a local community class.
46. Handwash your car.

Chapter 3

Dealing with Loneliness
by Paulette Liburd and Dan Cox

Paulette:

Loneliness is said to be one of the most universal sources of human suffering. It's not limited by race, color, or creed. Some of us first experienced loneliness as a child. For others, it began once they started attending school. Remember junior high? Or maybe it was during the years leading up to the time you met your spouse. Ultimately, though, when you got married, you thought—you *thought*—your lonely days were over.

To begin with, what if I told you that, according to a Meta Gallup survey, "Nearly one in four people worldwide feel very or fairly lonely?"[18] Clearly, getting married doesn't exempt you from feeling lonely. You can even be in a crowded room of friends or a stadium of fans and still experience loneliness.

Some may wonder, "How can you be lonely when you're in the presence of others?" Looking up classic definitions of loneliness, I found one that explains that paradox. Kendra Cherry, MSEd, writes, "Loneliness is actually a state of mind. Loneliness causes people to feel empty, alone, and unwanted."[19] In other words, loneliness isn't a matter of physical isolation; it's a matter of emotional isolation. I like this definition because it encourages me to figure out how to switch to a different mindset and to take action when I'm feeling lonely. And in this chapter, we'll use the word "loneliness" to refer to the feeling of disconnection from meaningful relationships after a divorce.

Whether you're the one who filed for a divorce, or the one who was served with divorce papers, some degree of loneliness is probably an unavoidable reality. A marriage relationship can be extremely difficult during its demise with escalating feelings of loneliness and bewilderment over issues such as, "Why aren't we on the same page anymore?" and "I can't live with you anymore, but I'm not sure I can live without you?" This is the pain of emotional separation.

Marriages usually end in divorce in one of two ways: Either the divorce comes as a shock to one of the spouses, or the marriage slowly disintegrates for both partners over time. If your marriage slowly disintegrated, loneliness probably began long before your

---

[18] Taylor Nicioli, "The Loneliness Epidemic," *CNN*, October 24, 2023, https://www.cnn.com

[19] Kendra Cherry, "What Is the Loneliness Epidemic?" *Verywell Mind*, December 5, 2023

divorce decree. But either way, in the aftermath of divorce, loneliness can become acute. The lack of meaningful connections, a feeling that no one "gets" you or understands your situation, and the feeling that you're an outsider looking in—all of these contribute to the feelings of loneliness.

Loneliness at its core is an indicator that something isn't right in our minds and with our relationships. That "something" needs attention. If loneliness isn't addressed, it can manifest itself physically as fatigue, migraines, trouble sleeping, and a weakened immune system. Emotionally, it can also manifest itself in unexpected ways such as social-media addiction, over- or undereating, or "retail therapy" (spending money in order to feel better). It can also lead to darker places of self-criticism and even self-loathing. But if it's addressed in healthy ways, loneliness can actually spur us on to make the alterations we need in order to nurture ourselves and engage more meaningfully with others.

This chapter will address some of the feelings of loneliness that accompany stages of grief in the aftermath of divorce, and we'll offer some practical advice on how to manage loneliness and foster connections so that your loneliness can become a doorway to healing and wholeness.

In our own situation, as a young Caribbean couple migrating to Cincinnati, my husband and I made friends who were also from the Caribbean and who were in the same life stage, namely "married with kids." Consequently, all of my close friends were also friends with my husband. After our divorce, I heard from none of them, and to me, this seemed to be a shaming silence.

To compound the problem, even though I'm very extraverted, because of the intense shame I felt, I didn't want to be around people who seemed to have their life together—especially couples. (Dealing with shame is addressed in our chapter on Self-Image.) Therefore, I intentionally isolated myself except for work and my children's activities. I nursed the loneliness "state of mind," and I resented that my spouse had left me with two children and no adult friends. I adopted a victim mentality.

Although you may have support from friends and family, loneliness during and after a divorce can feel like you don't have a friend left in this world, feeling stuck with a constant sense of deep isolation. Some days you may be anguished by an empty apartment or house. Other days it feels like there's no one to call, and there's no one calling to check in on you. There's just you and your own thoughts and your own questions, solving your own problems over and over.

I don't blame my friends for not reaching out. Rather, I believe they didn't want to choose sides, and they probably felt as awkward as I did. In the years since my divorce, I've learned that married couples often feel too uncomfortable to stay friends with both or even one of the divorcing parties. There can be a number of underlying reasons: They just don't know what to say; they don't want to be perceived as playing favorites; they don't know whose story to believe; they feel pressured by one of the parties to choose sides; it may increase the anxiety they feel about their own marriage, so, they default to just staying away.

In my own circumstances, that behavior compounded a different problem: My children had often been ridiculed for their Caribbean accent and how they didn't fit in culturally with their American peers. So, when the "just stay away" awkwardness hit us, I felt especially bad for my children because they lost contact with the only other second-generation American children with whom they shared their culture and dialect.

During a divorce or separation, loneliness can become more intensified by choices we make to withdraw from others. That was true for me, and I made excuses for my behavior. I felt like I always needed to answer for the big "D" that I perceived was stamped on my forehead. Therefore, to avoid explaining why my marriage had failed, I withdrew from my usual community of friends and family. For example, I stopped attending our local cricket games because I knew my ex-spouse and many other "couple friends" would likely be there.

I also stopped attending the church that our family had been part of, and I joined another church where no one knew me. I was convinced that the people at my former church perceived me as "less than." In that church, a single African American woman with two children stood out like a sore thumb in a congregation made up almost entirely of seemingly intact Caucasian families. While other families could comfortably waltz into the pews holding hands or walking close to each other, I felt like everyone was staring at my family when we had no man to walk beside me or to hold one of the children's hands.

My loneliness was on a rampage, and it was further complicated by fear and shame; fear because divorce and the many unwanted changes and choices that accompanied it had struck trepidation in my heart, and shame that despite going to counseling and reading many books on relationships, I hadn't been able to hold my marriage together. As I stated in the previous chapter, I had wanted to be an example to my extended family, a role model of a healthy marriage and family. So, it's probably not surprising that it took me three long months after I filed for divorce to finally let my extended family know. I was ashamed, thinking that my mother would gloat, "I told you so." And I was very afraid that, living in a city with no family, I couldn't survive as a divorced, single-again African American woman with two children.

The Christian pop duo King & Country sings about "…a kind of love that God only knows," and they say that that love is "…for the lonely, for the ashamed, the misunderstood, and the one to blame." Those lyrics perfectly summed up my mindset. I was very lonely with no spouse or family close by, and I felt very misunderstood. I heard comments like, "You're so sweet. How could this happen to you?" When you're going through a divorce, I think people make comments like that because they don't know what to say, they are naïve about why marriages fail, or they don't really want to talk about how you're doing. Unless they've been through a divorce themselves, they seldom have much understanding of the depth of hurt you're experiencing. And really, how could they?

It took a lot of courage for me to get out of my own way and begin to forge meaningful relationships again. I read a lot of books and articles, and I listened to a lot of Christian radio. The King & Country song that I mentioned goes on to say, "We can start over. God only knows what you've been through. God only knows what they say about you. God only knows how it's killing you."[20] I took to heart my need to draw close to the God who knows me and knows the way forward. For hours I also tuned in to radio and television speakers who tackled the subject of divorce. In listening to all these, I became a huge fan of Myles Monroe, Chuck Swindoll, Tony Evans, and Rick Warren. I read everything I could get my hands on that they authored. I became an adherent of Chuck Swindoll's book, *Life Is 10% What Happens to You and 90% How You React.*[21] I made that title a personal mantra. In my struggles, I would recite it over and over: "Life is 10% what happens to me and 90% how I react to what happens." That simple quote made a huge difference in how I approached my new status as a divorced mother of two.

Dan:

The period leading up to my date in divorce court made me painfully aware that I was alone. Facing the most difficult event of my life, all the moral support of, "Hang in there" and "I'm here if you need me" didn't really help. I was alone. Day after day, night after night, the soundtrack of my life seemed to be on repeat. At night I would struggle to go to sleep, then toss and turn until the radio alarm went off at 5:30 am; I always left the radio on, just to break the silence, hoping it would take my mind off the ever-present fact that my wife had just left me. I would get dressed, grab a cup of coffee, and head for work. (A side note: During that period of my life, the roads were always full of idiots who didn't know how to drive. As time went on, they got much better, but for a few months there…)

Very tired from lack of sleep, I'd eventually arrive at work to face all the stress of my job. Although some people at work knew my wife had left me, they didn't seem to understand what a big deal it was. Typically, I'd immediately be hit with a problem that somebody thought was major but seemed very insignificant to me. Part of me was glad about the distraction of being at work. On the other hand, I was angry that no one there asked about how I was doing. At the same time, if someone did ask about my divorce, it bugged me because it was really none of their business. I'm sure I wasn't a fun guy to be around. The unrelenting cloud that hung over me was the sense that I was very alone. From our early years, until the day we die, we're alone with the thoughts in our heads, but this new form of divorced loneliness felt different to me. I was hyperaware of being totally alone with my thoughts in what felt like a huge, windowless, cold warehouse. My thoughts seemed to echo, and they would race from one unsolvable scenario to another. While my brain was working overtime on way too many things, the feeling of how very alone I was would envelop me, like a shadow that wouldn't go away.

I explained to a pastor that I was struggling, and I felt somewhat abandoned by God. The pastor reminded me of the many times in my life that God had proved He was by my side even when I thought He wasn't. Now, I know that any therapist or pastor worth

---

[20] King & Country, *God Only Knows (Official Music Video)* YouTube

[21] Charles R. Swindoll, "Life Is 10% What Happens to You and 90% How You React," republished January 17, 2023.

their salt will insist that it's not their job to tell you what you should do. It's always better when a counselor can lead us to discover our own solutions to whatever problems we encounter. But I also believe there are occasions when we can be so stuck that it can be helpful when someone we trust provides some direct advice as a stop-gap measure. My pastor believed that as well, so he said, "Here's what I think would be good: Watch two funny movies every night for an entire week." His counsel caught me off guard, but I also felt relief. I could do this! Believing that this advice was God-inspired, watching funny movies was exactly what I did, and I discovered that I could still laugh. Honestly, I'd begun to wonder if I would ever laugh again, but in humor, I was able to remember who God is: the kind and loving Father who wants peace and joy for me. When I watched funny movies for a week, my sense of aloneness didn't suddenly disappear, but the humor reminded me that there was more to my life than just my divorce.

Divorce is an incredibly lonely and stressful experience, but through my rediscovery of humor, I encountered the reality of one of the key verses in the Bible: "The LORD is close to the brokenhearted." (Psalm 34:18) As we'll note in the Compass Scriptures chapter, God himself has experienced the heartbreak of divorce. Because He completely understands our distress, He's especially close to us in it. Furthermore, it's in His very nature; He cannot be distant; to be so would be a contradiction to Himself. You can trust God with your broken heartedness, because as Psalm 34:18 continues, "[The LORD] saves those who are crushed in spirit."

God gives you grace—undeserved favor and acceptance. Therefore, it's important to give yourself grace and do things that are just for your own wellbeing. During and for a while after my divorce, I was alone more than I wanted to be. Getting outside for a walk or finding a peaceful place to sit in the shade, or in the sun, reduced loneliness and brought clarity and hope. Learn to be comfortable when by yourself. Being alone, but not lonely, takes intentional action. Set aside time for activities you enjoy. They'll remind you that there's more to your life than just divorce. And laugh! Just because you're going through a divorce doesn't mean you're not allowed to laugh or enjoy yourself. Watch funny movies or funny video clips online. Your body and your brain will thank you. If you feel so stuck that you simply can't muster the energy to do anything, it might be time to see your doctor and discuss what medical options are available. The doctor might suggest meeting with a counselor, or you may need medication to temporarily help get you out of your quagmire. I've known some people who, through this process, discovered that they'd been dealing with undiagnosed depression or other psychiatric issues for quite some time.

Another type of loneliness I've had to deal with was the longing for someone with whom to share my life. After my second divorce, it was years before I remarried, and not by my desire. It just took a long time, a very long time, to meet the right person. I went through periods when I felt fine being alone, but as the years dragged on, the lack of a soulmate became harder and harder. Sometimes, when I took vacation days to work on my house, it would occur to me that I hadn't even spoken to or seen anyone for most of a week. I could have died, and my moldering carcass wouldn't have been discovered until somebody noticed that I'd never come back to work. During that whole period, I had a big family and lots of friends, but I had to fight to remind myself that I really wasn't alone.

Another tough time in dealing with loneliness was whenever I was sick. Some people want to be left alone when they're sick, but I'm not one of them. I fit the horrible stereotype of a male who thinks my nagging cough is equivalent to the pain of giving birth. Usually when I was sick, I wasn't so ill that I couldn't fix myself something to eat, or run out and grab some cough medicine, but when you're sick, it's nice to have somebody else to do those things for you. Any illness reinforced my awareness that I didn't have a mate.

One other situation when loneliness would get the best of me was when I was invited to some event where a "friend" wanted to introduce me to my perfect match. I know what you're thinking: I should have just said, "No thanks!" But I would always succumb to the temptation to accept the invitation, thinking that, just maybe, this time would be different. But you guessed it: My friends' ideas of my perfect match just made me question their opinion of *me*! Even though I tried not to let these offers get my hopes up, I would always end up disappointed, and my drive home would feel especially lonely.

Even with my own family, especially during holidays, being the only person without a spouse made me feel alone. Looking back now, I think I should have been more aware that I really wasn't alone; I was sitting in a room with fifteen people who really cared about me. Some of my loneliness could have been abated by a more thankful attitude for what I still had, instead of dwelling on the past and what I'd lost. As the Bible says, "Do not say, 'Why were the old days better than these?' For it is not wise to ask such questions" (Ecclesiastes 7:10).

Managing loneliness and getting comfortable being alone will not happen unless you *decide* to make them happen. I look back now and remember the early days of my divorce being some of the most meaningful times in my life. I became comfortable being alone by realizing that *I wasn't really alone*. God was always with me, and I had friends and family who were there for me too. I just needed to reach out. I had lots of talks with God, sometimes thanking Him and other times letting Him know that I wasn't happy with my perception of His laid-back management style.

Paulette:

Strategies for Managing Loneliness

Sometimes loneliness is just a fact of life. Married people can feel lonely, so having a partner doesn't guarantee a life free of loneliness. In any status, what helps the most is developing a deeper relationship with God, deeper friendships with the people you already know, and new friendships with those who share your interests and experiences.

Look at how a friend whom I'll call "Karla" expressed her need for support after her divorce, and how that led her to eventually experiencing comfort.

When I was first divorced, life didn't change much for me and my two daughters—until I injured my ankle. When it hadn't healed properly in a month, my doctor said my Achilles tendon was torn and needed surgery.

I was petrified because I was the sole provider for my daughters. I wondered how I was going to go through surgery and recovery and take care of all the things I needed to do as a mother. Furthermore, being an only child, I didn't have a family member to be my emergency contact.

I reached out to one of the pastors at the Vineyard Church to let her know my dilemma. She said she would be my emergency contact and take me to and from the surgery. Then one of the members from my Divorce & Beyond small group learned of my predicament and organized a team of people who helped our family after my surgery every single day for a month. They brought groceries and hot meals, and they helped me with other errands. Some of them took me to doctor's appointments and helped me around the house.

When Paulette asked me to write about how I experienced God's love during my divorce, I immediately knew what I would share. God is loving, kind, and powerful—and He works through His people. The period after my ankle surgery was a pivotal month in my life, and without the love of God and His people, I don't know how I would have made it. Blessed be God and His people!

In John 15:15, Jesus explains, "I do not call you servants any longer, because the servant does not know what the master is doing; but I have called you friends, because I have made known to you everything that I have heard from my Father" (NRSV). That is so meaningful. Jesus calls us his "friends." Jesus—with His divine companionship and comfort—is always close enough to hear our whispers. But even so, when Jesus sent His disciples out, He sent them "two by two" so they would have human companionship also. So, let's look at several more ways we can combat loneliness by cultivating health-giving friendships.

Dan:

Loneliness is compounded when we don't feel connected in a meaningful way to those around us. That's why you'll hear people say that they sometimes feel the loneliest in a crowded room. They might say, "There are all these people around me, but I'm not connected to anyone!" So, get connected! I discovered that even though I never knew it, some of my friends at work and some of my neighbors—people I had known for years— had gone through divorces before I met them. Some of them had valuable experiences and insights they were willing to share, and others were walking advertisements for things not to do when divorcing. But either way, it helped me to know that I could look around and see others who had gone through divorces and survived, and our shared experiences created more meaningful connections.

Paulette:

Unlike mine, your family may live nearby and is at least somewhat functional. If so, spend more time with them. Relationships with family can deepen during periods of grief. Sometimes in marriage, we can forget the importance of the rest of our family. Include family in your new routine, and don't be shy about asking for help and a hug when you need them.

Dan:

Be open to developing new friendships. If your case is like mine, your married friends may no longer be available, or they might not have the time to hang out with you very much. Perhaps they're busy with their kids all the time. So, explore relationships with other single people in situations similar to your own.

If you don't have many friends with whom you feel a meaningful connection, reach out cautiously, but with some vulnerability, and see who responds. You can't count on the random UPS driver showing up to fill the void. You have to take steps to put yourself in situations where you'll meet new people. Remember, you're not looking for a new spouse; you're just looking for some wholesome friends.

Do you like golf? Go drive some golf balls or go golfing. If you're at all open to it, you'll inevitably meet others who like golf as well. Do you have a certain hobby? Join a club full of other fanatics. But most importantly, if there's one available, join a divorce-recovery group in your area. Aside from the help the group will provide as you work through your divorce, there'll probably be other people there who are looking for new friends, and there may be gatherings and fun activities outside of the formal group meetings.

At the time of my divorce, I had one "best" friend who was married. I now have two "best" friends: my married friend and another friend I fell in with because he was also going through a divorce. My divorcing friend and I spent hours and hours talking about our situations and figuring out our lives. So, because of my divorce, my best friend count went up by one, and I added several other friends that I never would have met.

Likewise, after I'd worked through a lot of my emotional pain, I slowly developed new friends at my church. I was fortunate that a group of single people went out to eat after the service every week. The first time I joined them, it was awkward, but they were friendly, and in no time, I felt like I belonged. I made connections with people whom I still enjoy today.

Paulette and Dan:

Another antidote to loneliness that we've found very helpful is volunteering. Volunteering reminds us that we still have much to offer to others, and it enhances our sense of self-worth. It gets us out of our heads and into the lives of others, which helps to dissipate our loneliness.

If you've never been involved in volunteering, find a cause that resonates with you, ideally with a group that needs a special skill you can offer. Whatever interests you, there's probably a volunteer opportunity out there for it. Scan your church website, search online, or just ask around, and you'll be volunteering before you know it. Steve and Janie Sjogren, the founders of the Vineyard Community Church, used to say, "You only get to keep what you give away," and that certainly holds true when it comes to volunteering. You always seem to get way more than you give. Volunteering will get you out of the house and into a world that you may have forgotten existed, and it's another great way to make new friends. There's something very meaningful about helping people (or animals) who can't reciprocate and joining a team of other like-minded volunteers.

Paulette:

In conclusion, here are some actions that might help you find your way out of the dark place of loneliness.

- Develop a healthier inner life, centering yourself in God's truths, devoting time to enriching your soul, and encountering God in fresh new ways. The goal is to be able to say to God what the psalmist did: "I am always with you; you hold me by my right hand. You guide me with your counsel, and afterward you will take me into glory. Whom have I in heaven but you? And earth has nothing I desire besides you. My flesh and my heart may fail, but God is the strength of my heart and my portion forever" (Psalm 73:23-26).

- Identify an inner circle of two to four key friends or relatives who would be willing to take a call or text from you in the middle of the night, just to listen and help you process your thoughts and your situation. And when you're picking those special helpers, choose people from whom you would also be willing to *take* that call.

- Invest in a second circle of relationships of three to ten people. This could be a small group of safe people—folks who don't judge you. Get to know these people so well that when they ask how you're doing, and your response is "Fine," they'll know when to call you on it.

- Develop a lifestyle of community and service. You might plunge yourself into your children's school and activities. You might volunteer at church and in the community. You'll get more out of these experiences than you've ever thought.

Obviously, none of these suggestions will provide immediate fixes for your loneliness. However, cultivating any of them or a combination of them will help over time. Just because you've been physically separated from your spouse doesn't mean you have to be physically separated from the world. Invest in your inner life, get out there and make some new friends, invest more deeply in some old friends and family, volunteer, and don't be afraid to ask for a hug when you need one.

Questions to Ponder:

1. Loneliness can be predictable. What are the times of the day, week, month, or even year that you're most likely to experience loneliness? What steps could you take to head them off?

2. Some of the suggestions we've made in this chapter are probably things that you've already done. Which of them is the healthiest in your life?

3. Which one of the suggested behaviors needs the most attention and why?

Chapter 4

Compass Scriptures and a Biblical Understanding of Divorce and Remarriage
by Bill Koontz

Introduction

"God hates divorce." Many people who come to our Divorce & Beyond seminars believe that God hates divorce and consequently, are filled with dread at the thought of delving into what Scripture teaches about divorce. These have been people who were already reeling and weeping over the loss of their marriages, even though some of them had been mistreated or even abandoned by their spouses. These were people who already felt judged by others, and many of them had already struggled to come to terms with what the Bible teaches about divorce, so the words "God hates divorce" sounded foreboding to them. They anxiously wondered if, by extension, God also hates divorced people. And they wondered if our seminar was going to reinforce that stigma.

If you're feeling that kind of dread right now, just relax because this chapter is for you. In fact, the theme of this chapter is that the seriousness of our sin is no match for the totality of God's forgiveness. So yes, a sentence within several translations of a Bible verse does say that God hates divorce, but God loves you, period, no exceptions. God loves divorced people, period, no exceptions. So let down your guard. You won't need to defend yourself. Just be open to examining what it is that God hates, and why He hates it.

There are numerous views of what the Bible says about divorce and remarriage. This is a crucial chapter because many people feel trapped in guilt and even shame because of what they think Scripture teaches about divorce—or because of what other people have told them Scripture teaches. I'm convinced that some, if not many of those feelings of guilt and shame are unwarranted. So, I invite you to follow me just one step at a time here and see if we can get from "God hates divorce" to the conclusion that "God loves, forgives, and restores divorced people."

Here's a remark Jesus made to correct religious leaders on the purpose of the Sabbath, "The Sabbath was made to meet the needs of people, and not people to meet the requirements of the Sabbath" (Mark 2:27 NLT). I believe the same principle is true regarding marriage. Marriage was made for people, not people for marriage. And when we elevate the value of the institution of marriage over the people in the marriage, I think Jesus would correct us in the same way.

The power of perspective

A "perspective" is an established set of attitudes and beliefs about something. If our goal is to develop a healthy, godly perspective on divorce and remarriage, we have to recognize two criteria. One, that every one of us brings a unique perspective to this subject, and our differing perspectives can lead us to draw different conclusions from the same Bible passages. And two, our perspectives can have power over our emotional reactions and openness to changing our attitudes and beliefs.

The picture on this page is a famous illustration[22] of how powerful our perspectives can be. What do you see in this drawing? Some people look at it and immediately see a glamorous young woman glancing away. Just as quickly, other people see an old woman sullenly staring downward. Many people can see the opposite image if it's pointed out to them, but some people can't be convinced that there's any possibility other than the one they saw at first glance. I don't know what it means if you see the old woman first, or if you see the young woman, but the point is that each of us sees this picture through a lens that predisposes us to seeing the image one way or the other. In other words, we all see what our perspective conditions us to see.

In the same way, each of us sees divorce from a perspective that's been shaped gradually by our socioeconomic, cultural, ethnic, religious, and personal histories. Our perspectives have been influenced by how we've been touched personally by divorce and influenced by information and messages that we've stowed away in our minds from many sources. And if you're at all like the vast majority of the people I've talked to in the past thirty years, I can say with some certainty that the messages you've received about divorce, both directly and indirectly, have not all been accurate or well informed.

---

[22] Optical Illusion: Young Lady or Old Woman," *Bangtech.com*
https://content.bangtech.com/thinking/english/young_lady_or_old_woman_illusion.htm

Questions to Ponder:

1. What do you currently believe about divorce?

2. What beliefs do family members and close friends hold about divorce? Note any differences between them.

3. Take a few minutes to record your responses before continuing to the next section.

What has shaped your perspective on divorce?

Every one of us has a perspective on divorce that's been shaped by our prior experiences, and that perspective is deeply embedded in our psyche. To spur your thinking about the impact of your own prior experiences, I'm going to ask a lot of questions here. I don't expect you to get a profound insight from every single question, but when some of these questions hit a nerve for you, jot down the memories that have come to your mind. Then write a few sentences about how those memories have shaped your attitudes and beliefs about divorce and remarriage.

Let's think about childhood experiences first.

- *When you were a child, did your parents get divorced? How did you feel about that? Did you believe one of them was to blame more than the other?*
- *If they did, did one or both of them later remarry?*
- *If your parents weren't divorced, how did they refer to people who were?*
- *What attitudes did your family have toward people you knew who were divorced—or their children?*
- *If your family was involved in a church, was divorce ever discussed there in sermons or other kinds of teaching?*
- *How was divorce viewed by your church?*
- *How did you and your family feel about your church's teachings on divorce?*

Next, take a few steps back, and think about a bigger picture.

- *Over the course of your life, how many family members, close friends, or work associates have you known who've gone through a divorce?*
- *How challenging, contentious, painful, or even damaging were those divorces to the people involved?*
- *When those divorces happened, what kinds of feelings did they evoke in you? Were you devastated, angry, maybe even fearful? Were you sad, compassionate, empathetic, or some combination of these?*

Now let's consider the ongoing impact of your perspective on divorce in general.

- *How are you still affected by your feelings about divorce?*
- *If you have to tell someone that your parents, children, or siblings are divorced, do you feel a sense of shame? If so, why?*
- *How have other people's divorces affected your thoughts, attitudes, feelings, and opinions about divorce?*
- *Say the word "divorce" out loud. What thoughts go through your mind as you do, and what emotions do you experience as a result of saying that word?*

Now, if you're already divorced, or if you're presently going through a divorce, here are some more questions to ponder.

- *Prior to the failure of your own marriage, did you think differently about divorce than you do now?*

- *When you share with someone that you're divorced, do you feel a sense of shame?*

- *When you've been introduced to another divorced person, what thoughts have immediately crossed your mind? How have those thoughts influenced your view of the other divorced person? Were your attitudes toward the divorced person critical, relieved, angry, sympathetic, jealous, sad, disrespectful?*

- *Have your initial thoughts about another divorced person ever caused you to respond differently than if you'd met a person who wasn't divorced?*

Are you remarried? If so, here's one last set of questions to contemplate.

- *How do you feel when you reveal to someone that you're remarried?*

- *Do you watch other people's responses, especially non-verbal ones?*

- *How are your observations fueled by your own feelings about being remarried?*

- *Looking at the situation from the other side, when you meet someone else who's remarried, what are your initial feelings and thoughts?*

I've raised all of these questions simply to help you get in touch with how your current perspective on divorce and remarriage has been assembled from your accumulated beliefs, reactions, and wounds. Do you recognize them? It's very important that you do because this is part of your path toward healing, and toward helping others pursue their own healing.

On the other hand, I've found that divorced people almost universally report feeling like they have a big scarlet "D" stamped on them. While this self-perception is formed largely by the attitudes they've picked up on their own through different exposures and experiences, it's also partially formed by the attitudes other people project. In all probability, you've encountered people who've been insensitive or flat-out hurtful in their attitudes toward your divorce, and they may have left emotional scars on your heart. So, it's fair to say that not all of a divorced person's negative self-concept is self-induced.

All the same, we can't blame other people entirely for our own perspectives. As you've seen in this long list of questions, we've allowed all kinds of influences to shape our perspectives on divorce, and even if we're not aware of it, our perspectives have probably been tainted by some unhealthy thinking.

In my own case, when I think through the probing questions that I've posed above, I always have to linger over the ones that call to mind my tarnished childhood. By the time my parents divorced, many of the preceding years of their marriage had been conflictual to the point that I once had to physically separate them during a fight. So, in some respects, I was relieved when my parents finally parted. However, along with that relief, my self-confidence was shattered. Until they divorced, I hadn't realized how much my self-worth was tied to being part of a two-parent family. No longer having both parents with me at school functions, weekend activities, family gatherings, or church made me feel different, like a part of me was missing. And I also felt a sense of shame for the failure of my parents and consequently the failure of our whole family. On top of that, I felt that other people viewed me differently as well. I sensed that they thought of me as a child with a mark or strike against me—a kid who came from a failed family. All of these experiences shaped the perspective from which I eventually came to view my own failed marriage, and the results were devastating. But as we'll see in the next section, there was another big part of my perspective on divorce that pushed me to the very threshold of suicidal thoughts: Because I was estranged from my wife, I also estranged myself from God.

What molds your understanding of what Scripture teaches about divorce?

Maybe you've been part of a church that decries divorce as an all but unforgiveable sin.

On the other hand, many of us wouldn't need a priest or a pastor to convince us that God has ugly thoughts about divorced people. We're quite capable of convincing *ourselves* of that because we project onto God all the judgmentalism of our own distorted perspectives on divorce.

When I was lost in my anguish, why didn't I experience more of God's help? After all, I was a seminary-trained pastor. I knew God, didn't I? Yes, but now there was an obstacle between God and me. Because I was estranged from my wife, and my subsequent disappointment with God, I also distanced myself from Him. After all, if God had cared, He would have intervened to save my marriage and spared our children from the heartache they suffered.

At that time, I didn't really understand what was going on in my head, but since then, I've found an outcast priest named Brennan Manning, who put his finger on the actual source of my troubles when he wrote, "Remember the famous line of the French philosopher Blaise Pascal: 'God made man in his own image, and man returned the compliment.' We often make God in our own image."[23]

In any case, God wound up to be as uncaring, disappointing, and angry as I was. So, another vital question is, in your heart of hearts, what is God like to you? How do you personally experience Him? How do you think about Him to yourself, not how you necessarily describe Him to anyone else?

Another way to understand perspective is through the analogy of a lens. A lens shapes how we view what's before us. Before he retired, one of my neighbors was also my optometrist. At my annual checkups, I would sit in a chair, resting my chin in a somewhat awkward position on a cupped support. Then, one of the ways the optometrist would test my vision was by rotating a series of lenses of different powers in front of my eyes while asking me to read letters on a screen. Some of the lenses resulted in obscured images, but eventually the optimum lens would produce a sharp, crisp, easy-to-read letter. That's exactly what an optimum understanding of *God's character* does for theology. It's the lens that brings into clearer focus who God is and what He is communicating through His word.

Here's the bottom line: The only perspective on divorce that really matters is God's perspective, and the Bible is our best source for understanding God's character—who He is, what He's like, and how He views and feels about human beings, including you. We all need a way of reading the Bible that will put us in touch with God's mind and heart.

Of course, there are passages in the Bible (including those on divorce) that can be difficult to understand. In Chapter 3, "The Crisis Cycle," I wrote about "passages" in the Boundary Waters wilderness that were difficult for me to navigate in my canoe. And yet,

---

[23] Brennan Manning, "Did You Believe That I Loved You?" *YouTube*
https://www.youtube.com/watch?v=4AehcGSIkZw

I've found that, just as we have magnetic compasses that help us chart our way through the wilderness, we also have "Compass Scriptures" to help us find our way through the Bible. In the wilderness, the compasses that guide us always point toward the North Star, and in the Bible, the Compass Scriptures that guide us are the ones that point toward the "Lodestar of the Bible," which is the character of God.

The little-used word "Lodestar" originally meant "any star used to guide the course of a ship," but the word has also come to mean "a principle that serves as a guide." So, when I say that the character of God is the "Lodestar of the Bible," what I mean is that when we encounter difficult passages in the Bible, we can "navigate" them by consulting the guiding Compass Scriptures that direct our attention toward the character of God.

It was only after many months of shaking my questioning fist demanding answers from Almighty God, that I found a way to deal with that age-old puzzlement, "Why do bad things (divorces, for example) happen to good people?" I didn't get a full answer to that question, but I did get an insight that dwarfs it: God may have never completely explained why there is suffering, but in Jesus Christ, God not only bore our suffering, but also *entered our suffering.*

In His life on earth, Jesus experienced what it's like to be betrayed and abandoned by the people you've loved the most. Jesus experienced what it's like to lose a family member (His physical father) and close friend (Lazarus) to death, Jesus experienced what it's like to have your family think you're crazy. (See Mark 3:21). Jesus experienced what it's like to have people talk about you behind your back. Jesus experienced what it's like to be the victim of rejection even abandonment, injustice, hypocrisy, shaming, brutality, ridicule, poverty, lying, all these resulting in unfathomable pain. Especially in the last two days of Jesus' life, it's as if nearly every form of human sin came out to assail him. Jesus died, broken by the sins of the world. But then, when He rose from the dead, all of that sin and suffering was, as one commentator wrote, "swallowed by the ever-greater forgiveness and love of God."[24]

What a great discovery! In the life, death, and rising again of Jesus, we see a sweeping demonstration of the character of God. It surpasses any language we could use to describe it, but I will give you my best attempt.

I think nearly everything we need to know about His attributes can be summarized in eight words. The first three are, "God is love" (1 John 4:8), and the other five are, "full of grace and truth" (John 1:14), where "truth" refers to God's plainspoken principles of right and wrong, and "grace" describes the undeserved love and forgiveness that He grants us when we've failed to measure up to those principles.

This two-part maxim, "God is love, full of grace and truth," provides a wholistic description of God, warding off the temptation to overemphasize any one particular trait. I find it to be short, simple, and yet encompassing. It captures the climate of His Kingdom

---

[24] Robert Barron, "Why Did Jesus Have to Die the Way He Did?" *YouTube*
https://www.youtube.com/watch?v=CtcKV65-9uY)

and reminds us that the God of rigorous, life-giving truth, is also the God of benevolent grace. And on the flip side, the God of unfathomable love is also the confronter of sin. Without this balance, our view of God can become one-sided, losing sight of the forest and getting lost in the trees, or worse yet, getting lost in the weeds.

An illustration of the character of God appears in the Gospel of John when Jesus is confronted with a woman who's been caught in the very act of adultery. First, Jesus puts down a posse of hypocrites who've arrived on the scene ready to execute the wrongdoer (only one of the wrongdoers), and then Jesus has this little interchange with the guilty woman herself.

Jesus straightened up and asked her, "Woman, where are they? Has no one condemned you?" "No one, sir," she said. "Then neither do I condemn you," Jesus declared. "Go now and leave your life of sin" (John 8:10-11).

Truth: You are a sinner.

Grace: I don't condemn you.

Result: Change your pattern of sin

God is love, full of grace and truth.

In general, if what I teach offends everybody, I've professed truth without grace. And if what I teach doesn't offend anybody, I've professed grace without truth. Without a balance of the two, our view of God can become one-sided. But with a Christ-like balance in mind, we can get past our dysfunctional preconceptions and develop a healthy perspective on divorce, a perspective that matches God's own loving, grace-and-truth-based perspective on divorce.

I'll come back to this image of Compass Scriptures that point to the Lodestar of the Bible, but for now, I'll just observe that if a person has uncertainty or a blurred picture about what Scripture tells us about God, that can have a huge influence on a person's perspective on divorce and remarriage. I haven't been exempt from that uncertainty myself, but I've found that a humble self-awareness of my own uncertainty is the essential first step toward developing a biblical view of God and a godly view of divorce. Beyond this first step, I've found that a healthy perspective on divorce and remarriage develops best when our efforts are ongoing, when we're growing in self-awareness, and when our study is augmented by discussion in a caring community.

Unsurprisingly, for those of us who are divorced, it's important to wrestle not only with the question "How has your view of Scripture impacted your understanding of divorce?" but also with the opposite question: "How has your divorce affected your outlook on and experience of Scripture?" As I mentioned in the Crisis Cycle chapter, my disappointment with God, which fueled my anger and led to my depression, resulted in my being less motivated to read the Bible. And when I did read it, I found myself questioning and doubting it, especially the passages about God's character and his promises. The undercurrent of animosity that I felt toward God had a negative impact on my attitude toward what He had to say. Acknowledging that and grappling with the reasons underlying it were key steps in my recovery.

An "integrated" view of Scripture

At the beginning of this chapter, I said we would see if we can get from "God hates divorce" to the conclusion that "God loves, forgives, and restores divorced people." The first step in that progression has to be recognizing that God takes marriage very seriously. Consequently, we don't want to convey anything that would erode the purpose and sanctity of marriage. Nor do we want to encourage people who are struggling in their marriages to simply give up. Finally, we don't want to condone arbitrary divorce or "no fault" divorce.

On the other hand, I believe that, in the church today, the biggest mistake in dealing with divorce is a failure to apply a biblical balance of grace and truth. Many people have one or a few scriptures that they insist are the mind of God on divorce. Often, those verses are taken out of context and applied to all situations. Other people practice a type of 'line-item theology' that misses the larger view of a subject. While I know that biblical truth is simple, it's not simplistic. And too often in discussions of divorce, one verse of Scripture is used simplistically as a "black and white" law that tends to categorize people, even dismiss them.

Some people even insist that the Bible makes no provision for divorce, and that it unconditionally condemns and denounces it. They also insist that, if people go ahead and get divorced anyway (sometimes making an exception in a case of sexual unfaithfulness), they're sentenced to a lifelong celibacy. Perhaps you've been taught to believe that too, but in fact, Scripture tells us that every repented human failure is met by grace, healing and restoration.

To see how Bible verses can be used inappropriately, let me tell you a story. A few years ago, a man I'll call "Jeff," a counselor and one of the leaders in our Divorce & Beyond ministry, was asked to sit down with a couple who had some very serious marital issues. "Jeff" wrote the following report about that experience.

When I asked what was going on, the wife explained that she believed her husband had a severe drinking problem. The husband disagreed. When I pressed for how much alcohol he consumed on a regular basis, it surprised me how much he admitted to drinking, but his wife said it was even more. She said he became verbally and physically abusive when he drank, although only when he drank. He had recently disciplined their four-year-old daughter in a way that was verbally and physically abusive. The wife wrestled their daughter away from him and spent the night at her mother's.

Surprisingly, the husband seemed unaffected by any of his wife's descriptions of what he'd been doing. I asked him if he thought he was an alcoholic, and he said 'No.' I asked him if he would acknowledge that he had a drinking problem, and again he said 'No.' I asked him to at least talk to someone from Alcoholics Anonymous, but he considered that a waste of time. Then I looked at his wife and said, 'You need to pack your things and move out tonight.'

Well, that immediately changed his nonchalant attitude, and he loudly said, 'I thought this was a church, but you just told my wife to leave me?! And I've never been unfaithful!'

I assured him we were in a church, and I was a Christian, but the God I knew would never have people he loved stay in an abusive relationship. I made sure that the wife and daughter would be safe, and as soon as our session was over, I called one of our pastors. I explained that I had just told a woman to leave her husband and why. He said he would have told her the same thing.

I agree with that pastor and with that counselor. As Gary Thomas has written, "When a man preys on his wife and children, when he refuses to repent, when he essentially laughs at them and assumes that they can't escape his abuse because he hasn't given them a 'biblical reason' for divorce (usually described as being sexually unfaithful or abandoning them), and when he's subsequently supported by well-meaning Christians who essentially say that the shell of marriage matters more than the woman and children inside the shell, then I think we've lost the heart of God. If we're trying to preserve a shell by turning a blind eye to people being destroyed, the weight of Scripture is against us. God loves people more than he loves institutions."[25]

The objective of this chapter, then, is to simultaneously embrace both truth and grace. In other words, God's ideal purposes and lifelong design for the husband-wife relationship have to be "married" with his compassionate heart for those who are broken by the sins of one another. I don't claim to have the final answers on divorce and remarriage, and in fact, this chapter isn't intended to be a complete biblical treatise, but more of a pastoral application. However, I do believe this "integrated view" is representative of God's character and the principles of His Word and that this chapter provides Biblical guidance that'll be helpful to people dealing with divorce.

(For a more complete biblical analysis, I recommend Rubel Shelly's book, *Divorce and Remarriage, A Redemptive Theology*.[26] I will quote him a couple of times in this text.)

So as you read this chapter, I invite you to do so with an open mind and spirit, and a willingness to say, "Lord, I acknowledge that I'm bringing to this chapter a view of divorce and remarriage that's been formed by years of past experiences: the things I've studied and been taught, the things I've heard in interactions with other people, and the distorted views that I've picked up of what you are like. Use this chapter to help me to better understand divorce and remarriage from your point of view. I ask for your guidance through what I'm about to read."

---

[25] Gary Thomas, *When to Walk Away: Finding Freedom from Toxic People* (Grand Rapids, MI: Zondervan), p. 174.

[26] Rubel Shelly, *Divorce and Remarriage* (Abilene, TX: Leafwood Publishers, 2007).

Questions to Ponder:

1. Which of the questions provided insight to you?

2. How does your spirit respond to the Lodestar – God is love, full of grace and truth?

3. How do you respond to "Jeff's" story and the Gary Thomas quote?

Divorce in the Old Testament

The weighty "Law of Moses" is spread out across parts of four books in the Old Testament. In that very detailed legal code, the word "divorce" appears about nine times, and every one of those passages deals with a set of circumstances, like exactly what to do if a priest's daughter gets divorced before she has any children. To cover those passages comprehensively would result in another thirty pages that would include more details than most people would want to know. So, for the purposes of this book, I think it'll be more helpful for me to take an abbreviated route. If you want a comprehensive dissection of what the Bible teaches about divorce, I again suggest that you read an excellent book called *Divorce and Remarriage, A Redemptive Theology* by Rubel Shelly.

One of those precise laws is generally recognized as the foundational Old Testament passage about divorce, even though it too deals with a specific case. As we read this passage, it's critical that we do so with the heart of the Lawgiver in mind. In Old Testament times, the Law pointed out failure or sin, but its purpose was not to condemn, but to bless. So, with that principle in mind, read this foundational passage:

> If a man marries a woman who becomes displeasing to him because he finds something indecent about her, and he writes her a certificate of divorce, gives it to her and sends her from his house, and if after she leaves his house she becomes the wife of another man, and her second husband dislikes her and writes her a certificate of divorce, gives it to her and sends her from his house, or if he dies, then her first husband, who divorced her, is not allowed to marry her again (Deuteronomy 24:1-4).

The first thing we have to recognize about this passage is that it deals not with divorce and remarriage in general, but with a convoluted case of a woman getting bounced from one husband to another but then not back to the first. Our goal with this "foundational passage" isn't to figure out where that hapless woman should end up, but to find the general principles that are embodied in this Old Testament law. The following points summarize divorce from this "foundational passage".

- By the time Moses issued this law, divorce was already being practiced. Divorce was never God's intention for marriage, but when sin entered the world of relationships, divorce became a reality. The Law of Moses accepted that unfortunate fact. Nothing in this passage says, "Thou shalt not get divorced." Nor does he try to define exactly when divorce might be justified and when it isn't.

- Again, as a result of sin, estranged wives at the time of Moses were too often treated very unfairly. A man could divorce his wife, but a woman couldn't divorce her husband. A rejected woman would have likely been forced into poverty, begging, thievery, or even prostitution.

- This Law of Moses established requirements that if a man "put away" his wife, he had to give her a "certificate of divorce", after which he could then "send her from his house." That certificate marked the *permanent* separation of the couple. The Old Testament's prescribed divorce process prevented any hasty, whimsical decision by a man to simply "put his wife away." After a divorce, the man no longer had any claim on his ex-wife. And the certificate expressly gave both the husband and wife the freedom to get remarried. That freedom in the ex-wife's case was her best hope for a secure future for herself and her children.

- Also, when a bride got married in Old Testament times, her family provided her with a dowry—of money, goods, or property that would be put under the control of the groom to help get the marriage off to a solid start. Once again, though, because of sin, some men would ditch their wives and keep the dowry. And even though the Law doesn't say this directly, it was understood that when a husband issued a legal certificate of divorce, he also was to return the bride's dowry to help her make a new start in life.

All in all, we can see in this passage that, because of God's love for brokenhearted, crushed, and wounded people, He didn't ignore the contingency of divorce but instead gave it special attention. Specifically, in this law, Moses didn't forbid divorce; he just insisted that divorce had to be done in a way that was as fair as possible to the spurned women. As we'll see later, that's why Jesus said that Moses allowed divorce. And there's general agreement among Bible scholars that the explanation I've just given was the way the rabbis of ancient times interpreted the Law of Moses. There was no question of the lawfulness of divorce and remarriage. The only problem was some men's abuse of that allowance. Nevertheless, it's clear from this scripture that God does in fact make allowance for divorce and doesn't condemn or even denounce either party.

Divorce should never be anybody's first choice when problems develop in a marriage. But in this fallen world, God, and I, and probably you too, have seen situations in which divorce was the least evil, attainable conclusion to an irreparably damaged marriage.

Beyond Deuteronomy, there are two other significant Old Testament scriptures that deal with divorce. In the first one, God speaks through the prophet Jeremiah: "I divorced faithless Israel because of her adultery" (Jeremiah 3:8).

Yes, according to this verse, God himself has been through a divorce. In fact, He initiated it by giving a bill of divorce to "adulterous" Israel. The context is that for many years, in spite of God's repeated prohibitions, the Israelites had practiced idolatry, and the prophet was crying out, "Enough is enough. Your unfaithfulness has broken our covenant with God. You've committed the equivalent of adultery against God." And yet, even at that point, God said, "Return, faithless Israel. I will frown on you no longer, for I am faithful" (Jeremiah 3:12). But the Israelites, in the hardness of their hearts, turned a deaf ear to God's pleas. Consequently, God, more than anyone, knows the pain and the heartbreak of divorce. You can turn to him. He understands completely.

A side note: It must be recognized that the spouse who files for divorce may not be the one who has actually destroyed the marriage. The person who files the papers may have been sincerely trying to maintain the marriage or even seeking healing for the troubles that have been tearing it apart. But in recognition of the destruction that has and is occurring in the marriage and perhaps seeing no willingness on their spouse's part to take any sincere steps towards reconciliation, they finally decide to make legal the divorce that has already occurred relationally.

The second, and perhaps the most troublesome Old Testament passage about divorce is the one I quoted at the beginning of this chapter: one that's so often quoted by people who insist that Christians have no recourse other than remaining in marriages that have failed. Here's that sentence in context.

So guard your heart; remain loyal to the wife of your youth. "For I hate divorce!" says the Lord, the God of Israel, "To divorce your wife is to overwhelm her with cruelty" (Malachi 2:15b-16a NLT).

In this passage, the original Old Testament Hebrew word that's translated as "divorce" would be best rendered as "putting away." In fact, several reputable translations (the American Standard Version, the King James Version, Young's Literal Translation, and the Orthodox Jewish Bible) stay with that literal Hebrew to render the verse in English as, "I hate putting away." And as you'll recall, "putting away" was exactly what Moses had regulated back in Deuteronomy—no longer was a husband to put a wife out of the house without a certificate of divorce or the customary return of her dowry.

Beyond that, I think Malachi's reference to God "hating" divorce is explained by his next sentence where he insists that to "put away" your wife is to "overwhelm her with cruelty." Other translations render that sentiment as "deal treacherously with" or "do violence against" your wife. So, it seems most likely that Malachi is referring, not to God hating divorce in general, but to God hating a cold-hearted withholding of what He justly requires, a certificate, when the tragedy of a divorce occurs. In addition, from the wider context it's clear that Malachi is indicting men for putting away their Jewish wives without justification so they could marry foreign women—a particularly heartless maneuver.

What's more, the second reason for the "hate" in these verses was the impact that "putting away" had spiritually and emotionally. Spiritually, Malachi is indicting the men's cavalier attitude toward covenant, and covenant is always the central issue with divorce in the Bible. In addition, marrying foreign wives constituted unfaithfulness to God as well as unfaithfulness to the men's Jewish wives. Emotionally, the practice of "putting away" left deep and often permanent scars on a wife and her children.

Of course, in divorce, even when an estranged husband and wife manage to obey the letter of the Old Testament Law, God hates the collateral damage that divorce inevitably causes. In that spirit, I can say that I hate divorce too—and likely so do you. Even in the best of circumstances, the harm that divorce creates seems to continue on. Families of origin, children, and future families all pay a price for a failed marriage. In that sense, God has always hated the impact of divorce. He hates it now, but God loves the people who suffer because of divorce. He loves you! In fact, God hates divorce because He loves the people who are the casualties of divorce. Remember the lodestar, God is love, full of grace and truth.

Here are two Old Testament Compass Scriptures that reflect this lodestar.

- "The Lord is close to the brokenhearted and saves those who are crushed in spirit" (Psalm 34:18).
- "The Lord heals the brokenhearted and binds up their wounds" (Psalm 147:3).

Very few people, if any, are more "brokenhearted," "crushed," or "wounded" than those who go through a divorce. As such people repentantly come to God with their brokenness and woundedness, these Compass Scriptures assure them that God is close and that He heals and saves those in the valley of divorce.

A story by a woman who I'll call "Diane" illustrates how God relates to people who are literally "wounded" by divorce.

> *Soon after our separation, my husband received the initial paperwork regarding custody and support, and he didn't like the magistrate's orders one bit. He came to the house where the kids and I were still living. He broke down the door (after damaging my car), yelled uncontrollably about how I had ruined his life, pulled out a gun and shot me in the head. My mother believes that an angel kept him from killing me. Once he was outside, I somehow managed to call 911.*
>
> *My husband left before the police or ambulance arrived, but I watched news footage of his arrest from my hospital bed later that night. Several months later at his trial, he plead guilty to assault and attempted murder and was sent to prison.*
>
> *I went to the Divorce & Beyond seminar one month after I had been shot, and then to the follow-up support groups. I slowly began to understand how important forgiveness was for my own emotional healing and well-being. Forgiving my ex required a lot—more than I thought possible. But it was worth it to rid myself of the burden of carrying all that emotional baggage and to let healing take place.*

As evidenced by the separation in this story, "Diane's" marriage was unraveling. There may have been some strand of hope until the reprehensible action by "Diane's" ex-husband, but the fabric of what remained of their marriage totally shredded in that moment. Yet God who is rich in mercy (Ephesians 2:4), faithfully met "Diane" in the devastation of her marriage. What her ex-husband did was totally contradictory to the covenant, companionship, and consummation (Chapter One) of the marriage God ordained, and any suggestion that she would somehow sin by divorcing him when he hadn't had sex outside of marriage, seems completely incompatible with God's character and the nature of marriage. Did she have no recourse but to stay married to him? It seems clear that divorce, while always heart-wrenching, was "Diane's" and her children's best alternative. Similarly, do you think it's consistent with Deuteronomy 24 and Scripture's overarching theme of redemption to conclude that "Diane" would be living the rest of her life in adultery because of her eventual remarriage?

Using the Lodestar as I did in the story of the woman at the well in John 8, let's apply it to "Diane's" story as a way to summarize and connect the main points of these Old Testament passages.

Truth: "Diane's" marriage had been reduced to a rubble of broken ashes because of hard-hearted, sinful choices.

Grace: God makes an allowance for her and her children to exit from this destruction.

Truth: God "hates" the effect of these sinful choices on all parties involved.

Grace: God's compassion offers to forgive all parties, to bind up their wounds, and to heal the effects of their sinful choices.

Result: Restoration and the opportunity to be restored to a new marriage.

To summarize this streamlined discussion of divorce in the Old Testament, I'll quote Rubel Shelly: "The use of the Bible either to imprison people in unholy relationships or to deny them the freedom to move on with life as forgiven people in search of wholeness is … irresponsible."[27] What's more, I believe that the New Testament treatment of divorce and remarriage sheds further light on God's compassion toward people whose marriages have failed.

Questions to Ponder:

1. Have you ever considered that Moses directive was primarily to protect women? How do you emotionally respond to that?

2. Have you ever considered that God has been through a divorce? How does that speak to you?

3. Would you concur with me that 'I hate divorce?' Why or why not?

4. In light of "Diane's" story, what do you think about Rubel Shelly's quote at the end of this section?

---

[27] Rubel Shelly, *Divorce and Remarriage* (Abilene, TX: Leafwood Publishers, 2007), p. 87.

The New Testament Perspective

As I've mentioned, this chapter isn't intended to be an exhaustive study of what the Bible teaches about divorce and remarriage. For the New Testament perspective, I'm going to focus on the teachings of Jesus in the gospel of Matthew because that's the book most often cited regarding divorce. In fact, the New Testament verse that's most often quoted regarding divorce comes from the gospel of Matthew: "Anyone who divorces his wife, except for sexual immorality, makes her the victim of adultery, and anyone who marries a divorced woman commits adultery" (Matthew 5:32). But before jumping to conclusions, we need to make sure we read these verses in context in order to understand the way Jesus intended them.

Recall that just earlier in this same chapter, Jesus' Sermon on the Mount in Matthew 5 begins with more Compass Scriptures in verses 3-10, describing the heart and character of God:

"Blessed are the poor in spirit, for theirs is the kingdom of heaven."

"Blessed are those who mourn, for they will be comforted."

"Blessed are the meek, for they will inherit the earth."

"Blessed are those who hunger and thirst for righteousness, for they will be filled."

"Blessed are the pure in heart, for they will see God."

"Blessed are the peacemakers, for they will be called children of God."

"Blessed are those who are persecuted because of righteousness, for theirs is the kingdom of heaven."

Now, if there's any uncertainty about what Jesus teaches about divorce in Chapter 5 of Matthew, in the end our interpretation of it will need to be consistent with these powerful Compass Scriptures at the beginning of this sermon.

At the same time, we need to recognize that Jesus' first reference to divorce comes in the middle of a much longer passage, encompassing chapters 5-7.

I think it's fair to suggest that if we could talk to people who were present at that Sermon on the Mount, and if we could ask them what Jesus said, his two sentences about divorce and remarriage probably wouldn't be the first things to come to their minds. In fact, the context of those two sentences on divorce is so important that I think we need to read them together with some of the surrounding verses, as in the following abridgment.

"Do not think that I have come to abolish the Law or the Prophets; I have not come to abolish them but to fulfill them."

"I tell you that unless your righteousness surpasses that of the Pharisees and the teachers of the law, you will certainly not enter the kingdom of heaven."

"You have heard that it was said to the people long ago, 'You shall not murder, and anyone who murders will be subject to judgment.' But I tell you that anyone who is angry with a brother or sister will be subject to judgment."

"You have heard that it was said, 'You shall not commit adultery.' But I tell you that anyone who looks at a woman lustfully has already committed adultery with her in his heart."

"If your right eye causes you to stumble, gouge it out and throw it away. It is better for you to lose one part of your body than for your whole body to be thrown into hell."

"And if your right hand causes you to stumble, cut it off and throw it away. It is better for you to lose one part of your body than for your whole body to go into hell."

"It has been said, 'Anyone who divorces his wife must give her a certificate of divorce.' But I tell you that anyone who divorces his wife, except for sexual immorality, makes her the victim of adultery, and anyone who marries a divorced woman commits adultery."

"You have heard that it was said, 'Love your neighbor and hate your enemy.' But I tell you, love your enemies and pray for those who persecute you."

"Be perfect, therefore, as your heavenly Father is perfect."

This whole sequence of "you have heard it said" statements could be titled "Heaven's Dream." It's a picture of "Eden Restored." It describes the Kingdom values and relationships that have always mattered most to God. At the time of Jesus, the Pharisees, while ferociously dedicated to following the intricacies and their added nuances to the Law, had disconnected that Law from those Kingdom values and relationships, focusing instead on external observances of the Law. That's why Jesus said that the righteousness of His followers would have to exceed that of the Pharisees. Jesus was calling His followers to surpass the Pharisees by obeying God from the heart—not by just mechanically obeying the letter of the Law, and certainly not by dutifully obeying the hundreds of additions that the Pharisees had attached to God's Law. Jesus makes it clear that He hasn't come to abolish the Old Testament Law, but to fulfill it. So, He repeatedly instructs His followers to keep the Law, but more importantly to follow the *intent* of the Law, and not merely the *letter* of the Law. Jesus' mission was to transform the *hearts* of His followers; to sincerely love God, their neighbors, and even their enemies.

In the two following bullet points, I've paraphrased what Jesus said, just to emphasize the way He repeatedly contrasted "you have heard it said" with "I tell you."

- It's been said that murder is an offense against God, and that's true. But I tell you that even getting angry is a failure to demonstrate the heart of God.
- It's been said that adultery is an offense against God, and that's true. But I tell you that even looking at a woman lustfully is a failure to demonstrate the heart of God.

And now, in one more bullet point, I'll paraphrase the verses on divorce in a way that brings out the same pattern.

- It's been said that men can give their wives certificates of divorce, and that's true. But I tell you that breaking the covenant of marriage by divorce is as much a failure as breaking it by adultery and fails to demonstrate the heart of God.

Did Jesus say that anger is a very serious offense? Yes. Did He say that lust is a very serious offense? Yes. And did He say that breaking the covenant of marriage is a very serious offense? Yes. That is the truth. Just to clarify, God Himself does have ways of being righteously angry, but anger among humans is seldom godly.

But what about grace? How does Jesus relate to those of us who've gotten angry, those of us who've let our desires cross the line into lust, and those of us who've broken the covenant of marriage? Jesus answers those questions in another Compass Scripture that's right there in the same gospel of Matthew: Then Peter came to him (Jesus) and asked, "Lord, how often should I forgive someone who sins against me? Seven times?" "No, not seven times," Jesus replied, "but seventy times seven!" (Matthew 18:21-22).

Looking at the whole gospel of Matthew, we have to conclude that anger, lust, and breaking the covenant of marriage are sins against God, but God forgives repentant sinners. Yes, God takes sins very seriously, but this Compass Scripture tells us that if Jesus admonishes Peter to forgive seventy times seven, how many times does God extend forgiveness to us? Remember the lodestar: God is love, full of grace and truth.

But now, let's look at a literary device that Jesus uses in this sermon. This literary device is vivid in verses 29 and 30 where Jesus talks about gouging out eyes and cutting off hands. Take a second look at those two shocking verses.

"If your right eye causes you to stumble, gouge it out and throw it away. It is better for you to lose one part of your body than for your whole body to be thrown into hell. And if your right hand causes you to stumble, cut it off and throw it away. It is better for you to lose one part of your body than for your whole body to go into hell" (Matthew 5:29-30).

Reader, raise your right hand. Now put it down if you've never used it to steal, to strike a person, to falsely point and blame, have illicit sex, or to otherwise harm anyone. If you're like me, your hand is still up! And furthermore, your eye socket is empty! So, here's the unavoidable, ghastly question: Does Jesus expect us to conform to Kingdom values by hacking off our hands and wrenching out our eyeballs?

Keep in mind the Compass Scripture I just cited in Matthew 18. Obviously, this amputation imagery is an example of *hyperbole*—elaborate exaggeration that's used to make a point. Elsewhere in the gospels, Jesus used hyperbole when He said things such as, "Take the log out of your own eye" and "It's easier for a camel to go through the eye of a needle." And in this stark passage about hands and eyes, Jesus is again using hyperbole to very vividly and very memorably emphasize the values and relationships that are most important in the Kingdom of God.

Did Jesus really think it would be less of a problem to lose a hand or an eye than to lose the Kingdom of Heaven? Yes. He said that very directly. In other words, He is saying that by comparison it is better to lose a hand, or an eye than not to have your heart right with God and be cast into hell. But did Jesus expect His followers to have such purity of heart that their hands and eyes would remain intact? Or in contrast, did He expect them to hack off their right hands or wrench out their right eyeballs? No, or His followers would've been known for their absence of limbs and eyeballs! And we all know that they would have kept right on sinning with their left hands and their left eyes. So, Jesus wasn't telling people to dismember themselves. He was using the literary device of hyperbole to emphasize the seriousness of sin and that it is the heart of a person that matters most to God.

Now, remember that this amputation hyperbole is in the midst of where Jesus ranked anger with murder, lust with adultery, and so forth. Did Jesus think that anger is destructive to Kingdom values the same way murder is? Yes. That's what He said, even though their human consequences are very different. But did Jesus expect His followers would never again be angry? Would they never again be guilty of lust? Would they never resist the evil actions of another person? Would they always reconcile with others and always love even their enemies? The answers to those questions were as obvious to Jesus as they are to us and it's quite clear that those who followed Him for nearly three years didn't perfectly embody Kingdom values. Rather, Jesus was telling people to avoid anger in the same way that He was telling them to chop off their hands—not with an expectation that they would be able to do either one, but rather in a vivid, memorable use of hyperbole to emphasize the seriousness of sin, because of its effects on their heart and its consequences upon others.

So at long last, here's the key point that I want to make: The Lodestar of the Bible is that "God is love, full of grace and truth." God's *truth about* our sins is always coupled with God's *grace for* our sins. *The fact that Jesus called His followers to perfect love didn't mean He expected they would always be perfectly capable of it.* But God offers grace for our failures of anger, grace for our failures of lust, and grace for our hatred and vengeance, because it's grace that continues to transform our hearts, enabling us to become those who love more and more as God does. And this is the context of Jesus' remarks on divorce and remarriage. Should they be regarded any differently than all of our other failures?

Let's go back to those troublesome sentences about divorce in Jesus' sermon.

"It has been said, 'Anyone who divorces his wife must give her a certificate of divorce.' But I tell you that anyone who divorces his wife, except for sexual immorality, makes her the victim of adultery, and anyone who marries a divorced woman commits adultery" (Matthew 5:31-32).

If we apply the same logic here that we've applied to the rest of Jesus' sermon, we can conclude that, from God's perspective, divorce and adultery are two acts of the same type. They're both the result of very serious sins of the heart. (I address Jesus' "exception" statement in the next section, Matthew 19:3-9.)

But again, in light of the theme and the literary device in Jesus' sermon, (that both precede and follow these verses) it seems fair to ask, "Did Jesus expect that His followers would never get divorced, and did Jesus insist that getting divorced would *constitute* actual adultery?" To answer Yes to those questions means that anytime the followers of Jesus get angry, they're guilty of murder, and every time His followers engage in lust, they're guilty of adultery (which would then be reasons for divorce or even stoning).

As Rubel Shelly has noted, "Nowhere is it harder to keep the nature and purpose of the Sermon on the Mount clearly in mind than in [Matthew 5:31-32]."[28] Shelly contends that we tend to run to these two verses with the wrong questions, and consequently, we tend to come back with the wrong answers. In other words, we try to learn from these verses whether it's morally permissible to get divorced or remarried when that's just not the question that Jesus was dealing with when He spoke these sentences. Instead, Jesus is calling attention to the seriousness of divorce. Jesus is underscoring what a divorce is: a breach or violation of the marriage covenant. And by comparing divorce to adultery, Jesus is emphasizing the gravity of this sin. This understanding of our two disconcerting verses is consistent with Jesus' central theme of "the heart of sin" as well as His repeated use of hyperbole.

Furthermore, note that Jesus is addressing the man in the marriage, not the woman. Women were not permitted to divorce a husband, which was the reason underlying Moses' decree: to protect women. How can the wife become a "victim of adultery" (NKJV) unless the husband has committed adultery first in the act of divorce? Keeping the context of His sermon, Jesus is exposing the man's heart and accompanying motives. Why? Because the husband's action of divorce begins in his heart. It is there that he begins adulterating or breaking the covenant of his marriage. Then his action of divorce becomes the outward expression, resulting in the violation of his marriage covenant.

Divorce is not the failure of the marriage but rather the acknowledgment of a failed marriage. The adulteration or pollution of a marriage dilutes its commitments over time, and the "mistress" or "other lover" can be many things besides another person, such as addictions. Adultery then is the illegitimate dissolution of a marriage first in the heart and then in action, which in this passage, Jesus says then makes her "an adulteress", that is, a victim of adultery. (Not that she commits adultery.) Again, keep in mind the continued use of hyperbole. Just prior, lust was equated with adultery. Now Jesus is using the same hyperbolic style, equating divorce with adultery to emphasize the seriousness of the man's action.

Remember that earlier in the Sermon on the Mount, Jesus specifically states that He doesn't come to abolish the Law, but rather to fulfill it. So, He's not replacing the rules Moses set up for divorce and remarriage in Deuteronomy 24. Jesus doesn't retract the necessity of issuing a certificate of divorce in irreparable situations. And Jesus doesn't condemn a divorced woman to a lifetime of stigma as an adulterer. To believe that Jesus

---

[28] Rubel Shelly, *Divorce and Remarriage* (Abilene, TX: Leafwood Publishers, 2007), p. 83.

did would be to believe that Jesus discarded the Old Testament rules in favor of a more narrow, strict, and legalistic set of rules. That would conflict with the spirit of Jesus' teaching that it is our heart and our motives that matter most to God.

Let's try to apply this understanding of Jesus' teaching in a real-life situation. Consider "Daniel's" story:

My wife had grown up in a family with an alcoholic, rageaholic father. He would abuse his wife and his children and then take them to church and act as if they were a 'normal' family.

That rageaholic father died six months into our marriage, but the counselors we had seen throughout the course of our marriage concurred that my wife still had unresolved anger issues toward him. What's more, she was transferring that anger onto me. For more years that I want to remember, I was on the receiving end of outbursts of anger, hostility, quarreling, lying, physical abuse, emotional abuse, and spiritual abuse—all hidden under the facade of a Christian marriage. It got to the point where I could no longer live that way. That's when I made the decision to walk away from a toxic marriage and end the abuse.

No marriage is easy. Every marriage must overcome instances of hurt, pain, and sin. But can we agree that the problems in "Daniel's" marriage weren't the common struggles of living with a common sinner? Tragically, "Daniel's" wife was the victim of a traumatic childhood, and like too many victims, she consistently chose to scuttle her own happiness and the happiness of her marriage, rather than pursue the healing that God's grace and Christ-centered modalities, such as counseling, groups, etc. could have provided. As you've probably observed, when spouses aren't truly repentant of blatant, ruinous behavior, they don't change.

And that brings us to the pivotal question: Would it seem consistent with Jesus' teaching to say that "Daniel" committed an offense against God by divorcing his deeply wounded, hard-hearted, abusive wife, even though she hadn't betrayed him sexually? Was "Daniel" completely innocent of any wrongdoing in his marriage? Of course not. But is it God's intent to lock people into destructive relationships and deny them the freedom to move forward with their lives? Does God want to block men and women from living as forgiven people and continuing to grow into who God created them to be? Does it honor God's intentions for "Christian marriage" to force a couple to prolong an unchanging, devastating relationship that's slowly squeezing the life out of both of them? I'm convinced that Jesus said what He did about divorce to *protect* abused, exhausted spouses in destructive marriages, not to imprison them.

Rubel Shelly concludes, "Jesus is not 'trying to tighten the screws' on people, as if that would eliminate unrighteous behaviors. He did not take the attainable prohibition against murder and ratchet it up to an impossible-to-obey command against anger. Neither may we reasonably understand him to teach that lust is as bad as adultery. Yet we have succumbed to the mistake of equating divorce and remarriage with adultery. Anger, lust, and failure to stay married may all be repented of and forgiven."[29]

---

[29] Rubel Shelly, *Divorce and Remarriage* (Abilene, TX: Leafwood Publishers, 2007), p. 92.

In summary, in his inaugural sermon, Jesus is emphatic about three themes:

- God's Ideal: "Be perfect, therefore, as your heavenly Father is perfect." In our hearts, Jesus calls us to never curse another, never lust, never harbor anger, never divorce, never hate enemies, never resist reconciliation, but none of us reaches this standard. Only Jesus fulfilled the law.

- Our Reality: What's real is that in our hearts we all curse one another, we all get angry, we all lust, we seldom love our enemies, few of us reconcile, and many of us divorce. Perhaps an analogy would help. Say the ideal standard represented jumping across the Ohio River at Cincinnati, a span of over 1200 feet. None of us could do it. An Olympic athlete might get 25 feet out, some of us only five feet, and I would probably trip at the riverbank! Regardless, we'd all fall perilously short. When we fall short spiritually, confession and repentance are always the most appropriate responses to our reality.

- God's Grace: God, rich in mercy, has provided a solution, Jesus, who bridges the shortfall, whatever the distance! We reach the opposite shoreline because we have accepted Jesus' offer of the bridge of forgiveness and restoration. God views us as having accomplished the Ideal because Jesus did it in our stead. The apostle Paul calls this "justification." (See Romans 3:24, 4:25, 5:1, 9, 18.) As others have, I like to refer to justification as being "just as if I'd" never sinned.

In addition to this new position of justification, the process of applying God's mercy and grace to our failures results in us growing closer to God's ideal, and this growth is theologically called "sanctification." In reference to jumping across the Ohio River, God's grace can enable us to "jump farther" and then even farther as time goes on. We continue to heal and become more like the people God created us to be. But we will never be able to cover the complete distance. We will always need Jesus to bridge our shortfalls. I'm convinced that the stage of sanctification can include another marriage. God's solution to our failures is His perfect love, and that solution covers even the failure of divorce, and the possibility of re-marriage.

Matthew 19: 3-9

Now let's carry this forward and review another situation that Jesus encountered later in the Gospel of Matthew. (This same incident is recorded in Mark 10:1-12.)

Some Pharisees came to [Jesus] to test him. They asked, 'Is it lawful for a man to divorce his wife for any and every reason?' 'Haven't you read,' he replied, 'that at the beginning the Creator made them male and female,' and said, 'For this reason a man will leave his father and mother and be united to his wife, and the two will become one flesh" So they are no longer two, but one flesh. Therefore what God has joined together, let no one separate" (Matthew 19:3-6.)

This passage is the beginning of Jesus' longest (seven sentences!) treatment of divorce. Interestingly, Jesus didn't initiate this discussion, but rather it began in response to a trick question from the Pharisees. The whole conversation takes place in the geographical area where John the Baptist was arrested, imprisoned, and beheaded for confronting Herod Antipas and his wife Herodias about their illicit marriage. (Herod married Herodias after she was divorced from his half-brother, which was a violation of the Old Testament Law.) It appears that when the Pharisees asked their trick question, they were trying to set a trap, hoping that Jesus' response would get him in trouble with Herod and result in the same outcome as Herod had mandated for John the Baptist. Essentially, the Pharisees were devising a plan to accomplish their goal of killing Jesus, through Herod.

Observe that the question the Pharisees confront Jesus with is only about the *reasons* a man can divorce his wife, not about the *legitimacy* of divorce itself. It's especially shocking that the Pharisees were so picky to observe the Law, even to the point of creating all kinds of other traditions to ensure that they didn't even come close to transgressing the Law, and yet, when it came to divorce, their dominant view was that a man could divorce his wife for her failure to cook or clean well, or for a myriad of other trivial reasons. So, in responding to their question, Jesus brought the Pharisees back to God's original plan for marriage, as presented in Genesis 2.

The Pharisees had come to regard marriage as merely a contract, one that could easily be torn up and broken. They thought divorce was merely the tearing of a *parchment*, and they hard-heartedly neglected to realize that it was actually the tearing of a *covenant* with another person. But Jesus turns the tables on them. He emphatically reminds them that marriage is first and foremost a covenant ordained by God, and that God's intention from the beginning was that the covenant of marriage would last forever. (That is, in fact, why the failure of a marriage is so painful.) Jesus also states that whatever violates the "leave, cleave, one flesh" mandate has the effect of separating what God has joined together.

Returning to the next verse of our Bible passage, we see that the Pharisees then try to trap Jesus by goading Him into saying something against the Jewish law that had been set down by God through Moses hundreds of years earlier in Deuteronomy 24.

> 'Why then," they asked, "did Moses command that a man give his wife a certificate of divorce and send her away?' Jesus replied, 'Moses permitted you to divorce your wives because your hearts were hard. But it was not this way from the beginning' (Matthew 19:7-8).

At this point, it's clear that the Pharisees had totally whiffed on the primary purpose of Moses' instruction. Rather than realizing that it was to protect the rights of women, they had reduced it to serve their own desires: to divorce a wife for nearly any cause. Essentially, Jesus declares that no one has the right to be faithless to their spouse. Debate over. But because men throughout history allowed their hearts to grow hard and put away their wives frivolously, Moses had set up a law to protect women. Likewise, what Jesus said about divorce protects women; it doesn't imprison them.

Ultimately, Jesus identifies *hardness of heart as the foundational cause and universal reason for divorce.* From the beginning, God never wanted marriages to fail, but hardness of heart was why they did. Jesus didn't wade into all the nuances of why marriages fall apart. He didn't have to. We all know what people do to each other when their hearts are hard: they hurt each other with their words and actions. The forms that these words and actions take are numerous, but they're all harmful and damaging.

At this point in Jesus' discussion with the Pharisees, He declares, "Whoever divorces his wife, except for sexual immorality, and marries another woman commits adultery" (Matthew 19:9). It is imperative to bear in mind here that Jesus specifically addresses the actions of the husband, just as He did in Matthew 5:31-32. Jesus' response is revolutionary. As in Matthew 5:31-32, He includes the phrase, "except for sexual immorality." It's clear that Jesus pinpoints sexual immorality as a unique act of destruction against the marriage. It violates all three C's of marriage: covenant, companionship and consummation. Therefore, Jesus recognizes its extensive damage and that it is severe enough that the victim can be released from the one flesh relationship.

Let's briefly examine the word "adultery." The Greek noun form is *moicheia*, and it means "a breach of covenant." That's the word that's used here. Therefore, to commit adultery is to violate a person's marriage covenant. In context, it seems clear then, that the word "adultery" isn't necessarily a reference to sex, but to men hard-heartedly breaching their covenant of marriage to marry another woman. Again, Jesus is calling attention to the intent and motives of the heart. That understanding is consistent with Jesus' teaching in Matthew 5 and for that matter, throughout His ministry. The phrase "commits adultery," then, can be understood figuratively, not descriptively.

Given this understanding, the unjustified dissolution of a marriage covenant constitutes adultery, whether a remarriage ever occurs or not. There are certainly instances when a person's hardness of heart leads to affairs of the heart, which then starts to dissolve their marriage covenant. In our modern world, social media and artificial intelligence technology can be used to entice affairs of the heart more easily than ever, feeding our ego and enticing us to believe "the grass is greener on the other side". A friendly gesture can quickly enflame relational desires and lust. Similarly, abuse can destroy a marriage, and so can addictions, not only to alcohol or drugs, but also to things like work or violence and the destructive behaviors that result from any of these. These behaviors begin to violate or adulterate the marital three Cs over time and can result in the heart becoming so hard that divorce becomes the better alternative than the destruction of the people involved. Even so, can men (or women) be forgiven for this covenant breaking? Our Lodestar says, of course they can. In fact, Jesus' clarification of divorce as adultery at a point in time makes it clear that repentance is the gateway to remedy—forgiveness and healing—which then opens the possibilities of health and growth for each party.

Let me illustrate how unexpectedly God's remedy can work out in action: There was a woman who came to a Divorce & Beyond seminar and then participated in the follow-up groups. Her husband had been sexually unfaithful, and consequently she had filed for divorce. But as she began the journey of forgiveness (see the Forgiveness chapter), God began to heal her wound of betrayal. Her heart began to soften toward her soon-to-be ex-husband. As she prayed for him, she began to sense that it wasn't yet time to file for a divorce. So, just days before they were to appear in court for the divorce to be granted, she withdrew the paperwork.

Many years later that woman and her husband were reconciled! I honestly can't imagine the patient, but painful, ordeal she went through. She told me that she had believed it was God's healing that had kept her heart tender toward her estranged husband. She had a sincere conviction that she should wait, but that if her husband wanted to remarry, she would grant him a divorce. He never did want to remarry, and neither did she. It wasn't because she didn't think she could divorce him, but because God had given her a peace to wait and see if her husband would someday repent and want to reconcile. I want to quickly add that this kind of outcome isn't common, and I'm not trying to suggest to anyone whose spouse has committed infidelity that they should follow the same course. Rather, I'm just emphasizing that repentance, forgiveness, and healing in both parties can indeed provide the power for potential reconciliation.

What's more, I resist the notion that sexual unfaithfulness constitutes inflexible "grounds for divorce." Please understand that I'm not glossing over the pain of sexual betrayal. As Jesus indicates, it violates the covenant of marriage like no other insidious act can, but the idea that sexual adultery requires divorce isn't found in scripture. Rather Jesus says that it is because of "hardness of heart" that Moses, on behalf of God, allowed or permitted divorce. As a marriage deteriorates, the hearts of both parties become harder toward the other. That's what happens when love has spoiled. Both spouses play a part. Yes, usually one spouse's heart is harder and begins to commit more damaging hard-hearted acts toward the other. But when one announces that they have "grounds for divorce," it more likely reveals their own hard-heartedness, however understandable it may be. That doesn't mean that divorce shouldn't be the result. It's just important to realize that it's in the healthiest interest of each spouse to deal with their own heart condition.

Prior to the remarriage of either partner, reconciliation of the parties to their covenant can remain an option. But remarriage of either party ends any possibility of that, as Moses declared in Deuteronomy 24:1-2. Therefore, remarriage is the demarcation, "the point of no return." The assumption in both Testaments is that both the man and woman will remarry and that doing so is not "living in adultery." In fact, repentance from the attitudes and actions that led to the ending of a previous marriage can pave the way for a healthier second marriage. Therefore, a subsequent remarriage is a real marriage, not an ongoing case of "living in adultery."

In the Greek language, the verb "divorce" literally means "puts or sends away." I think that is a word that describes what is actually occurring, first in the heart of one or both spouses, and eventually when a divorce is filed. Divorce is the sending away, the rejection of the covenant of marriage by the people involved. This is important because it highlights what is happening in one or both hearts that must be recognized in order to be healed by the grace of God.

As we have already seen, God's remedy included each of the following:

- Out of love for imperfect, fallible people, God provided an exception to His original decree of married people permanently becoming "one flesh."

- Out of grace and mercy, God allowed Moses to make this exception to keep His people from destroying each other.

- We are always expected to make a commitment to the ideal, but God acknowledges and provides for the reality of failure, which leads to redemption and the possibility of re-marriage.

By the way, I believe the value of marriage counseling would be enhanced if it explored the question "How have your hearts become hard toward one another?" As each spouse identifies the attitudes and actions that are resulting from that hardness, and displays a willingness to acknowledge, confess, and repent of those, first inwardly, and then to the other, real healing can occur.

Questions to Ponder:

1. What insights did this section have for you to consider?

2. Which story(s) was the most meaningful? Why?

Conclusion

A man I'll call "Adrien" participated in a Divorce & Beyond seminar and follow up group. His heartbreaking story illustrates how a marriage can slowly become "adulterated," (also, unclean, poisoned, contaminated, spoiled, ruined).

I got married shortly after college. My wife and I were part of a church-planting team. Our commitment to God and our joint purpose formed a solid bond between us. Our marital conflicts were quickly forgiven. But in the pace of life and ministry, we didn't spend much time understanding how our personal brokenness affected our relationship.

A move across the country and a ministry of planting a new church paved the way to our next logical step: children. The many new connections and opportunities to lead people into relationship with Jesus were very fulfilling for me. However, in the midst of my rewarding work, and raising our four children, my marriage was not thriving.

At this point, I began to discover more about myself—what I liked, what I wanted, and what I needed. I started individual counseling to explore the impact that my childhood history of being adopted had on my behaviors and motivations. I ultimately decided with my board of directors that it would be best for me to set aside my church-planting work, and our family pursued another direction. With four kids in tow, my wife and I moved to a new city, and I joined the staff of a large, fast-growing church.

The new position was a dream job that leveraged my skills and passions. But I spent long hours away from home, leaving my wife with now five young children. My new job nourished my needs for success, identity, and purpose in life, but aspects of my brokenness pushed me toward workaholism, poor boundaries, and neglecting the overwhelmed condition of my wife. Her own wounds compounded the situation, and we each needed to take responsibility for the breakdown of our relationship. (A wise friend once said this about dysfunction in relationships: "My problem is me; your problem is you.")

For many reasons, including an attempt to save our marriage, I resigned from my ministry job, and we went to marriage counseling. In what turned out to be our final appointment, the counselor emphatically said to me, "Don't you get it? She's done with you!"

The unraveling of our relationship had been in process over a number of years, and tragically our marriage was beyond repair. Divorce was simply an outward acknowledgement of what had already happened inwardly. My feelings of rejection, failure, and loss were overwhelming. The implications to our children and our friendships were staggering. The consuming shame and the assault on my very being were utterly debilitating.

From birth to adulthood, we accumulate wounds from parents, family, teachers, and peers. These wounds may come through abuse, comparisons, criticism, jealousy, putdowns, rejection, resentment, shame, and other hurts. In Chapter 1, I used the analogy of a bag of rocks to depict these wounds. God's design is that the bag we bring into marriage would get lighter because of the healing power of love that spouses experience from one another. However, in a failed marriage the rocks in our bags multiply in number and weight due to the adulteration, and maybe infidelity in the marriage.

But regardless of the size or number of your personal rocks, when they're acknowledged, confessed, and repented of, Jesus forgives and redeems them with the goal of healing and restoring you! Every account of Jesus' forgiveness is accompanied by a new beginning—restoration to a fresh future. Regardless of the reasons for divorce, from sexual unfaithfulness to the most trivial, redemption awaits. Regardless of whether you have deliberately destroyed your marriage, or your coldness of heart was much more subtle, renewal by God's grace can prevail. His purpose is to liberate you to be who He intended you to be. But acknowledgment, confession and repentance are the keys that open up God's treasure chest of healing.

Repentance from the particular ways you contributed to the breakdown of a failed marriage is in fact critical for *your* spiritual and relational health. It paves the way for healing and wholesome relationships, with family as well as others. It's a sort of cleansing. Without this trio of keys, rocks that continue to accumulate and grow will undermine a divorced person's future, blocking the healing that brings freedom—the freedom to be who God uniquely intended you to be. You can likely identify some of your own acquaintances who, after a divorce, continue to carry burdensome "rocks" in their lives and relationships. Tragically, it's known that second marriages fail more than first marriages mostly because of this reality.

More Stories

In my own case, some of the rocks that were either enlarged or added through the divorce process and in the months that followed were: fear of relational and emotional intimacy and its resulting mistrust, fear of not enough (primarily love and money), cynicism, and shame. Candid counseling, support groups, and in-your-face friendships helped me to identify these; as I repented, I began to re-tenderize my heart. One vivid example of this came to light while I was dating Laura. We had dated for about nine months, and our relationship had become serious enough for us to begin discussing what our future together might look like. She revealed that she was looking forward to having children. (She hadn't been married before.) Suddenly, an alarm sounded in me. Children?! Naively, the thought hadn't crossed my mind, but now that it was on the table, I wanted it off. Laura had unknowingly poked one of my large rocks, and my immediate impulse was to guard it. This rock had been formed by the wounds I carried from the breakdown of my relationship with my two children from my first marriage. I was emphatic that I didn't want to risk the hurt of having more children—so much so that Laura and I broke off our dating relationship.

But God was gracious. He used the pain of our breakup to help me recognize (acknowledge) this rock and the origins of its presence and power. Over the next four months, I came to grips with its dysfunction and determined that I wanted to be free of it. I confessed it and repented of it and began to experience God's healing, enough that I humbly asked if Laura would re-engage our courtship with the agreement that we could plan to have children. She graciously did, and we were married nine months later. When we were expecting our first child, I once again encountered that rock. That happened when we were attending a church service that was focused on personal renewal. I sensed the Spirit probing my heart, and it became apparent to me that I was still protecting my heart from our child that Laura was carrying. The persistence of this rock had been unknown to me. I could tell that it was smaller and less powerful now, but nevertheless its influence was still there. I began to experience what the Bible describes as "Godly sorrow," and I started to weep. Confession and repentance followed and once more applied a healing salve to my heart.

Most rocks of any size don't disappear in one episode. Rather, at specific times, they are chipped away, and each time they are, our hearts grow a bit more tender and whole. Together, Laura and I now have two adult children, both of whom I deeply love. Over time, God has used them to further chip away the remnants of that rock and usher in more of His healing.

Now for another story. The primary character in this one is the woman Jesus met at the well in John Chapter 4. You'll see she was carrying a massive bag of rocks! Here's how that story might have unfolded as it's been depicted in the book *Encounters with Jesus* by J. R. Hudberg.

The sun at its peak made the heat nearly unbearable. Not the ideal time for manual labor. But the early morning hours for drawing water were not an inviting time for everyone, at least not for her. It hadn't taken many mornings for her to decide that suffering the heat and sun was preferable to the scorn and ridicule of her neighbors. She felt like she had five scarlet "Ds" stamped on her forehead.

With a jar on her shoulder, she left her home. She looked around as she made her way to the well. The side stares were normal. She still noticed them, but routine has its benefits, and she no longer cried. She stopped when she saw the figure sitting at the well. A moment's indecision held her. With a sigh, she steeled herself. A man at the well in the middle of the day wasn't simply unexpected; it was unprecedented. She would keep to herself, get her water, and get home.

He spoke and asked for a drink. Despite the brief conversation being a bit odd – the way he spoke of living water was strange – this was going better than she could have imagined. This man was warm and caring. He didn't seem to mind the differences between them that had first concerned her. Until the conversation turned personal. He asked her to bring her husband. The uneasy and intrusive question was easily sidestepped. "I have no husband." Painful but true. What he said next tightened her chest and turned her stomach. He knew. He knew about her, and not just her present, but her past as well. Knowing her man was not her husband was surprising, but not completely implausible. But how did he know about her past? Did he know the full story? He was clearly a prophet, and so he may well have, and the thought of bringing those issues into open conversation was like opening a mortal wound.

She learned he did know her. He knew her like no one else did. And he revealed why. He was the Messiah![30]

The woman in this story had been married five times and wasn't married to the man with whom she currently lived. Recall her cultural context: Five husbands had divorced her. Imagine the pain of that compounded rejection. And now likely out of financial desperation, she had chosen to now succumb to living outside of marriage with a man, and she was bearing the shame that came with that choice. There's no mention of children. Perhaps she was barren, which would only have heaped more shame upon her, and it may have been a reason that she was divorced by her husbands. This was a very broken woman whose life was clearly out of control—precisely the kind of person Jesus loved and sought out. Jesus simply called out her situation and behaviors. He didn't condemn or denounce her behavior, past or present. He didn't say she was living in adultery. He didn't tell her to "marry or move out." He simply offered her the transformation of living water by identifying who He was.

Her response was to stake her life on that very discovery, as evidenced by the way she went back to her village and proclaimed, "He told me everything I ever did." Did you catch that? "He told me everything I ever did." *There's a profound freedom in her boldness.* It was a far cry from "He judged me for everything I ever did." The townspeople already knew "everything she had ever done." There can be little doubt that she had been judged, labeled, and ridiculed for it. So why did so many of the townspeople come out to see if this man at the well was indeed the Messiah? It must have been the compelling nature of her transformation and declaration. John the gospel writer says, "Many believed in him because of the woman's testimony: 'He told me everything I ever did.'"

This woman's narrative testifies loud and clear of our Lodestar, "God is love, full of grace and truth." Redemption and restoration result from an encounter with that truth and grace, and this woman demonstrated that so convincingly that many came to see Jesus for themselves. "Could this be true? How could this woman's life be so dramatically transformed?" The people whom she used to avoid, whom she knew used to cast pitying glances toward her and speak unkind words about her, now came to her. Because of Jesus, she found a new place in the community and a new faith in the Messiah. Although they stayed an additional two days, John makes no mention of what became of the relationship of the woman and the man she was living with. Evidently, it wasn't important enough to mention. Would it have been to you?

What the Law can't do, Grace can!

As we near the end of this chapter, I hope you've tasted God's message and can conclude with me that divorce is not a sin in its own special class that requires a lifelong penalty of

---

[30] J. R. Hudberg, *Encounters with Jesus* (Grand Rapids, MI: Our Daily Bread Publishers, 2021), pp. 30–35.

any kind—shame, or probation, or remaining celibate. It's inconsistent with the Compass Scriptures to believe that there's no biblical option other than living forever with the failure of a marriage. Think about it: Would it be consistent to believe that Jesus can heal any physical, emotional, and spiritual condition, forgive any sin, and restore any hard hearts, even of those who murdered Him, but not those who have divorced? He redeemed them to live new lives with new possibilities, but He would not heal, forgive, restore, and redeem those people who have failed in their marriage? *What the law cannot do, grace can!*

"He heals the broken hearted and binds up their wounds" Psalm 147:3 Yes, every divorce is the result of sin, and every divorce is an act of adultery against the covenant of marriage, but as I've said, divorce is not a sin in its own special class that requires any kind of lifelong penance such as remaining single. Rather, it seems most consistent with the Compass Scriptures that divorce, although serious, can be forgiven under any circumstance. Divorced people can get back on their feet, heal, and pursue God's ideal. In fact, the Bible is written by people God redeemed from massive failures and blessed with new life and opportunities. If all the books of the Bible written by a murderer or adulterer were removed, all that would be left is a skinny remnant.

When He launched his public ministry, Jesus quoted the prophet Isaiah:

The Spirit of the Sovereign LORD is on me, because the LORD has anointed me to proclaim good news to the poor. He has sent me to bind up the brokenhearted, to proclaim freedom for the captives and release from darkness for the prisoners, to proclaim the year of the Lord's favor (Isaiah 61:1-2).

Another Compass Scripture. Let's apply this promise to those who are divorced: those who are poor in spirit, brokenhearted, and captive, and those who are imprisoned in the darkness of their sins and the sins of a former spouse. To them, Jesus declares a period of "the Lord's favor" when the Savior will…

…comfort all who mourn and provide for those who grieve in Zion—to bestow on them a crown of beauty instead of ashes, the oil of joy instead of mourning, and a garment of praise instead of a spirit of despair. They will be called oaks of righteousness, a planting of the Lord for the display of his splendor. (Isaiah 61:3).

In Jesus, our Savior and our "year of the Lord's favor" have come.

At this point, I want to specifically speak to those who are remarried or considering marriage again. You are in a demographic group whose marriages are statistically likely to lead down the path to divorce, but that doesn't need to apply to you! That reality does require you to face the fact that you were party to a failed marriage. I don't say that to shame you, but to doubly invite you to embrace the truth that God wants to restore to you the ability to make choices that will lead to health and wholeness in your current marriage—a marriage that can last until "death do you part". That gift of opportunity begins with you asking for and receiving God's forgiveness for the failure of your previous marriage(s). It requires that, with relentless honesty, you identify, acknowledge, confess, and repent of the attitudes and actions that contributed to the downfall of your previous marriage(s). Making a list will be beneficial, but only so your cleansing and washing is complete, leading to a deeper experience of God's healing and, therefore, health in your current marriage. (This may also be an opportune time to pursue counseling to be more thorough.)

Yes, God hates divorce, and so do most divorced people, but as we have seen, the central message of Scripture isn't condemnation, but redemption and restoration, *with no exceptions for divorce.* The Lodestar of the Bible is always telling us that God offers to re-establish us. It always leads us closer to the One who created us for the display of His splendor! In fact, after the downfall of humankind in the third chapter of the Bible, the main theme of the remaining 1,186 chapters is God's relentless efforts to invite us back into relationship with Him and the wholeness He designed us for.

One last recommendation: Just as context is imperative to more clearly understanding the guidance the Bible provides on divorce and remarriage, so is the context of this entire book up to this chapter. Other chapters identify additional Compass Scriptures and reveal more instances of the intersection of the grace and truth of God's character with the numerous human stories we've gathered. Critical themes like confession, repentance, forgiveness, hope, and healing are vividly portrayed in the other parts of this book, augmenting those in this chapter.

Questions to Ponder:

1. List all the insights you had from this chapter

2. Which of them would be helpful for you to retain, to remind and encourage yourself?

3. How does this chapter change your perspective and how you view yourself or others who are divorced?

Chapter 5

Forgiveness

by Bill Koontz

>———————■———————◄

Introduction

Forgiveness.

How do you feel when you read that word? What does "forgiveness" mean to you? What does it trigger? Do you in anyway feel: Repulsed? Afraid? Angry? Overwhelmed? Hopeless? Intimidated?

Forgiveness is likely the most difficult but most critical aspect of divorce recovery. The journey of forgiveness is like no other. Its difficulty is rooted in its pain. In this chapter, you'll be guided through the following: misconceptions of forgiveness and then what forgiveness is and isn't, signs of unforgiveness, receiving God's forgiveness, challenges to tackle in forgiving, practical steps, and the relational power of forgiveness. It concludes by unlocking the door to gaze into the future that forgiveness forges.

Perhaps one of the most vivid and striking movie clips portraying the difficulty of forgiveness is from the classic movie, *Forrest Gump*©. The scene starts with Forrest and his childhood friend Jenny strolling by the empty house where she grew up and was abused. Although we viewers can't see her face, it's apparent that Jenny is staring at the house intently. She stands frozen, the intrigue builds, and we're beckoned to join her in a slowly developing scene. What is she feeling? What memories are flooding her mind? What emotions are being triggered? The intensity builds as Jenny begins to walk toward the dilapidated house with its peeling paint, cracked windows, sagging roof, and a crumbling porch with ruined furniture scattered across it. The house seems to mirror Jenny's state of being.

Suddenly Jenny picks up a rock and hurls it at the house. Then another and another until she finally strikes one of the windowpanes, breaking it. She falls to the ground, physically and even more so, emotionally exhausted. As she sits there, we viewers can't escape being drawn into her heartache. She's overwhelmed, and so are we. Forrest in his innocent way slowly approaches her, kneels, and mutters, "Sometimes I guess there just aren't enough rocks."

Trauma is complex, particularly childhood trauma, and I don't mean to trivialize it or the process it takes to heal from its scarring effects. However, healing from trauma is possible. Though childhood trauma and the trauma of divorce are quite different, many people who have dealt with the ending of their marriage state that this experience was the most traumatic of their lives. If this is true for you, it does not need to negatively impact the rest of your life. Healing and forgiveness are possible.

If you could see an x-ray of Jenny's soul, what do you think it would reveal? Unresolved wounds from many forms of abuse—deep, bloody, and infected. Wounds that continued to impact, even haunt her in powerful ways, ways that she replayed into adulthood. But was she doomed to a life of painful resentment and bitterness? What would be your advice to her? How could her life take a different path?

Likewise, what would an x-ray tell you about your own soul? Are there wounds (pre- and/or post-divorce) that continue to fester in your thoughts and emotions? Has painful abuse from your childhood and/or marriage taken root accompanied by emotions like anger, jealousy, resentment, bitterness, guilt, shame, unforgiveness? Often when we experience painful events as an adult it triggers past wounds that were never dealt with, and our emotions can reach a tipping point. If so, these emotions command an immense amount of desperate, exhausting energy. The wounds haunt, but could you ever have enough rocks to retaliate? Would retaliation even be healing? Hebrews 12:15 counsels us to not miss the grace of God so that no bitter root grows up to cause trouble. How could your life take a different path? How could these roots experience the grace of God?

I'm going to suggest that a primary way to escape bitterness and heal these wounds is through the grace of forgiveness. But before I can do that, I'll need to dispel some cultural myths about exactly what constitutes forgiveness. There are many quite common misconceptions about what forgiveness is and isn't. For example, you can probably finish the phrase in each one of the following cultural myths about forgiveness:

- Let bygones (*be bygones*).
- Don't get mad (*get even*).
- Forgive and (*forget*).
- Sticks and stones may break my bones, (*but words will never hurt me*).
- Time (*heals all wounds*).

These are just some of the cultural myths associated with forgiveness. It's apparent that they're all fallacious, and you may think you don't believe them, but subconsciously, do you? Ask yourself that question as you read that list again. Consider how you react when you believe you've been mistreated in some way. Is your natural impulse to ignore the offense, to stuff it, to try to get even, or to seethe over it? Regardless of what your first impulse is, it's probably one that you've internalized from our cultural norms. And when it comes to getting even, there's even a website that offers to "help" people with that fruitless endeavor.

ThePayback.com is your home for all your revenge needs… Your spouse lied to you when he said that he would never cheat on you? Well, you know the saying "Don't get mad, get even." Get Revenge On People Who Have Done You Wrong! We stand ready to help you get revenge and let these individuals know exactly what you think of them! [31]

Over the years, I've collected excuses that people have given me for not being willing to try forgiveness. Have any of these phrases ever passed through your mind?

- I would just be sending the message that they can do whatever they want and get away with it.
- This would mean that I've got to bury my anger.
- If I forgive, it means they win, and I lose.
- I guess I'll just have to put a smile on my face and say everything is all right.
- I feel that I'm being required to go soft on something that's severely wrong.
- One more time, I must play the good guy while the bad guy just skips on their merry way.

Is there one of these excuses that you've mentally nursed or held closely to you? Have you yearned for a friend to listen to your heart's cry?

In the Crisis Cycle chapter, I used the analogy of a "marked trail" that winds through a wild and untamed place but follows a proven way. Similarly, this chapter will be like a marked trail—a map rather than a set of instructions. Personally, I resist instructions, but I love maps. Maybe you're the same way. A map gives us the lay of the land and water, but it still leaves us with the challenge of making the choices of how to traverse the landscape that's ahead of us. A map is a blueprint that gives us the freedom to decide how to best navigate the journey before us. It's not a formula that dictates how to do it. It's simply a guide that those who've come before us have made available to help us on our own journey.

The "contour lines" on a hiking map alert us when we're approaching steep terrain. Likewise, this map of the forgiveness journey will point out terrain that's more difficult, sometimes seemingly insurmountable. But just as a hiking map shows that there's an end to the steep terrain, so it is with this map of the forgiveness journey. It'll help you to keep going when you can see that hope is just beyond the next ridge. So, don't give up, never give up. View this chapter as an overall roadmap, and not as a detailed prescription for every step you need to take. A map doesn't tell you about the speed at which to move; the speed of the forgiveness journey will differ for each person, but it's critical you don't allow yourself to get stuck in one place for too long.

In the ensuing pages, I'm going to share four stories from people I've met over the years. While no story can include every detail of what happened and each story is just that person's perspective, these stories will provide insights into navigating the forgiveness

---

[31] "The Payback," accessed February 27, 2023, www.thepayback.com.

roadmap. As said in the Introduction, out of respect for them and their families, names have been changed and they remain anonymous.

The first story is from "Dave."

About ten months after our divorce, I found out that my ex had remarried. I remember that night very clearly. I sobbed uncontrollably. I was devastated, and I still carried a huge amount of guilt.

I shouted to God, 'Why?' And in a rare moment of clarity, I sensed God saying, 'What possible answer could I give you that would make you feel like everything you've been through makes sense?'

And there it was: I was using 'Why'—an unanswerable question—to remain stuck. I think subconsciously I thought that once I got the answer to 'Why,' it would be easy to forgive and move forward. But no explanation could possibly change the pain that I felt. Then I realized that I needed to let go of the fantasy of being compensated for the pain my ex had caused. I realized the unforgiveness I thought she deserved was wrong, and it was only hurting me.

In my unforgiveness, I'd even devised a scoring system, assigning points to each of us to help me prove she was worse. So long as I kept the score decidedly in my favor, I didn't need forgiveness, and I certainly didn't need to forgive my ex. The problem with this arrangement was that I was the only one keeping score. God wasn't keeping score. My ex had already moved on and didn't even know I'd assigned points to her. I realized that very night that I needed to ask God to forgive me for the scores I'd been keeping in order to justify my grudges. And I needed to ask God to forgive me for my part in our divorce, to help me forgive my ex, and to accept His forgiveness.

I came to understand that the breakdown of our marriage was our fault. When my ex needed me, I was too often worn out, and I made myself emotionally unavailable. Meanwhile, my ex kept a running list of everything I did wrong and went to a coworker to look for understanding.

While I don't want to minimize our challenges and all the pain they created, I do want to share what helped me choose to forgive. I would imagine that my ex and I were two years old. I pictured us in a room full of toys, arguing over one particular toy. Both of us were crying uncontrollably, screaming, and pointing at each other as the cause for our tears. Then in my mind, I walked in as an adult and realized that neither of us had a clue about life, or how silly we looked trying to blame one another. I think that's how God sees us—as a bunch of two-year-olds pointing our fingers at one another. Would God forgive those two-year-olds? Of course. I think in his eyes, we're all a bunch of kids. And if God can forgive us, can we forgive our own two-year-old selves? Of course.

All of this happened about 27 years ago. Hopefully, I'm no longer just two years old in God's eyes. Most of the time, I feel like a pretty mature three-year-old.

Offenses that lead to divorce are far from trivial in their effect on our entire being. Something inside us yearns for justice. Often our desire is for the perceived offender to be hurt more than us and to be paid back with interest. The impulse to get more than even is overwhelmingly strong, to see our ex suffer even more, and to extract a type of justice. While a desire for justice isn't wrong, demanding it on our own terms is.

But there's a dilemma. How is justice achieved? As you'll read in all the stories in this chapter, justice is forever elusive. The score can never be evened. There's no payment sufficient, and the search for it typically turns into bitterness and even revenge. In his book *Forgiveness*, Gary Inrig writes, "Forgiveness challenges our natural instincts; revenge feeds on them. It is very seductive and powerful… toying with revenge is like playing with dynamite."[32] This is perhaps some of the most vitally important guidance on our road map. This is what those who've come before us have learned, often through agonizing years and bitter tears.

That's why this chapter is so critical. Forgiveness is the gateway to resolving this craving for justice. Forgiveness alone is the remedy for our unhealthy quest for revenge. It's forgiveness that holds the keys to unlocking healing for the wounds, and to spiritual, mental, and emotional freedom.

Recall "Diane's" story in the Compass Scriptures chapter, in which her husband barges into the home and shoots her in the head. Its impact and illustrative value about forgiveness are worth remembering.

Can you imagine being shot and "Diane's" difficult journey of forgiveness? As C. S. Lewis observed, "Everyone says forgiveness is a lovely word, until they have something to forgive."[33] But as "Diane" attests in her story, forgiveness is possible in even the most extreme circumstances. Unfortunately, most people assume that forgiveness is impossible, simply because they don't understand what the word "forgiveness" really means.

Questions to Ponder:

1. What are the wounds that continue to fester in your thoughts and feelings?

2. What myths or excuses about forgiveness have you fallen prey to?

3. What are your immediate mental and emotional reactions to the word "forgiveness"?

4. What's the most extreme offense that you've ever needed to forgive?

---

[32] Gary Inrig, *Forgiveness* (Grand Rapids, MI: Our Daily Bread Publishing, 2021), p. 178.
[33] C. S. Lewis, *Mere Christianity* (New York: Scribner's, 1952), p. 89.

Misconceptions and Truth About Forgiveness

In the quest to discover what forgiveness really is, it can be helpful to examine what forgiveness *does not* mean. Don't speed-read the following clarifications. Rather, take your time, let them soak in, and ponder each one.

Forgiveness *does not* mean forgetting or excusing an offense.

Forgiveness *does not* mean accepting that the way you've been violated is OK. Furthermore, forgiveness *is not*:

- Agreeing to become friends with the wrongdoer.
- Allowing others to continue to disrespect your needs and boundaries.
- Lying down and becoming a "doormat." Forgiveness is not weakness.
- Burying, ignoring, or denying an offense, or pretending to go back to normal relations as if nothing happened.
- Minimizing or trivializing an offense or pretending that the past is no longer significant or relevant, and everything's fine.
- Denying the pain that's been caused by a wrongful deed.
- Agreeing to move on, but only in response to an apology.
- Easy.

If we're laboring under any of those faulty descriptions of forgiveness, then forgiveness may very well be impossible. For example, it's impossible to accept an apology when no apology is ever offered. Along the same lines, it's impossible to deny real pain once it's been inflicted on us.

On the other hand, a workable definition of forgiveness would have to directly confront the hurtful things that have actually been done to us. Forgiveness must be something we can do, if need be, without any cooperation from the person we're trying to forgive. Real forgiveness must be robust enough to persist even when we again feel negative emotions associated with the wrong that's been done to us.

While it's true that forgiveness is never easy, here's a definition of forgiveness that's tough enough to deal with our most painful hurts, and yet realistic enough to be within reach, even in the worst circumstances.

Forgiveness is canceling and releasing the debt owed to you; it is marking "Paid in Full" on the offender's bill of indebtedness. Forgiveness involves facing the facts of an offense and choosing to let go of our demand for repayment, and our perceived right to resentment, or anger. To forgive means to release rather than retaliate—to let go of the desire to get even. Forgiveness is granted, not deserved. And let's be honest: Forgiveness is hard and costly. With those descriptions in mind, forgiveness then begins with the words, "I forgive you".

Morally and justly, the debt of a person's offenses can be resolved in one of two ways: The first option is for the offender to acknowledge the guilt and pay the penalty. That's cold justice, which usually can't be enforced. The alternative is for the offended person to release the offender and what the offender did. That's forgiveness.

Here's how one woman who went through our program described her own breakthrough with forgiveness:

A couple of years after my divorce, I signed up for the Divorce & Beyond seminar followed by a 13-week group. They played a significant role in my healing, particularly by changing my understanding of forgiveness. I had always thought that to tell someone I forgive them meant that I was resigned to say to myself, 'It's okay.' But forgiveness doesn't mean that at all. After all, the things that were done to me were NOT okay. But at the age of 48, I finally learned that real forgiveness involves not excusing the terrible things that a person did to me but releasing that person from a debt they could never repay—just as Christ did for me on the cross.

In a divorce situation, an initial period of emotional numbness (remember the denial stage?) might feel like forgiveness. Quick closure can be tempting, but it's not real forgiveness, and ultimately, it'll prove to be unsatisfying. The other extreme is waiting to feel like forgiving. Obviously, that doesn't help either.

Between those two extremes, though, there's a way of approaching forgiveness that does work: Wait an appropriate amount of time to grieve and then begin the process of forgiving. A number of factors influence how long the waiting period needs to be. Some of the most crucial factors are: a) the length and depth of intimacy, b) the type and duration of the offenses, and c) the outcomes of any previous experiences in extending forgiveness. The key to success is to just keep the map in mind. Don't try to sprint ahead before you're really ready, and don't give up and stop. Just maintain your movement.

Usually, forgiveness has layers. The first layer may seem trite, even superficial. But choosing to forgive, or asking God for the will to forgive, are especially important first steps. Making that choice will be the doorway to a forgiveness that penetrates every chamber of your heart. It won't happen instantly. Therefore, it can be helpful to record your beginning date. Then during the journey, which may be lengthy or sporadic, you can always look back at the specific date when you began and remember it as the decisive beginning of your commitment to forgive.

There's no contradiction between choosing to forgive and then feeling the anger or associated emotions that come back when they're triggered by an unpleasant memory. Feeling anger doesn't mean that you haven't forgiven; it just means that there's still a neurological connection between the memory and the emotion. It means that you've come to another layer on the onion of the offense that you've remembered. But even in the midst of that troublesome memory, you can choose to forgive. And choose to forgive again. Easy? Not at all. Possible? Yes.

Fred Rogers once said, "Forgiveness is a strange thing. It can sometimes be easier to forgive our enemies than our friends. It can be hardest of all to forgive people we love."[34] Or loved. But our roadmap says there's a way, and each layer that you peel back will bring you more freedom, the freedom that forgiveness forges.

For "Diane," the woman who was shot, the path of forgiveness contained many layers. She forgave, then remembered more and forgave more. More powerful emotions would surface, and she had to forgive even more. The ramifications of a ruined marriage continued, and so did the need to forgive, but because of the thoroughness of her forgiveness, she healed to the extent that she has once again taken vows of trust and faithfulness in remarriage.

Forgiveness involves letting go of your dream from the past, and of the desire to make the offender pay some sort of penalty for shattering it. In "Diane's" case, she realized that even if he asked for forgiveness (which he never did), there was nothing her ex-husband could have ever done to make up for shooting her. Instead, it was only her own decision to forgive that could open the door for her to heal and have a better future.

The following story from a woman who I'll call "Cyndi" involves different offenses, but it again illustrates both how overwhelmingly difficult and critical it is to forgive.

I was a Christian in my late 20's and hadn't met the 'Christian man of my dreams.' I was both disappointed and angry with God. Then I met a guy at work who caught my eye. Although he didn't share my faith, I allowed myself to fall in love with him. Despite not having a peace about this decision, I married him.

We both had a lot of surface things in common: career aspirations, a hard-work ethic, great families, and good friends, but it was very apparent that our values weren't aligned. Even so, we lived the classic suburban dream. He was a VP of sales, I was in technology sales, and we enjoyed a prosperous young couple's life.

However, things were dramatically different from how they appeared. My husband traveled for work, and during our fifth year of marriage, he had an affair with his secretary. I was shocked and devastated, but I decided to reconcile.

It was a painful, slow process, and it required a huge amount of forgiveness. I leaned heavily on God to give me the strength and to clear my mind of the recurring thoughts regarding his infidelity. Forgiveness is a step-by-step process, and daily I had to choose to take a step forward. It was a two-step-forward, one-step-backward journey. But finally in my heart by the strength God gave me, I decided I would release my husband from the cattiness I felt because of the damage and turmoil he'd caused in my heart and our marriage. I let go of the debt I believed he owed me.

Our marriage relationship healed to some degree, but after two more years, things grew cold again. My husband promised throughout many counseling sessions that he would never

---

[34] Fred Rogers, *Wisdom from the World According to Mister Rogers: Important Things to Remember* (White Plains, NY: Peter Pauper Press, 2006), p. 41.

cheat again. Instead, if he were ever dissatisfied with our marriage, he would just tell me that he wanted out.

Then one day he announced he wanted a divorce.

At that point, I started investigating our financial records, and what I discovered blew my world apart. My husband had been sleeping with prostitutes. It seemed like I was living in a bad movie. I was shocked and horrified, and I began to suffer from what I later learned was PTSD.

My marriage had turned out to be a complete lie. Eventually, more shocking news surfaced. During the divorce process, I discovered that my husband was also dating a woman in another city, and she was pregnant. What a living nightmare! In the middle of my grief, pain, and extreme anger, I also knew that I had to forgive again. I knew that unforgiveness would keep me tied to my ex-husband forever and eat me alive. I didn't want the rest of my life to be defined by what he had done to me. At the same time, I didn't WANT to forgive him. He was a monster, a liar, and a cheater—and he DESERVED my wrath and hate. My anger came in huge waves threatening to overtake me.

I had to choose to forgive, but how? I simply couldn't see a path forward to letting go of all my anger and unforgiveness. It was a mind/heart game that I couldn't win. So, I asked God to help me. Repeatedly, I prayed for help with forgiveness. One of the biggest encouragements that helped me during those dark days was scripture. One particularly helpful passage was 2 Corinthians 10:5. It came alive for me like never before: 'We take captive every thought to make it obedient to Christ.' Another was the second part of Ephesians 4:32: 'Forgive each other, just as God in Christ forgave you' (NCV).

I began to visualize my ex-husband's secret life of pornography and prostitution, so that I could picture his offenses being laid at the foot of the cross. Slowly over the months and years, God began to soften and mold my heart to again have forgiving thoughts. Slowly I began to understand that the mercy God had extended to me should also be extended to my ex-husband.

My story ends in freedom. Freedom to cancel and let go of what my ex-husband could never repay, so that I could live a whole life—unencumbered by the past—through the God-given miracle of forgiveness.

In most divorces, there are many specific things to forgive. Don't try to forgive everything at one time. Identify events that left a specific wound and forgive each one. For example, if your ex often lied to you, do you remember particular lies that were the most hurtful? Forgive your ex for each one individually. Or did they have multiple affairs? Forgive them for each one. Bunching them all into one (for example, "I forgive you for all your lies") minimizes their effects.

You may have been deeply mistreated. Taken advantage of. Abandoned. Betrayed by the one person you thought you could trust. Perhaps you carry a pain that you think will never heal until you're dead. You feel like a powerless victim. You lament, "If my life is any evidence of the mercy of God, then I'm not impressed."

But the evidence of God's mercy toward you doesn't come from *your* life. The evidence of God's mercy toward you comes from *God's* life—the mistreatment, misunderstanding, betrayal, and abandonment that He, in Jesus, suffered in your place.

Because God sent His own Son to walk through the valley of condemnation, rejection, and even hell, you can trust Him as you walk through your own valleys. As "Cyndi" discovered, forgiving those who have deeply mistreated you (and created a rubble of your life and family) can actually become a real possibility. Even if your ex has betrayed you and shown no sign of remorse, forgiveness can be extended, and it can lead to hope and healing. Besides, what could your ex ever do to make up for everything that's happened?

Refuse to live in the past or to let it control your present. Refuse to pick at the scabs. Refuse to rehearse the ugliness. Regardless of the massiveness of the sins that have been committed against you, God's grace is bigger, deeper, richer. And you can choose to live in that grace.

"Cyndi" had a choice: She could let her ex-husband and all that he had done control her, or she could choose to let God control her. Her choice eventually led to her healing and becoming a leader in a ministry.

Forgiveness is hard. It's always a struggle because it begins with personal pain, and the divorce experience can be the most intense pain a person has ever encountered. We don't want to forgive our ex; we want payment for the pain. Our natural feeling is, "You hurt me, you owe me."

But we all live flawed lives, prone to selfishness. Therefore, in divorce, *there's always fault on both sides*. There's always hardness in each heart; it's just hard to see it in ourselves. Perhaps your faults alone would not have led to a divorce. But it isn't a score-keeping affair. Even if it's true that your ex was more responsible for the failure of your marriage than you were, all you can control is whether or not *you* grow from the experience.

A prayer like this penetrates the heart of the matter:

Father, I release (name of your ex) into Your hands. I lay down any attempt to get even. Whenever bitterness or revenge try to captivate my attention, I refuse to brood over them. Rather I entrust them to Your mercy and justice. I resolve not to repay evil for evil. Father, You know all the offenses (lies/vicious words/actions) that have wounded me. I now bring (name of your ex) before You and each offense that has deeply hurt me. Father, I now want to begin to forgive (name of your ex) for each offense. (Identify each one, and after each one continue with) I release to You the impulse to demand repayment, to harbor resentment, or to strike out with anger. Instead, I choose to forgive (name of your ex) and each offense.

Questions to Ponder:

1. What misconception(s) about forgiveness have you fostered?

2. Which of the following descriptions of forgiveness do you find to be most helpful? Most challenging?

   a) Forgiveness is canceling and releasing the debt owed to you.

   b) Forgiveness involves facing the facts of an offence and choosing to let go of our right to repayment, resentment, or anger.

   c) To forgive means to release rather than retaliate—to let go of the desire to get even.

   d) Forgiveness is granted, not deserved.

3. What's another layer of forgiveness that you need to extend to someone?

4. Would you agree with Fred Rogers, "It can be hardest of all to forgive people we love" (or loved)? Why or why not?

5. Are you ready and willing to make the closing prayer your own?

Signs of Unforgiveness

People often ask, "How do I know if I've forgiven someone?" One way of determining the answer to that question is to ask yourself if you still show any symptoms of unforgiveness. There are four common signs to look for.

The first indicator of unforgiveness involves trying to make the offender feel guilty by your actions and words. Typically, this takes the form of snide remarks such as, "You're late again." "It's always about money, isn't it?" "Been keeping your pants on these days?" "When are you going to grow up?" "Why don't you take some responsibility for once?" Underlying these putdowns is resentment. Sarcasm can give you a delusional sense of power, as if, somehow, at some point, the result will be getting even. But we don't get even and never will.

Along the same lines, putdowns can be a way of maintaining an upper hand by trying to keep another person in a position of owing a debt that they can never repay. But replaying offenses over and over in your mind will only keep the hurt alive and your blood pressure up.[35] It's toxic, like drinking poison and thinking the other person will die. This kind of toxin corrodes the container it's kept in—our own hearts. And that creates chronic anger and stress. Who ends up paying? Suffering? Being imprisoned? We do!

Unforgiveness keeps you behind your own bars of bitterness, indignation, and judgmentalism. Are you better or worse for it? Nursing grudges and recycling resentment will consume far too much emotional energy that could be better used on other issues. Forgiveness is the key that unlocks the prison cell of a judgmental heart and the handcuffs of hardness. Forgiveness gives us the power to break the chains of resentment that would otherwise keep us in something like an emotional purgatory.

Finally, unforgiveness as a means of wielding guilt can also be used as a weapon of protection to keep your ex-spouse away. This can be especially true if you felt a lack of power, or even a complete powerlessness, in your marriage. Unforgiveness can seem like a form of power, but this weapon will turn and inflict its wounds on you. At some point, I learned an acronym that helped me remember how vital it is to let go and forgive. The acronym is called "The Four H's": Harboring Hurt Hardens Hearts.

If the behaviors that trigger you to make caustic remarks are recurring issues, it's probably best to address them with the goal of remedying them rather than just rehashing them. After careful consideration, determine whether the issues are even yours to address. If they really are, then the goal of remedying them would most likely be accomplished by some very carefully chosen words delivered privately, or in writing, or in the company of another person.

The second indicator of unforgiveness involves what you write in social media, emails, texts, and the like. For example, what do you post about your divorce and ex-spouse— #exspousealouse? For some people, posting such communications can seem like a "safe"

---

[35] Gary Inrig, *Forgiveness* (Grand Rapids, MI: Our Daily Bread Publishing, 2021), p. 110.

outlet for their anger—a place of punitively striking back, getting a pound of flesh, without immediate consequences. But venting anger in this way can become a sort of security blanket, and we need to recognize it for what it really is: passive aggression. It's okay to stand up for yourself, but lashing out in anger on social media simply doesn't work for that purpose. If you really do need to stand up for yourself, the only approach that has any hope of succeeding is to communicate in a healthy way directly and privately, at an appropriate time, and in an appropriate manner. But once again, it may be that the fault you feel compelled to criticize is no longer an appropriate issue for you to even comment on. In any case, broadcasting your ex's dirty laundry on social media is a definite indicator of unforgiveness. And remember your ex's dirty laundry, more than we usually realize, is yours too. It's simply *never* a good idea to try to air that out in cyberspace.

Along the same lines, one of the most hurtful forms of unforgiveness is gossip, which can be defined as "conversation, mainly involving derogatory details, intended to put another person down." No one likes to think of themselves as a gossip, but the hard reality is that too often when an ex-spouse is spoken of, gossip is often the best word to describe what's going on. Gossip is part of the impulse to blame (a form of anger), and gossip not only deepens judgments about one's ex but also leads others to form judgments about them. Again, this is unfair to all parties.

The third indicator of unforgiveness involves trying to influence children, family members, and other people against your ex. This is inappropriate because complaining and blaming are destructive to everyone involved. There's an African proverb that portrays how conflict in and after divorce can impact children: "When the elephants fight, it's the grass that suffers." In fact, it's actually dangerous to a child's psyche to hear you saying things like, "You know dad/mom is always late." "You know how forgetful dad/mom is." Or "You know how he/she is about money."

Children are half you and half your ex. Consequently, when you put down your ex in front of your children, that's also a blow to the kids. Along the same lines, when your side of the family makes disparaging remarks about the children's other parent, that can have a variety of impacts on the kids, none of which is good. Among those negative impacts are guilt on behalf of the other parent, shame for the family, defensiveness for the other parent, anger at the person speaking, anger toward you for putting them in a place where such things are said, and feeling self-conscious or even attacked because half of their own pedigree is being picked on. Instead, children need to hear about the qualities of the other parent from which they have directly benefited. For example, "You have your father's good sense of humor." Or "You have your mother's sense for organization." These kinds of statements affirm your children and give them your permission to love the other parent.

Of course, if the other parent is not safe for your children, or simply absent, explain their absence in an age-appropriate way, giving the minimum amount of information necessary. And even in those situations, it's valuable to point out the good qualities of your ex, as opposed to repeating their negative traits. Children need to understand that everyone has good qualities, and that can empower them to amplify those good characteristics.

A fourth sign of unforgiveness is trying your hardest to "wall" that person out of your life, by refusing to be around them. Too many times, I've heard children lament that their parents stonewall any occasion when they might cross paths with their ex. Once again, this puts children in the middle of their parents' ongoing resentment, an emotional "catch-22" for them. Remember the Anger phase of the Crisis Cycle? I identified that one of the ways anger is manifested is withdrawal. Attempting to "wall off" your ex from yourself and even your children (unless your ex jeopardizes your safety or the safety of your children), is allowing your anger to fester ill will, leading you to make decisions that physically keep them away.

Actually, this will prove to be futile. While you may be able to physically separate them from your life, mentally, emotionally, and spiritually you can't. They will pop up in your thoughts and conversations, feelings will be triggered by some event or circumstance, and they will even show up in your dreams. As I wrote at the beginning of this chapter, while you don't need to be friends with your ex, you will only be free if you forgive them, choosing to release them from any debt they owe you. And this forgiveness releases you to then be around them during holidays, children's events, and social gatherings when friends want to invite both of you. In short, continuing unforgiveness will inevitably have an unhealthy impact. That impact may be unrecognized for a while, but it won't remain hidden.

Our trash or garbage gets picked up weekly. In our home, taking it out is on my list of responsibilities. If I forget to do it, it's an odorous eyesore. Not a pretty picture. Unforgiveness is like letting the trash accumulate in our hearts. Like physical garbage it smells and spills over. Others can sense it, if not actually see it. The obvious question is why hang onto it? Emotionally, we may feel like there's some kind of advantage. But let's be honest, there isn't. Today is garbage day. Take out the trash. Leave it out. Resist the temptation to rummage through it.

Yes, all four of these forms of unforgiveness *may* make your ex squirm, but they'll *certainly* gobble up your own heart. Unforgiveness will surface in your thoughts, words, actions, and even dreams. The Bible says it well: "See to it that … no bitter root grows up to cause trouble and defile many" (Hebrews 12:15).

On the contrary, when forgiveness has been granted, the impulses to make an ex feel guilty, to criticize them in writing, to influence others against them and wall them out will wane. Forgiveness means, "I will not rehearse it, review it, or renew it (with you or myself)."

It's certainly not wrong to be heartbroken for a time, but don't let that anguish overstay its welcome. Just as is the case with unforgiveness, when you hold onto heartbreak for too long, it weighs you down and prevents you from moving forward—like running a race with a heavy backpack slung over your shoulders. Unfortunately, what happened in the past will remain. We can't change the past. But we *can* decide to move forward in… forgiveness.

What's more, in addition to being sincere, forgiveness must be thorough. Here's an illustration of why thoroughness is important. After my second wife Laura and I built our first home, our lawn looked great for two years. Inexplicably, in the third year, my green grass began to develop brown patches. Mystified, I examined them closely. There was no visible, apparent reason for the decay. So, I grabbed my shovel and began to dig. "Clunk." Just inches below the surface, my shovel struck a rock. Returning with a pickaxe, sure enough, I found that a large rock the same size as the brown spot had risen nearly to the surface, killing the grass. This proved to be true for each of the brown spots on the lawn. Buried rocks, left behind in the ground from construction, were slowly making their way to the surface and throttling the lawn's root system.

What an analogy of our lives! And it's one that I alluded to in Chapter 1. Over time, people can learn how to cover up the "rocks" in their hearts. But the fact remains that we each bring sub-surface rocks—hard places in our hearts—into marriage. Because of the nature of the marriage relationship, over time—sometimes a matter of months, other times a matter of years—the rocks work their way to the surface of our lives and damage this relationship.

We need forgiveness for the wounds those rocks create in us, and the wounds they create in our spouses. Then we need to extend the same forgiveness to our spouses for the wounds that their rocks inflicted on us. Sure, their rocks are different from ours, and so are the resulting wounds. Nevertheless, forgiveness is the only antidote that can bring healing to both parties.

On the other hand, unforgiveness *enlarges* our rocks. The pain of broken promises, withdrawal, and even infidelity multiplies the size and effects of the rocks. The "bag of rocks" that we've brought into the marriage, as well as the rocks that get added as the marriage breaks down, will get heavier and heavier. All these rocks, both old and new, will wreak havoc on our mental, emotional, and spiritual health. As a result, our self-esteem and self-image will begin to suffer. The gradual enlargement of these rocks will open the door to anger and depression and their side effects.

Questions to Ponder:

1. What signs of unforgiveness can you identify in your life?

2. What motivates you to withhold forgiveness?

3. What are the consequences of withholding forgiveness?

Accepting God's Mercy

Perhaps you have difficulty receiving the rich mercy of God in Christ, not because of what others have done to you, but because of what you have done to torpedo your own life, maybe through one big, stupid decision and/or maybe through hundreds of them. You've abused God's mercy, and you know it. Your family suffers because of your choices. You're feeling crushed under the load.

Do you know what Jesus does with those who abuse His mercy? He pours out more mercy. God is rich in mercy. That's the whole point of the Gospel.

Regardless of whether we've ended up in misery because of our own sin, or because we've been sinned against, or both, the Bible says that God is not tightfisted with mercy but openhanded. Not frugal but lavish. Not poor but rich.

The richness of God's mercy means that your regions of deepest shame and regret are not hotels through which divine mercy passes, but homes in which divine mercy abides. God's mercy means:

- The things about you that make you cringe the most, make God hug you the hardest.

- His mercy is not calculating and cautious, like ours; it's unrestrained, flood-like, sweeping, and magnanimous.

- Our haunting shame is not a problem for God, but the very thing He loves to work with. Mercy means that our sins don't cause His love to take a hit. Our sins cause His love to surge forward even more.

Shame is nearly a universal experience in divorce. Conviction says, "I did something bad." Shame says, "I *am* bad." Whispers of shame and condemnation are not the voice of God. They're lies, either from the Adversary or from our own darkened subconscious minds. Refuse and refute both. Shame is addressed more fully in the chapter on Self-Image.

By the same token, grief can be tricky, especially when it results from life-altering choices. Scripture describes two kinds of grief: worldly and godly. Worldly grief turns our focus onto ourselves and our feelings. It becomes a "Woe is me" attitude. We think that if we can just feel bad enough or punish ourselves enough, we can make up for what we've done wrong.

On the other hand, godly grief realizes that, first and foremost, our sin choices are spiritual. They're transgressions of God's direction and desire for us. Therefore, when we're experiencing godly grief, the primary focus is on making things right with God. Godly grief produces a repentance that leads to the experience of forgiveness. Once that process has begun, godly grief leads toward making things right in our own hearts and toward the other people involved. This then leads to freedom. A powerful equation of the mind and heart emerges: Forgiveness plus Freedom equals Healing.

The roadmap in Scripture provides this model: "I acknowledged my sin to you and did not conceal my iniquity. I said, 'I will confess my transgressions to the Lord,' and you took away the guilt of my sin" (Psalm 32:5 CSB). God forgives your sin and removes the guilt of your sin. Talk to him honestly about how you feel. Confess, pray, and surrender every emotion. No matter the situation, you are already known to God. You are seen. You are not forgotten or forsaken. You are not done. You are loved. You are forgiven. Psalm 103:12 tells us that God separates our sins from us "as far as the east is from the west" (CSB). In other words, there's no limit to God's forgiveness.

Be aware, though, that being forgiven doesn't mean that we'll never remember and regret our old sins. That's normal and expected, but many people get lost in regrets from the past. Here again, the difference between helpful remembering and harmful remembering is our focus. When our heads are turned looking backward, we inevitably veer into the ditch of regret. It's hard to move forward when we're looking mostly at the rearview mirror. Regret will never serve you well, but be assured that God doesn't let you remember your mistakes in order to condemn you. Far from it! He enables us to remember in order to be delivered from our old ways. Repentance isn't feeling sorry for our choices in the past; repentance is turning the other way when we're faced with the same circumstances in the present. Look forward, not backward.

When ongoing feelings of shame, guilt, or regret interrupt your thinking, determine their source (the lie that caused the feeling), and replace that false belief with a specific truth from Scripture that applies to it. There's no easy formula for doing this. The process calls for more of a continual surrender of our thoughts to the Lord, and it's described in more detail again in the chapter on Self-Image. In her story, "Cyndi" mentioned how 2 Corinthians 10:5 provided a pathway: "Take every thought captive and make it obedient to Christ." Allow yourself to be "transformed by the renewing of your mind" (Romans 12:2). Use Scripture as an offensive weapon—"the sword of the Spirit, which is God's word" (Ephesians 6:17). One technique for doing this is to arm yourself with notecards of verses that will serve as "thought reminders and replacements."

Remember, though, that this process is not a "lone ranger" venture. God never meant for any of us to try this alone. He never meant for any of us to be alone. Fill your life with relationships and activities that are life-affirming—reinforcements that God can use to encourage you when the mental and emotional terrain is rugged.

The previous story mentioned the value that Scripture had in redirecting "Cyndi's" thoughts. Maybe you've never read the Bible. If not, I suggest you start by reading the Psalms. There you'll find a king named David and quite a few other people who graphically recount their struggles as they pray to God. They needed empathy. They needed to know that God was with them. A list of suggested Psalms is found in the Crisis Cycle chapter in the Recovery section at the end of the Spiritual Renewal segment.

On the other hand, you may regularly read the Bible, and you may even know some verses. In any case, in your pain, don't just read or recall scripture, but search the Bible for answers to the feelings and dilemmas you face. Verbalize to God that you want to listen.

There are probably many voices in your head competing for attention. Practice setting them aside while asking God to help you hear His voice through His Word. This may not come naturally, but as you continue, you'll hear Him. Verses in the Bible will come alive. Those that you've read previously will take on new insight and application.

"Dave," whose forgiveness journey is in the beginning of this chapter, shared this with me:

> I had read John 3:16 more times than I can remember. But one evening, out of nowhere, I read it again and began to cry. It was like I just realized in that moment that every rotten thing I had ever done was forgiven. I already knew that was true, but at that moment, it became even more real. And if I had been forgiven for so much, how could I withhold my forgiveness from anyone else?

Questions to Ponder:

1. What's the difference between conviction and shame? Worldly and godly grief?

2. What's a scripture you can memorize that would aid you in experiencing God's forgiveness?

3. Which of the Psalms was most meaningful for you? Why do you think it was?

Forgiveness Forges the Way Forward

The final story in this chapter describes the impact that "rocks" have on a marriage, the crushing blows that result when "the elephants fight," and the ensuing mountainous terrain of forgiveness. A man whom I'll call "Demar" conveyed this:

Our marriage lasted 15 years, but we faced challenges as soon as the second month of our marriage when my wife informed me that she was leaving the next day with her old boyfriend. She changed her mind and decided to stay, and over the ensuing years, we met with counselors, went to marriage retreats, and received prayer. Eventually, my wife went to counseling, but maddeningly, that turned into an affair. Other affairs followed until I found her at another man's house. Following that discovery, she filed for divorce.

Now before you jump to the conclusion that our divorce was entirely her fault, understand that I brought issues into our marriage too: stuffing anger, being leery of the hurt that can come from relational vulnerability, and dismissing the emotions of others. I discovered those issues after our divorce, through introspection, reflection, and counseling.

I learned that one of the greatest gifts I could give myself was to ask the question, 'How did I contribute to the breakdown of my marriage?' I became a better person as I was willing to dive into that question with an honest willingness to grow. I learned that my fear of vulnerability kept me guarded, stuffing my anger blocked emotional understanding, and my dismissing the emotions of others short-circuited any problem-resolution.

My story continues. We had an elementary-age child. A month after she filed for divorce, my wife accused me of sexually abusing him. That's an accusation that totally changes your life. People tend to assume that you're guilty until proven innocent. And for some, there's no 'proving' that you're innocent. There was no accusation that could have been more shaming to me—and to our child.

As a result of the accusations, I was stripped of all my parental rights, and I wasn't allowed to see our boy for three months until just before Christmas. Little did I realize that Christmas would be the only time I saw him until the following June, despite there being no evidence to corroborate the charges. I was formally arrested with the indignities of mugshots, fingerprints, and all the rest. A trial date was set. To this day, I recall times of mourning the loss of my relationship with my child—crying over his confusion about who I was and wasn't.

My acquittal mattered little. I was beaten up and wounded. My marriage was destroyed. My relationship with my son was undermined because—while there was never any evidence to substantiate my ex-wife's claims—in my absence, she had successfully convinced him that I was guilty.

So, for the next 13 years, when I was sporadically with my son, that story was the elephant in the room. I received mail from him calling me an abuser, followed by a year or two of refusing to see me. I sent presents, left voice mails, and wrote cards and letters – all to no avail. When my son turned eighteen, he changed his last name to that of his stepfather.

Finally, when he was in his twenties and had been through his own divorce, he accepted my suggestion to re-examine his beliefs. I flew to where he lived and spent the weekend with him. We poured over why he believed those lies about me. He acknowledged that he'd never had any actual memories of sexual contact with me. He listened to my story, and he examined the evidence, which included a video tape of a Children's Hospital interview, all pointing to my innocence.

I flew home hopeful that a change of heart was beginning. One month later, my son called to say that after reviewing and reflecting on everything we'd read and discussed that weekend, and after asking God for clarity and truth, he'd decided that I was indeed innocent. The next 15 years were a journey of immense healing in our relationship. In fact, today we both agree that few fathers and sons have as close a relationship as we do.

As you might imagine, forgiveness came very slowly for me. I was extremely angry with my ex-wife, but just as angry—maybe angrier—with God. I couldn't help asking, 'God, why did you let this devastation happen, especially to my child?'

It took 10 years for me to resolve this question. I argued over and over, it's not fair. God, how can I forgive my ex, and how can I ever trust you as deeply as I did before the divorce? How can I praise a God in whom I am so disappointed? Finally, I let go of my angry inquisition of God, and I surrendered to his love for me, my child, and even my ex. I figured out some answers to the 'Why?' question, but I realized that if I made figuring everything out a pre-requisite to forgiving my ex and fully reconciling with God, I would continue to be a prisoner to my wounds. My brokenness would go with me to my grave.

There could be no more waiting until 'I felt like it.' Instead, I wrote a letter detailing all the hurt my ex had caused me and our son. I didn't send it. Instead, I poured over it, feeling the pain, expressing the anguish, crying the tears. The wife of a couple from my support group agreed to be a 'stand-in' for my ex-spouse, and in tears and sorrow, I read the letter to her. Substituting for my ex, this wife then asked for my forgiveness. While it wasn't the same as my ex asking, it was a pivotal and powerful moment as I said, 'I forgive you.' A short while later, as I continued to reaffirm my forgiveness, I was ready to burn the letter. As I watched the flames devour it, I continued to forgive what my ex couldn't repair or repay even if she wanted to. These steps of forgiveness paved the way for me to move forward, refusing to let anger and unforgiveness consume me.

Then I consciously began to revisit the value and love that God had for me. When Jesus said, 'Father forgive them for they don't know what they're doing,' I knew that I was first in line in the need for forgiveness. And as I experienced God's forgiveness, I found that I could even more deeply extend 'I forgive you' to my ex. Over the ensuing days, months, and years, I've had to repeat that phrase over and over, until now there are just faint scars where the gaping wounds used to be.

This story illustrates why Jesus' teaching on forgiveness is so straightforward. Jesus knows how vital forgiveness is to our well-being. In the Lord's Prayer (the only place in the gospels where Jesus gives such specific directions on how to do something), he teaches us to pray, "Forgive us for our sins, just as we have forgiven those who sinned against us" (Matthew 6:12 NCV).

Later in Matthew, Peter comes to Jesus to try to justify not forgiving someone who has repeatedly wronged him: "'Lord, how often shall my brother sin against me, and I forgive him? As many as seven times?' Jesus said to him, 'I do not say to you seven times, but seventy times seven'" (Matthew 18:21-22 RSV). In other words, Jesus expects us to forgive beyond anything we could ever keep track of.

But not only did Jesus teach forgiveness; he also lived it, most dramatically while hanging, dying on a cross. Even while he was in excruciating pain and gasping for every breath, Jesus eyed his calloused perpetrators and unbelievably uttered, "Father, forgive them, for they do not know what they are doing" (Luke 23:34).

That example is for all of us as well, and our ex-spouses need the same. There's a real sense in which all of us are ignorant of the full extent of our sins. I need the Father's forgiveness for all my wrongdoings, including those that I've done and don't even realize.

It's so freeing to follow Jesus' example and extend forgiveness in our hearts to our ex-spouses. A shining example of that kind of forgiveness comes from Corrie ten Boom, who was the lone member of her family to survive the Holocaust. She once wrote, "When the actions of others alter our life, we must remember this truth: Our lives, no matter how difficult the circumstances, are in God's hands. Regardless of the sin, we all need God's mercy. No one is exempt. It isn't our duty to understand or to shift blame. It is our responsibility to keep our hearts clean, to walk in God's compassion."[36]

To borrow an illustration used by Barry Long in his book the *Ocean Swimmer's Prayer*, when a person experiences the richness of God's forgiveness, it's like they begin lounging in a river of his mercy and love. And as they dwell there, it becomes easier to splash others with the living water of forgiveness.[37] And rather than the splashing being annoying, it is welcomed, even celebrated, because forgiveness does all this:

- Breaks the chains of the past.
- Releases the weight of vindictiveness.
- Enables us to love beyond what we can comprehend.
- Brings victory from the jaws of defeat.
- Opens the door to a new future.
- Declares confidence in God.

Questions to Ponder:

1. Which of the scriptures about Jesus' teaching on forgiveness above most deeply penetrates your heart?

2. Which of the results of forgiveness do you most yearn for?

---

[36] Corrie Ten Boom, *God is My Hiding Place* (Grand Rapids, MI: Baker Publishing Group, 2021), p. 132.

[37] Barry Long, *Ocean Swimmer's Prayer* (Self-published, 2022), pp. 57–58.

Practical Steps to Forgiveness that Heals

From the preceding stories and my own experience, it's clear that the journey of forgiveness in divorce is intensely challenging. To help, here are some practical steps in forgiving that can be gleaned from these stories.

- Select several scriptures about Jesus' teaching on forgiveness. Memorize them or write them on cards and reflect on them daily. Then search for other scriptures on forgiveness. If you aren't that familiar with the Bible, search online for the word "forgiveness" in the bible.

- Experience the value and love that God has for you. You're probably familiar with John 3:16, "For God so loved the *world*." Replace the word "world" with your own name and realize that nothing you have ever done or will do is beyond God's forgiveness. Your scarlet "D" is no match for His scarlet robe. He always receives you and never treats you as you deserve. Trust Him. You're safe in His hands. His purposes for your life haven't ended. Rather, they're continuing in what may be unrecognizable ways.

- This leads right into prayer. Thank God for His immense forgiveness for you—past, present, and future. As you experience His complete and total forgiveness, realize that God loves your former spouse just as much as He loves you. Go ahead, put their name in the John 3:16 scripture. "For God so loved ____." Yes, nothing they have ever done or will do is beyond His forgiveness. Ask Him to give you the strength and courage to begin to extend your forgiveness to your ex-spouse: "I forgive you." Go ahead, say it out loud: "I forgive you." Say it again. I know that may be almost excruciating, but it's possible. By God's Spirit, you can do it. Then commit to repeating "I forgive you" as often as the incriminating thoughts about your ex come to the surface. Challenge yourself to battle negative thoughts and hurtful memories. Whenever those thoughts enter your mind, release them to God. Remember, letting go of them is for *your* spiritual, mental, and emotional health.

- Part of what will help is accepting and understanding the situation that you're in, and your ex, just as they are. Release unrealized expectations. You both brought rocks into the marriage, and maybe, like you, your ex wishes their rocks weren't there either, but they were. In your ex's most vulnerable moments, when they're alone with their thoughts, maybe they regret the words and actions that wounded you. Their pride may never let them acknowledge any fault on their part, but deep down they know they played a role.

- Realize that your ex also wishes that things would have gone differently, otherwise they wouldn't have married you in the first place. They too regret that the marriage has been destroyed. Perhaps they too desire the present to be better.

They may even want forgiveness, even though, because of the animosity and division between the two of you, they may never be able to acknowledge that. And even if they don't accept any responsibility for the hurtful things they've done, they alone—like you—are responsible for who they are and who they will become.

- Write a letter detailing all the hurt your ex inflicted on you, but don't send it. Sending a list of grievances is neither the intent nor the value of this exercise. Just read and reread your own letter. Feel it. Let the layers of emotions flow—the heartache, the pain of wasted years. Reflect on your letter. Beyond that, it can help to share what you've written. Hopefully, you've joined a divorce recovery/support group or have a trusted, mature friend who you can confide in. Read the letter to them, not as an act of vindictiveness against your ex, but as an exercise in bringing healing to yourself.

- If you have a trusted friend, ask if they will help you follow the guidelines listed below. If you don't have that friend yet, hopefully you will and can come back to this. These guidelines are based on Galatians 6:2 and James 5:16, which say that there is power in carrying one another's burdens and in confessing our sins and then being prayed for. In fact, confession and prayer are big parts of being healed. What you're looking for is a friend who will accept your request to pray the following for you:
    - Recognize God's very presence wherever two or more believers are gathered.
    - Acknowledge the pain that you've been suffering.
    - State an assurance of God's forgiveness for you.
    - Ask that you'll have the strength and the will to grant this same forgiveness to your ex.
    - Thank God for the healing, restoring work He is doing and will continue to do.
    - Thank God for the future that's ahead of you—one of freedom and blessing.

- Plan ample time alone for what is to follow. Build a fire in a fireplace or outside. Have a place to sit. Re-read the letter that you wrote in the previous steps. Sit with it. Inhale deeply, and exhale slowly. Allow yourself to express your emotions. Label them with words. Then decide to cancel and release the debt of each offense that you've itemized. Do that by forgiving the offenses that your ex can never repay.

That's the God-given mechanism for moving forward and growing, no longer letting anger, hatred, and unforgiveness consume you. Let your ex go. This exercise won't be easy, but it will be freeing, certainly for you and perhaps, in some measure, for your ex.

Then when you sense the time is right, toss your letter into the fire. The use of a fire is important. The process of preparing and building the fire is therapeutic in itself. (If you are unfamiliar with starting a fire, ask someone to help you before you begin, so your fire will be ready to start when you are.) Seeing its light amid the surrounding darkness, feeling its warmth, and hearing its crackling can be such a profound, vivid experience. It's visceral. Ceremonial. Perhaps you'll want to burn sections of the letter one at a time, all in one evening or spread out over a period of days or even weeks if that's what it takes. But be intentional about burning the whole thing.

As you watch your letter burn, observe the ashes. See how they vanish into the sky or fireplace. Watch as the letter slowly becomes nothing. Stay there. Don't be too quick to leave. Perhaps there are words you'll need to say aloud or even shout. Perhaps there'll be silence and tears. Or maybe you'll need to physically express what you're feeling. If so, get on your knees, raise your hands, throw something, or simply pace around—whatever you need to do while you release everything that's been pent up inside of you. Be aware of what's transpiring physically, emotionally, spiritually. In the end, pray. Express your heart to the Father God, your Creator, the One who loves you deeply.

In time, a sense of healing and wholeness will emerge. The stingers infecting your wounds will dissolve. Scabs will form and eventually fade into smaller and smaller scars. If you later recall something that was listed in your letter, quickly remind yourself that you've already forgiven that offense, and you no longer carry that burden. The letter and all its contents are no more.

Questions to Ponder:

1. Who are you willing to invite to walk the forgiveness journey with you, to pray for you and help guide you?

2. What's a date you could set to begin or continue taking steps of forgiveness?

3. What goals do you hope to accomplish by forgiving?

The Relational Power of Forgiveness

Over the months, maybe years, of following this roadmap to recovery, you'll probably recognize some ways in which you could have been a better spouse. As I wrote earlier, we all live flawed lives, prone to self-centeredness. There's always fault on both sides of a divorce. There's hardness in each heart, and it's pivotal that you take responsibility for yours.

So, what were your contributions? There are examples of contributions in some of the stories in this chapter and in other places in this book. Here's a starter list of what can undermine marriages.

- Failing to deal with your own relational weaknesses, such as not making your spouse the top priority over every other human being, including children or any other relationship.
- Being chronically absent because of over-involvement in work, recreation, hobbies, or other outside interests.
- Withdrawing from conflict instead of working through it.
- Holding grudges and allowing them to accumulate.
- Intimidating other people with anger or allowing others to intimidate you with their anger.
- Failing to deal with (or even recognize) co-dependency.
- Being too passive as a marriage partner, especially in decision-making.
- Fearing emotional or physical intimacy.
- Seldom apologizing for mistakes, intentional or unintentional, and failing to ask for forgiveness.
- Succumbing to flawed motives for marrying in the first place.

For any of these flaws, or many others like them, face the reality of how they've hindered or even broken you, as well as your marriage.

After you've done this self-assessment, discuss your discoveries with a trusted friend, a counselor, or your divorce support group.

This recognition of your shortcomings will probably be accompanied by defensive thoughts of rationalizing, excusing, blaming, and even self-pitying. Avoid these. As you identify the contributions you've made to the failure of your marriage, take ownership of them, confess them, and repent of them. The value of this process can't be overstated.

- Take ownership of your contributions. Learn to be starkly honest with yourself and accept the insights of others. These are critical to your future growth and relational health.
- Confess your contributions. That simply means to admit or acknowledge these flaws to yourself and then to God.

- Repent. What comes to your mind as you read that word? Probably an assortment of images and feelings, mostly with negative connotations. Unfortunately, "repent" is a term that has gotten some lousy press, but scripturally, it's a word with rich meaning. In its simplest form, "repent" means "to turn from," and that's how I'm using it in these paragraphs. To "repent" is to "turn from" the detrimental relational characteristics that surfaced in your marriage. To dig out the "relational rocks" that I previously compared them with. The desire to "turn from" needs to emanate from the chambers of your heart.

- Finally, receive God's forgiveness, because experiencing His forgiveness is what can most empower you to leave those mistakes behind.

During this Own-Confess-Repent-Receive process, guard against the warning issued by Soren Kierkegaard: "Sudden quick repentance wants only to down the bitterness of sorrow in a single [gulp] and then hurry on. It wants to get away from guilt, away from every reminder of it."[38]

At the same time, be aware that God doesn't give extra credit for owning more than your fair share of blame or comparing yourself to an unreachable standard of perfection. Be realistic. Some of us tend to either downplay our shortcomings (out of pride) or overemphasize them (out of guilt). You want to come out of this process with a clean slate.

When you avoid these two extremes, you experience the fullness and richness of God's forgiveness and His cleansing. You can be washed as white as fresh-fallen snow. Tell God that you want to change. Ask Him for the power to change. Then consciously begin to incorporate changes into your relationships. Involve your trusted friends, your recovery group, your family, and/or a counselor. Ask them to pray for you and with you. Your relationships will improve qualitatively.

Hopefully, at some point you'll be able to acknowledge to your ex-spouse how you think you contributed to the problems in your marriage. I say "hopefully" because there are situations in which an ex-spouse is so dysfunctional that this kind of discussion would be unlikely to have any value for either of you. Advice from a professional (or a person who knows both you and your ex) can provide any needed counsel on whether this kind of interaction would be workable. If it's not, I'll explain below how you can still forge a path toward forgiveness. On the other hand, if you can reasonably expect that your ex will respectfully listen to you, the goal of this kind of an encounter is to simply demonstrate your intent to have a cleaner heart toward your ex. And for both of you, that demonstration will foster growth in healing and wholeness.

Begin the process by writing down what you want to communicate to your ex. In taking ownership of how you injured your marriage and your ex, your motives are to

---

[38] Gary Inrig, *Forgiveness* (Grand Rapids, MI: Our Daily Bread Publishing, 2021), p. 223, quoting Søren Kierkegaard, "Emissaries from Eternity: Repentance and Remorse," accessed October 7, 2004, https://www.bruderhof.com.au/articles/Emissaries.htm

unencumber your heart and be a salve to theirs. Refrain from any excuses such as, "I didn't mean to, but I think I probably hurt our marriage." And refrain from vagueness such as, "If I've ever done anything to hurt you…." And yes, stating the hard truth about yourself will be humbling, especially if it was primarily your ex's actions that triggered the divorce.

Next, decide how to communicate this information. The top priority is for the exchange to be safe for both of you. If your ex's dysfunction prevents that, sit down with a trusted friend, and read your confession out loud. Discuss what you wrote, and then in a little ceremony like the one described earlier, burn your document as a way of bringing finality to your confession.

If you're going to directly communicate with your ex, your options are obviously mail, email, video conferencing, or meeting in person. The best option is determined by your perception of how your confession will be received. If you're unsure, it can be instructive to get the opinion of someone who knows both you and your ex.

Ideally, this kind of encounter would be face-to-face. If the relationship you now have with your ex is amicable, and you've already had fruitful conversations about other topics, then perhaps the conversation can happen organically. If so, simply look for an opportunity to introduce the topic.

On the other hand, if a casual approach isn't realistic, then try to initiate the process by communicating with your ex-spouse about the purpose of the conversation that you want to have. Agree on which avenue of communication to use. If the two of you agree to meet in person, also agree on a location, probably a public place, where both of you can feel comfortable. Inviting a mutually agreeable third party may also be helpful. In any case, the actual conversation should be short. And if, at any point, it starts to deteriorate, it's better to bring it to an end than to create any new issues.

In any kind of face-to-face encounter, in person or via electronic media, adhere to the following guidelines:

- For the sake of brevity and clarity, rehearse what you want to say with someone you trust, and ask for feedback.
- Be conscious of your tone of voice, eye contact, and body language, any of which can speak louder than words.
- Use only "I" statements and be specific.
- Don't mention any of your ex's actions.
- Do not grovel.
- Ask for forgiveness. If you don't think you can do that, then you're simply not ready for this stage in your recovery.
- End with a "thanks for meeting and listening."

If you meet, here are some responses that you'll need to be prepared for:

- Perhaps your ex will want to share their own contributions to the breakdown of the marriage. That can be good, but make sure the interaction doesn't deteriorate. If it does, graciously bring it to a conclusion.

- Perhaps your ex's response will be some form of "I forgive you." If that's the case, listen carefully and thank them. Your ex may feel a compulsion to say something else beginning with "But...." If that happens and it begins to get uncomfortable, gently suggest that it might be best to continue at another time.

- Also be prepared for the possibility of an unhealthy response such as, "I'm sure glad you're finally realizing what I've been telling you for years." Or "It sure would've been nice if you'd realized that sooner." If you get that kind of response, swallow the urge to strike back. Don't become defensive or say anything that could undermine what you've shared. You may be able to say something like, "Yes, but I'm sorry now, and I want to move forward." Don't get drawn into a conversation about why your ex can't forgive you, or what you would have to do for them to forgive you. That kind of conversation won't be fruitful. Along the same lines, your ex may stubbornly let you know that they'll *never* forgive you. In any case, it's up to them to decide what to do with your apology.

- One other possibility that you need to be prepared for is that your ex may not respond at all. There could be many reasons for this. Therefore, guard against pointlessly speculating about the possibilities.

If a third party has been part of your meeting, then debrief with that person immediately, or at least as soon as possible. Or if there was no third party involved, discuss the conversation with the person you rehearsed it with. Reaffirm to yourself that you've genuinely owned your personal contributions. Recognize that acknowledging your faults and asking for forgiveness are huge steps toward healing, regardless of how your confession has been received.

After this exercise, do a little self-assessment. Do you feel lighter in your spirit? Unburdened from guilt? Know that apologizing for your part in the failure of your marriage, affirms that you have a clean slate in God's eyes. Journaling about it can also assist in cementing the value of this encounter. Finally, renew your commitment to the future. As Maya Angelou said, "Do the best you can until you know better. Then when you know better, do better."[39]

If your former spouse is the one who initiates a conversation about forgiveness, suggest that you both use the guidelines above. Listen humbly. Accept the degree to which your ex owns their faults, even if you believe they don't go far enough. Simply listen, don't try to help them remember things they haven't mentioned. If they ask for forgiveness, the next step is up to you. Don't say you forgive them if you haven't. If that's the case, simply respond that you're working on it. Then, work on it.

---

[39] Debbie Moore, "DBA Get Together – Good Food, Good Friends and Good Fun," *The Bastrop Advertiser*, June 6, 2013, p. A8, col. 6.

Questions to Ponder:

1. From the stories and the list of possible ways people contribute to the breakdown of their marriages, what are some that apply to you? Are there others you can identify?

2. Own, Confess, Repent, Receive – what steps of growth can you take?

3. Could you share your contributions to the breakdown of the marriage with your ex-spouse? Do your closest supportive people concur?

4. What way of communicating with your ex-spouse would produce the healthiest outcome?

Forgiveness Unlocks a Better Future

Now for a pep talk. What is your preferred future? Do you want to re-tenderize your heart? Do you want your family to flourish? Do you want to become more of the person God created you to be, the version He intended? Are you willing to make decisions to grow into that future? Forgiveness is how. It's the pathway to a different future, one of blessings. Don't wait to forgive until you "feel like it." If you do, you may go to your grave still waiting. Forgiveness is an act of the will that can overcome the afflictions of the heart. It will open the door to healing.

True forgiveness is a process of deliberately deciding, again and again, to let go of the impulse to get even. It's like peeling an onion one layer at a time. Every time another layer of hurt or vindictive thought reaches the surface, go through the steps again. Start today. *Even now!*

If you do, you'll begin to come out of your heartbreak. Dawn will begin to break. God will meet you. Your character will grow. You'll become more hopeful and forward-thinking. You'll become wiser.

The actor Jim Carrey attests to the character-building that forgiveness forges. In a speech he delivered in June 2022, he testified that,

> *Ultimately, I believe that suffering leads to salvation. In fact, it's the only way. We have to accept, not deny, but feel our suffering and feel our losses. And then we make one of two decisions: We decide to go through the gate of resentment, which leads to vengeance, which leads to self-harm, which leads to harm to others. Or we go through the gate of forgiveness, which leads to grace.*
>
> *You've made the decision to walk through the gate of forgiveness to grace—just as Christ did on the cross. He suffered terribly and was broken by it, to the point of doubt and a feeling of absolute abandonment, which all of you have felt. And then there was a decision to be made, and the decision was to look upon the people who were causing that suffering, or the situation that was causing that suffering, with compassion and with forgiveness. And that's what opens the gates to heaven for all of us.*[40]

As Romans 5:3-4 attests, "…suffering produces endurance, and endurance produces character, and character produces hope…." (ESV).

The stories in this chapter remind us that there are no straight-line journeys through life, only journeys with many twists and turns, but through forgiveness, Jesus transforms what appears to be an ending into a new beginning.

If another marriage is a new beginning that you would like to be prepared for, the more thorough your forgiveness journey, the more likely it is that your future marriage will succeed. More second marriages end in divorce than first ones. When I first read that, I was surprised and curious. Why? You would think that people entering a second (or

---

[40] Jim Carrey, on the power of forgiveness and grace, *YouTube.com*, featured by *HomeboyIndustries.org*.

third) marriage would be more insightful in selecting another mate and more aware of their own tendencies to negatively influence the relationship. You would expect people to get better the next time around. But that doesn't seem to be the case. I think one of the reasons for repeated failure is that many people in second marriages still harbor unforgiveness and the woundedness that it creates. And they don't ask the tough questions of themselves or their new spouse: "How did I contribute to the breakdown of my previous marriage?" "What have I learned about myself and about marriage?" "How have I grown. How have I changed?"

I'll conclude this chapter with the lyrics of a song written by Mike Campbell, Don Henley, and John David Souther. They wrote about forgiveness in a song called *Heart of the Matter©*, and their words are as impactful today as when they were first penned. It's obvious from the song that, at some point in his life, Henley went through a serious break-up or divorce; the lyrics repeatedly emphasize the need to forgive in order to move forward. The song begins:

> *I got the call today, I didn't want to hear,*
> *but I knew it would come.*
> *An old true friend of ours was talkin' on the phone,*
> *she said you found someone.*

Over the years, I've heard many stories about a phone call like that. The pain, the anger, the sadness, and sometimes the reminder of failure that the phone call brings can be overwhelming. The lyricists point out that if we put our faith in people, it's inevitable that we'll be disappointed.

> *There are people in your life who've come and gone,*
> *they let you down, you know they hurt your pride.*
> *You better put it all behind you baby, 'cause life goes on.*
> *You keep carryin' that anger, it'll eat you up inside.*

The singer also admits his own part in the breakup.

> *Oh pride and competition cannot fill these empty arms,*
> *and the work I put between us, you know it doesn't keep me warm.*

Finally, at the end, the singer describes how difficult it can be to forgive, and he adds that forgiveness is a matter of the will. He mentions that while he's doing his best to choose to forgive, his thoughts can scatter. I wonder if his thoughts are about all the hurt that caused his anger? The song closes with:

> *I've been tryin' to get down to the heart of the matter,*
> *but my will gets weak, and my thoughts seem to scatter.*
> *But I think it's about forgiveness.*

He repeats that word, forgiveness, over and over, perhaps because the repetition is needed to penetrate the depths of his own heart and soul. Forgiveness really is that simple, and that hard, but freedom from the past is given only to those who forgive. "*Even if you don't love me anymore.'*[41] If freedom is the goal, there can be no exceptions to who or what you'll forgive.

The rocks we've accumulated and dished out can persist for many years, as can our need to experience and extend forgiveness, but it doesn't have to take years to experience the healing power of forgiveness in our lives. Take the time to listen to this song. You might even want to use it as a mantra to keep you moving forward.

I'll close this chapter with a prayer, and I invite you to make it your own:

Father, I feel as if there's no way for me to be free from the thoughts that imprison me. The pains of rejection and heartache feel like more than I can bear. My mind is overcome with negative feelings. They're so powerful, and all my struggling and complaining bring no satisfaction or release. I come to You wanting and needing to experience Your love for me. I admit that I've tried to keep my ex-spouse in a prison of my resentment, but the person I've ended up imprisoning is me. So now I release the people I've tried to keep captive. I invite You to show Your love to my ex-spouse and to any others who I've allowed to trap me in a prison of my own making. I acknowledge that it's only Your love that can set me free. I lay down my arguments and resistance and extend forgiveness. Heal me, and may Your love take the throne of my heart.

Are you willing to leave the past behind and embrace the choices that will lead to the future you desire? You'll never know God's love so intensely as when you finally let go of unforgiveness toward yourself and others.

Questions to Ponder:

1. What are the choices that will lead to the future you desire?

2. Are you willing to embrace those choices and leave your brokenness behind?

---

[41] Mike Campbell, Don Henley, and John David Souther, "The Heart of the Matter," lyrics, *Sony/ATV Music Publishing LLC* and *Warner Chappell Music Inc.*, 1989.

Chapter 6

Self-Image – Healing and Rediscovery

by Paulette Liburd and Bill Koontz

➤━━━━━━━━━━━ ✖ ━━━━━━━━━━━◀

A s anyone who was raised in the United States knows, D-Day refers to June 6, 1944, the day this country and its Allies stormed the beaches of Normandy. But as anyone who's been through a divorce knows, we have other meanings for "D" Day. A woman I'll call "Latricia" wrote this:

> *My first personal "D" Day was Divorce Day, which was bad enough, but then came Discovery Day: the day I discovered that the person I thought I was had been uprooted like a tree in a hurricane.*
>
> *I'd never really thought much about my self-image before. Who I was had been largely defined by my roles as a wife and mother. Moving into those roles had been a slow evolution, but like a good ole broken-in pair of jeans and a comfy T-shirt, my roles had come to feel like they fit me just right. There were growing pains along the way, of course, but nothing that would cause reason for alarm.*
>
> *But once that "D" Day hit, life as I once knew it was never the same. What followed that day was a whirlwind of emotional tidal waves and life-changing decisions for me and my children. And as those waves crashed into my head and heart, I was thrust into the tailspin of a self-image crisis.*

As "Latricia's" story illustrates, one of the biggest revisions a person has to face during a divorce is the revision of their self-image. In this chapter, we'll discuss two distinct facets of self-image. First, there's our *identity*, which refers to *who* we believe we are, and secondly, there's our *self-worth*, which refers to *what value* we believe we have. Putting them together, *self-image* involves who I believe I am and what value I believe I have.

This chapter explores the maze of questions that result from all the significant changes that are occurring in your self-image because of your divorce. It's an invitation to view the upheaval as an opportunity to rediscover and redefine your unique self-image. That is, it's a chance to learn to see yourself, not through someone else's eyes, but as the person God created you to be, and to recognize the value that identity brings to your life.

Remember the question raised in the first chapter of this book: Why is divorce so hard? In delving into that question, you read about the three Cs of marriage: covenant, companionship, and consummation. The dissolution of covenant, companionship, and consummation shakes a person's self-image to the core. Understandably, as a person whose marriage has failed, you may now feel conflicted about certain aspects of your identity and value. You may well be wrestling with questions like:

- Who am I, now that I am no longer a wife or husband? Now that my marriage has failed, what value do I have moving forward?
- What does the revised me look like?
- Will the revised me be able to make new friends?
- And perhaps the paramount question: Will the revised me ever be able to love again, or be loved?

In addition, there may be significant changes in your social and socioeconomic status that have rocked your world. Be assured, this isn't unusual. You're in the "normal" camp.

Source of Self-Image

To set the groundwork for rebuilding, let's first examine where our identity and self-worth commonly come from, and where they *should* come from. Unfortunately, all too often we allow our self-image to be defined by others but think about the power that puts into the hands of the people who define us. If a significant other has controlled our self-image, and if that significant other has held us in high esteem but no longer does—and even worse, if that person has begun to assign negative value to our self-image—then the results can be debilitating.

On the other hand, if we embrace who we are in Christ, our self-image will reflect our identity and the enormous value that God places on us. In the Old Testament, Psalm 103:4,8 declares that God abounds with love and shares His abundance with us through redeeming us and crowning us with love and compassion. In the New Testament, 1 Peter 2:9 describes us as "God's special possession," and Ephesians 2:10 says that we are "God's masterpiece" (NLT). Instead of trusting the belittling lies that we may have been told during an argument, we can put our hope and trust in the One who has said, "See, I have engraved you on the palms of my hands" (Isaiah 49:16).

At our Divorce & Beyond seminars, to illustrate the constancy of our value to God, Bill uses an analogy of the value of a $20 bill. He takes out a $20 bill and humorously asks the person closest to him to verify that it's real. Then he states that he's going to give the $20 bill to someone in the next three minutes, and he invites all the participants to raise their hands if they'd like to receive it. All but the most cynical do. He then crumples the bill into a ball and says, "If anybody doesn't want this $20 bill anymore, put your hand down." All hands remain raised. Then he drops the balled-up bill on the floor and crushes it under his shoe and asks the same question. All hands remain raised. Then he pretends to spit on it, and he asks the audience once more if they would still like to receive the $20 bill as a gift. Nearly all of the hands stay raised! Why? Because no matter what is done to the $20 bill, its identity and value remain intact. It still has its identity as a $20 bill, and it still has its value of $20. And that's how it is with our self-image.

Regardless of what we've gone through in our lives and during the process of divorce: the name calling; the hurtful attacks; the lies that have been spread about us; the times we've felt crumpled, stepped on, and spit on, nothing has changed who we are in Christ, and what we're worth to the God who created us. One particular psalm on that theme is very clear and dear to me. Speaking to God, the psalmist says, "…you created my inmost being; you knit me together in my mother's womb; I am fearfully and wonderfully made; your works are wonderful … how precious to me are your thoughts, God!" (Psalm 139:14,16). When we realize that we've been "wonderfully made" by Almighty God, we can be certain that our identity and our value are unchangeably secure. "What shall we say about such wonderful things as these? If God is for us, who can ever be against us?" (Romans 8:31 NLT).

"Doug" is an alumnus of The Divorce & Beyond seminar and follow-group, who now serves as a table leader at the seminar and has co-facilitated some of the follow-up groups. He writes:

Darkness like I had never known enveloped my life. Being betrayed, abandoned, and deceived left me feeling embarrassed, ashamed, and emotionally crushed. Since I was so sensitive to what my ex and others thought of me, my self-image plummeted. Depression, loneliness, and despair soon followed. There were nights when I felt like it might be easier to end my life. But then I read this in the Bible:

'Today I have given you the choice between life and death, between blessings and curses. Now I call on heaven and earth to witness the choice you make. Oh, that you would choose life, so that you and your descendants might live! You can make this choice by loving the LORD your God, obeying him, and committing yourself firmly to him. This is the key to your life.' (Deuteronomy 30:19-20a NLT).

Wow! I found that scripture to be powerful. I began to reestablish my self-image on this spiritual foundation in what I called my 'coming out of hiding' phase. I jumped into recovery with both feet. I attended the Divorce & Beyond seminar and then the follow-up support group.

There I discovered that I was codependent: I was always trying to meet other people's standards in order to gain their approval. That was the only way I could feel good about myself. The problem was that those standards would constantly change and therefore approval was always just beyond my reach. I was very critical of myself over the most minute details, and I would second-guess almost every decision I made. I felt guilty about never being good enough, and I felt angry with myself for being such a failure.

In my support group, though, I learned how to get out of this trap: I could base my self-image, not on other people's expectations, but on God's acceptance and forgiveness. The Bible says, 'Therefore, since we have been made right in God's sight by faith, we have peace with God because of what Jesus Christ our Lord has done for us' (Romans 5:1 NLT). Understanding this truth—along with gaining freedom from co-dependence—led me to self-acceptance.

When I finally understood codependence and how it had governed my choices, the newfound freedom saved my relationship with my sons. I learned to stop trying to live their lives for them, and I was able to let them be the men God designed them to be. The same change has also enabled me to have better relationships with my mom and my brothers, as well as helping me develop other more authentic, godly relationships.

Along the way, I learned that closure on what had happened in my marriage was not about asking, 'Why' it had happened but rather 'What do I do to move forward?' I learned something else that's really helped me. I'd always had a tendency to put things off rather than dealing with them. But I learned that procrastination can be an expression of resentment, and it's often an indirect way of showing anger. So instead of hiding behind my lifelong pattern of procrastination, I started to learn how to express my anger in appropriate ways and toward the appropriate targets without being crippled by a fear of retaliation.

In addition, I began to understand that I tended to hide behind logic (or intellectualization) rather than dealing with the emotions that bothered me. Whenever someone asked me how I felt about a situation, I'd always give them an intellectual opinion about it rather than expressing how I actually felt about it. But in my recovery group, I learned that when I buried my bad feelings, my good feelings got buried too—and burying all of my feelings left me hollow and numb. The way I learned to break this pattern was to 'Feel it to heal it.' As I learned to go ahead and let myself experience bad feelings, the good feelings began to float to the top. I felt joy and true happiness for the first time in years.

As if all that wasn't enough, being involved in a recovery group helped me find healing in another unexpected way: In our group sessions, I found much freedom in confessing my sins and failures to others. I found a huge sense of relief in realizing that other men could accept me in spite of my failures. I'd been filled with shame for my financial mistakes and my broken marriage, but in our group, I was accepted in spite of my failures—just as God has accepted me in spite of my failures.

Before long, when people asked me how I was doing, I could honestly say that I felt like the best years of my life had begun. At first, I thought that my life had just suddenly gotten better, but since then I've realized that, in fact, my whole life had been great. I'd just had too much worthless stuff in my way to see that. The recovery process helped me see the precious parts of my life instead of the worthless.

In the Bible, the prophet Jeremiah asks God, 'Why then does my suffering continue? Why is my wound so incurable? Your help seems as uncertain as a seasonal brook, like a spring that has gone dry.' And this is how the Lord responds: 'If you return to me, I will restore you' (Jeremiah 15:18-19 NLT). Those verses are where I took my stand.

I'm not saying that all of my problems suddenly went away. In fact, my wife served me with divorce papers in early December, and in order to meet the filing deadline, I had to fill out divorce paperwork on Christmas Eve. Ho, Ho, Ho! I'm not going to pretend that I had a merry Christmas. But I did have a new perspective on my situation. I could see that my broken marriage reflected the two broken people who'd been in it. Brokenness is really broken thinking, and my own broken thinking had led to many unwise little decisions that in turn *led to bigger problems including bankruptcy and the accompanying stress. But because my brokenness was being healed, I realized that the failed marriage wasn't all my fault and that I wasn't doomed to spend the rest of my life in despair.*

What I'm saying is that my mindset has been transformed by being renewed in God's Word. I've found so much freedom, and to me, 'The name of the Lord is a strong tower' (Proverbs 18:10 NRSV). I've found that I no longer have to hide from God's love; rather, I can hide in his love! It's unconditional and readily available! This recovery process has led me to many victories.

My advice to people going through divorce is to remember who you really belong to, and therefore who you are and how valuable you are. You have a choice: You can keep developing your spiritual foundation and moving forward, or you can go back to where you were. This could literally be a life-or-death decision. You're being called every day, sometimes every hour, sometimes every minute, to choose life—to separate the precious from the worthless, and to tell your story to help others do the same.

The Divorce & Beyond seminar and follow up group helped me heal my broken heart and serving in this community is one of the most fulfilling things I've ever done.

In this story, "Doug" describes all kinds of growth he experienced when he took a constructive approach to divorce-recovery, but I want to emphasize that his 180-degree turnaround started when he learned to align his self-image with God's truth about him. When "Doug's" story is condensed to a few paragraphs, it might sound as if he just internalized some key Bible verses, and those truths brought about a complete transformation of his self-image. That is the heart of what happened, but I can assure you that the process is seldom quick or simple. In addition, these high impact verses needed to be lived out in relationships with others to become fully transformational. Many of us need to admit that we don't want to change; we want everyone else to change, but this opportunity to change is where we can leverage the trauma of divorce to work for us instead of against us.

The failure of a marriage inevitably forces a recalibration of our entire self-image. How can it not? For one thing, divorce produces changes in our family, changes in our friends and circumstances, and many times, it evokes feelings of guilt and shame. You may have taken on the family name of your ex-spouse. It's a constant reminder that part of your identity is no more. For example, I was no longer a wife. Being single again brought these changes to a climax, because I had to start thinking of myself as a single mother with two children. Transitioning from a married family to a single-parent family would shake and confuse anybody's self-image. In fact, just moving into a new set of life circumstances and a new group of friends can cause us to feel unsettled. Especially if your self-image wasn't entirely healthy coming into marriage, the post-divorce adjustments can be very difficult.

The search for a more durable self-worth can be guided by Saint Augustine's famous insight: "You have made us for yourself, O Lord, and our heart is restless until it rests in you."[42] If we embrace Christ, as "Doug" described in his story, our self-image will reflect our true identity and the enormous worth that God places on us. We are accepted as His children; we belong to Him. The Bible says, "See what great love the Father has lavished on us, that we should be called children of God! And that is what we are!" (1 John 3:1). Divorce hasn't separated us from this truth. We belong to God! Instead of trusting the belittling lies we may have been told during arguments, we can put our hope and trust in the One who holds all things together.

I led off this chapter with a story from a woman I called "Latricia" who described how "D Day" (Discovery Day) had sabotaged her self-image, but there's much more to "Latricia's" story:

Once I broke away from the murmuring internal and external voices, the endless tears, and the fog-filled days, I resolved to align myself with people who could guide me into the next steps of recovery. Just as losing myself in my deteriorating marriage was a slow fade, so was the process of finding my way back to myself. It doesn't happen quickly, but I can say that it's painful and beautiful at the same time. Ultimately, God's hand pulled me out of a voracious whirlwind and guided me to Divorce & Beyond. That ministry's seminar and the support group that followed it were steps that were instrumental for me. They provided steppingstones to help me rediscover just who I am. Pastors, a professional psychologist, and many Christian books were also instrumental in my journey of rediscovering who I am.

As my inner strength grew, so did my confidence. Then one day it happened: As I was taking a walk outside on my lunch break, I had an overwhelming feeling of curtains opening and the sun beginning to shine. It was as if a new day had dawned, and I just knew I was going to be okay. For months, I'd been searching to find myself—trying to find out who I was, other than the person who'd been defined by my failed marriage. What I realized was that the person I'd been looking for all along was... me! And not only did I find her, but I also realized that I liked her! That turning point was just the beginning of rediscovering my self-image. Each and every day, I'm still seeking God's guidance to be more like him and to know that my identity is found only in him. Knowing that I am God's daughter will keep me grounded.

Jesus promised, "Whoever follows me will never walk in darkness but will have the light of life" (John 8:12). And in her story, "Latricia" described a moment when the "light of life" dawned on her. But let's face it: Sometimes the night can be awfully long, and the darkness can be awfully bleak. Were you called derogatory names during the demise of your marriage? Did that name-calling bring up ugly, repressed childhood memories? The people we've known and loved the most are the ones who can see where we're most vulnerable, and in divorce, they can sometimes use that knowledge as a weapon. A small nugget of truth about a shortcoming can be amplified far beyond reality. Over time, you may have slowly accepted, succumbed to, and come to believe some of the hurtful, negative things that were said about you. Is your mind stuck, rehearsing those horrible comments? Do you feel broken-down, ugly, fat, disgusting, boring, unloved, and even

[42] St. Augustine, *Confessions*, trans., (Lib 1.1–2.2.5.5: CSEL 33, 1–5)

unlovable? Do you wonder, "Who could love me?" There's a name for that soul-crushing emotion. It's *shame*.

Dealing with Shame

A pastor whom I deeply respect wrote the following paragraphs about shame and how it affected him during his divorce:

> *Shame: It's probably the most mind-bending, heart-rending, and spirit-breaking pestilence that hits during divorce. Dealing with shame is like wrestling with an Olympic champion—humiliating and defeating. Shame is groomed as we grow up because it is a part of the devil's playbook as seen from the very beginning, after Adam and Eve succumbed to temptation to eat from the tree of good and evil in Genesis 3:7 'At that moment their eyes were opened, and they suddenly felt shame' (NLT). While there are other divorce wounds in need of the salve of healing, shame may be the most difficult one to medicate to its roots.*

One reason why shame is so problematic in divorce is that it's one of the most prevalent "rocks" we carry into marriage to begin with (as portrayed in previous chapters). For many of us, the roots of shame have long been firmly embedded in how we think, feel, and respond to others. Then divorce multiplies shame's effect, driving its roots even deeper and wider. Like an iceberg, the majority of a person's shame lies beneath the surface and wields a disproportionate influence on their life. Therefore, it can be challenging to sufficiently apply God's healing grace and truth to shame's pervasive presence.

Since much has been written on how to deal with shame, I won't delve into that here, but it's imperative for you to recognize and treat shame. If you would like to learn more about shame, Bret Lyon and Sheila Rubin's book *Embracing Shame* (Sounds True, 2023) is a good resource. Likewise, Gary Sweeten's RelationalPeace.org website has an article titled: "Relax and Enjoy Life—We Are on Vacation from Shame," and also on that website there are many other resources for personal growth, as well. Along the same lines, Brené Brown has a Ted Talk titled: *Listening To Shame*©. Although it was recorded in 2012, her observations are still relevant. As in everything, awareness is the beginning to overcoming shame.

"Blake's" story highlights how shame can begin in the parent-child relationship.

> *Here's my journey through the maze of shame. As is sometimes the case, shame begins in the parent-child relationship, especially if guilt, blame, or rejection are used as a means of controlling a child's behavior. Through most of my elementary years (at the end of which my parents divorced), my father would preach, 'Children are to be seen, not heard.' Childish mistakes were often overreacted to. Affirmation was given sparingly. 'Not being good enough' was the unspoken theme. As a result, my relationship with my father was distant, especially after their divorce.*
>
> *To be fair, my Dad was born at the beginning of the Great Depression in the mountains of West Virginia. 'Not enough' was an unfortunate reality in his early years. His family never had enough money or resources. They celebrated Christmases in which the only gifts were pieces*

of fruit that were considered luxuries in their home. But often overlooked and even more sinister in my Dad's family was that there was not enough attentive love. So much time and energy were focused on making ends meet that Dad's self-image languished, especially under the weight of peer rejection and abuse. Like me, his unspoken belief was, 'I'm not good enough.' Not surprisingly, he carried this belief into his marriage and parenting.

My own struggle with shame was intensified because I never really identified it until after my divorce. As is often the case, I subconsciously felt shame about shame. That is, shame had such a demeaning effect that I didn't recognize (perhaps didn't want to recognize) its presence and the effect it was having on my relationships, my work, or any of the other realms where I sometimes experienced failure. To me, failure meant, 'My performance wasn't good enough. I didn't love enough. I wasn't wise enough. I didn't think fast enough. And therefore, I wasn't good enough.'

At times though, there were healthy breakthroughs. One occurred at age 27, about seven years after I committed my life to Christ. I sensed the Lord leading me to try to rebuild my relationship with my Dad. It was intimidating and seemed risky, even though he had also become a Christ-follower. I mused over it for a few months. Dad and I shared a passion for fishing, and I thought about a cottage in Canada that had been the site of a couple family vacations. I decided to approach my father with a big ask: 'How about if we take a fishing trip to that cottage in Canada we used to go to?' He asked, 'Who else will go?' I sheepishly replied, 'I was thinking it would just be the two of us.' I could tell that idea unsettled him. I braced myself for what he might say next, but to his credit, he agreed.

It was a twelve-hour drive to the cottage, and our first several hours in the car were awkward for both of us. There was a lot of silence. Then, at the end of our long drive, getting to this cottage required parking at a marina, unloading our gear into a sixteen-foot aluminum fishing boat, and navigating a five-mile maze of windy, rocky rivers and lakes. Dad brought his small motor to attach to our rented boat. Having steered through this region a number of times, Dad drove the boat. It was tricky avoiding the slightly submerged rocks and making the correct turns, but he did it flawlessly.

If this was going to truly be a rebuilding time, conversations about our disconnected relationship were necessary. We were both conflict avoiders, so the level of discomfort felt like scaling a 50-foot wall with no safety harness. Furthermore, I knew it would be on my shoulders to initiate such topics. On the second evening, we enjoyed the delicacy of a fresh caught walleye dinner. With satisfied palates and stomachs, I began to scale that 50-foot wall. Dad followed. I sensed the Holy Spirit was at work answering my prayers (along with the prayers of others who were supporting this reunion). The long periods when Dad was MIA (missing in action) were the main lapses that I needed to discuss: Dad's absence during my foreboding, formative years of middle school and puberty. His absence during my high school football, baseball, and basketball games. His absence while I was trying to figure out college. There in our fishing cottage, Dad listened. At times he was defensive, but when I reminded him that I just needed to talk, he respected that. This was new and challenging ground for both of us, but particularly for him. Our conversations continued into the following day.

The next evening, I childishly said, 'Dad you're a really good storyteller, and one of the things I missed growing up was bedtime stories. Would you tell me one tonight?' It was a weird request, and he reacted accordingly. But then he smiled, the tension melted, and he told me the story of David and Goliath. I fell asleep before it ended. There was something healing about that story time for both of us. We repeated it the next night, and again I fell asleep before he finished the story.

A pivotal moment occurred the next day when we ran out of the propane that powered the cottage. In an effort to prove my manly competence, I insisted I could pilot the boat through the circuitous waterway back to the marina. But on the way I made a wrong turn into an unfamiliar lake, and BAM, I struck a rock that was slightly under the surface. The impact broke one of the blades on the propeller. Full speed was reduced to half speed. I finally arrived back at the cottage an hour later than I should have. Dad was waiting on the dock. I felt the shame of having failed. I didn't want to face him, certain of his disappointment and his rebuke. I stepped onto the dock, trying to avoid eye contact, and I began to explain what had happened and that I was sorry. I mumbled, 'Please forgive me.' In one of his finest godly gestures, Dad embraced me. He said he forgave me, and that the most important thing was that I was okay. Shame's grip loosened. We hugged for a long time as healing pulsed so strongly through our hearts that it could be felt throughout our bodies. It was an important initial breakthrough, and thankfully it wouldn't be our last. But the pathway to healing my shame would still be a long journey.

Some years later, in spite of the healing that had begun, my divorce revealed deeper elements of my shame. The failure of our marriage was like an explosion with shrapnel that wounded every person in our family. The 'what if' questions plagued my mind and undermined my self-worth. But thanks to my recovery journey, over time, these open wounds also began to heal.

Today I can say that shame has lost some of its grip, but not all. In fact, in the past twelve months of this journey, I've discovered yet more patterns of thinking and responding that are still emanating from a place of shame. I welcome the continued healing that I know will come.

In this story, "Blake" describes some very creative approaches to healing the shame that had blighted his relationship with his father for many years. One of the other methodologies he utilized was something called, "The Five S Method." It's an effective way of chipping away at shame and experiencing healing. Below he briefly unpacks the steps it entails, each of which begin with the letter "S"—hence the name "Five S Method."

Spot – This is the critical first step. It's the recognition, the spotting of the "stinkin thinkin" that leads to the feeling of shame. Actually, in my own experience, I usually recognize the feeling of shame first and then quiz myself on the thoughts that led to it. Whichever comes first for you, getting to the source of the "stinkin thinkin" is what matters. For example, if someone's statement to me triggers a sense of shame (it may even be a few or many hours before I realize that), I reflect on that incident, what was said, and what I felt, and then I explore the beliefs that underlie my feeling of shame.

Stop – Once the "stinkin thinkin" is spotted, this second step is the conscious decision to stop it. That's not as easy as it sounds because I've probably been stuck in the "stinkin' thinkin" for a long time, and it's second nature to me. In other words, it's a basic, underlying belief that's hard to change. When I find myself up against this kind of barrier, it's often been effective for me to pray, "Lord, I want to stop this pattern of thinking. In fact, I repent because it's not true; it doesn't reflect the truth of Your Word."

Stand – I invite God's truth to dwell in my inmost being and become the basis of my beliefs about myself. I stand on God's truth about me—not what I've come to believe about myself. I may even say to myself—out loud if I'm alone—"In the name of Jesus, I reject the belief that I'm weird, out of step, a failure, not good enough, (fill in your own misbelief), and I stand on Your truth. Period. End of story."

Substitute – This step involves purposefully replacing the "stinkin thinkin" with God's truth about me. For example, I might pray, "I know, Father God, that I'm fully accepted and loved by You. My identity is that of Your child, and while I'm not complete, by Your grace I'm on a path to completion, and I know You'll be faithful to lead me forward on it. Furthermore, when I say 'forward,' I mean the 'forwardness' that's defined first by You and second by those who reveal Your truth to me, and not the 'forwardness' that's offered to me by people who don't."

Seek – This step involves taking actions like reading or reciting passages of Scripture that describe the truth about me, listening to music that reflects that truth, reading a book or enrolling in a class that presents God's truth about me, or maybe sharing with others the "stinkin thinkin" I've discovered among my beliefs so they can encourage and pray with me and for me.

For many people, this "Five S Method" has been a valuable tool to combat shame. And healing shame is critical because that very healing is the gateway to a deeper and more affirming relationship with God, as well as a greater confidence in who you are and what you can meaningfully contribute. What's more, the "Five S Method" can be equally valuable in overcoming any kind of temptation or unhealthy habitual thinking.

During the emotional devastation of a divorce, some level of despair is probably unavoidable. One option that's open to you is to surrender to that despair and to languish in hopelessness, resentment, and shame. The other option open to you is to begin a journey to rebuild your self-image, to get free from the effects of unwanted changes, to get free from obsessive fears and anxiety, and to move toward a meaningful life, believing that the world needs you and the value of your contributions. If you select the second option, the following strategies will be instrumental in your healing.

Rebuilding Strategies

1. Accept that you are unconditionally loved. This love starts with God, is received by us, and is experienced in some measure with others. Just talking with God at the beginning of your day can change your perspective of yourself and others. When you wake up in the mornings, what sort of messages come to your mind? Too many times, we're our own worst critics. Because of our circumstances, we tend to harbor self-doubt about our worth and abilities. We believe we have to be approved and accepted by other people, and especially by the opposite sex, in order to feel good about ourselves. We think of our failures as judgments of ourselves, and we tend to think, "I'm stuck. I can't change. I'm hopeless." But the Bible says that you (you personally!) are loved by and valuable to God. You are "the apple of his eye" (Zechariah 2:8). You are a whole being; you don't need a marriage to define your worth. In my own case, I often tell myself that if I someday get another spouse, so be it. But if not, I'm still a precious, beloved daughter of the Most High!

2. Focus on your attributes. Experiencing unconditional love clears the fog of our self-doubt and enables us to gain a different perspective on our attributes, personality, temperament, strengths, talents, skills, and gifts. We are unique! View yourself the way God says He sees you. As we've already seen, Psalm 139:14 declares, "I am fearfully and wonderfully made." You are perfectly imperfect, created by the God of the universe who loves you unconditionally. You, all of you, and all of your attributes and even baggage can be used by God. You can be single and whole. If you are having trouble with celebrating your own attributes, there are two books that I've found to be very helpful: *The Purpose Driven Life* by Rick Warren published by Zondervan and *Living Your Strengths* by Albert L. Winseman published by Gallup Press.

When I learned to focus on my attributes instead of my deficiencies, there was one very special surprise for me. In the midst of the challenges of becoming a single parent, I gained a deeper confidence in my abilities to raise my children. That also put me in a place to realize that God loved my children more than I ever could, and most importantly, that He would be a father to the fatherless.

3. Surround yourself with people who affirm you, who encourage you, and who speak the truth to you in love.

Traumas are events that affect the most basic parts of the brain and confuse how the brain processes emotion, thought, physical well-being, and behavior. One who suffers a truly traumatic event can feel they are not themselves; they say or do things without knowing why; they may forget, be unable to listen, feel anxious, and feel sad. For some, divorce seems to be a trauma with an extra, burdensome social stigma attached to it, which can make recovering very difficult and distressing. Those who do recover with greater success often have a significant relationship in which they can emotionally process the trauma in real time.

Divorce recovery is a great opportunity to build a team of relationships that you want and love. Your team or allies don't need to be limited to family and existing friends, but might include colleagues at work, or a recovery group, as well as new friends.

For me, in seeking out new allies, I chose to attend a new church and immediately got involved in ministry. In addition to expanding my community, this also had an unanticipated major benefit. Serving unleashed my buried passion for community work. Working with families who were less fortunate than mine gave me a needed "kick in the pants" to focus on others and, in the process, climb out of my own "woe is me" rut. Also, I reacquainted myself with my love for gardening and dancing, and for financial stability, I went back to work full-time. Eventually, from all of these avenues, I gained an entire community of new allies, including some who have become life-long friends.

Although your self-image may have been shattered leading up to and during your divorce, the steps above will help you rebuild what's been broken. It's quite possible that your self-image will end up being healthier than it ever was before. As Isaiah declares, God can "bestow on [you] beauty instead of ashes, the oil of joy instead of mourning, and a garment of praise instead of a spirit of despair" (Isaiah 61:3).

Finally, here's one more very motivating thought: Having a strong self-image is a benefit not only to you, but also to those around you. Your children, family, friends, and future mate, if there is one, will all be better because of the work you do now. Remember, you're the apple of God's eye. He wants nothing but the best for you.

Questions to Ponder:

1. Before your marriage, what cracks were present in your self-image?

2. How did those cracks become more pronounced during your divorce?

3. What role can your faith play in strengthening your self-image?

4. What are some concrete steps you can take to strengthen your self-image?

Chapter 7

New Lifestyle –
Facing Transitions and Fears

by Paulette Liburd

➤━━━━━━━━━━━━━━━━◆━━━━━━━━━━━━━━◀

How do you react to scary situations? Let me tell you honestly how I'm inclined to react.

A few years ago, I was happily living my life without physical limitations. My dog and I took long daily walks, and I enjoyed dancing—especially in a Zumba® dance/fitness class. But then I started having pain in one knee, and the doctor decided I needed surgery to repair some cartilage. The doctor called it minor surgery, but the way I see it, minor surgery is when they operate on *you*, but it's major surgery any time they operate on *me*. I put off the knee operation for as long as I could endure the pain, but ultimately I had to go ahead with it. That surgery helped, but a few years later, my knee pain returned. To make a long story short, the doctor told me that I needed a total knee replacement. Yikes! I was terrified by the prospect of that much bigger surgery and its grueling rehab. I looked into every alternative I could find to try to avoid the operation until the pain eventually got so bad that I had to give in to having the surgery. But you guessed it: My knee-replacement surgery wasn't successful, and before long my pain was worse than ever before. Then, as scared as I was, I finally had to agree to yet another knee operation on the same knee! Now, you might not be as phobic as I am about surgery, but isn't it true that most of us choose to keep living with our familiar pains until they finally get worse than the pains we think will come from making a change?

What do bad knees have to do with divorce? In my experience, they both create a roller coaster of pain with ups and downs that come in wave after wave and seem to never end. That pain elicits fear and its best friends, stress and anxiety. Until the pain of our current reality gets worse than the anticipated pain of making a change, our fears can keep us from making the moves we need to eventually find healing.

As has been said many times in this book, divorce is devastating for all involved, and persevering through it is difficult and usually exhausting. In the Crisis Cycle chapter, the last stage is entitled "New Goals – Fashioning Your Future". This next question is central to accomplishing that stage.

How does a person pick up the shattered pieces of life, face the fear of an unknown future, and confront the changes to become well-adjusted and productive again? First of all, believe me when I say that it will *not* help to sit back with an attitude of "This too shall pass". (That's a "famous Bible verse" that just isn't in the Bible at all.) I firmly believe that accepting the reality of divorce and transitioning through it requires conscious effort. The sooner you accept the reality of what has happened, as unfair as it might have been, the sooner you can begin the transition to enjoying life again. By making a realistic assessment of the pain involved in changing, and by confronting the fears that accompany that anticipated pain, you'll begin to see the possibilities of the future, or what we call the "beyond" of Divorce & Beyond.

By the way, as you begin this transition, take comfort in this truth: Regardless of the reasons for your divorce, this transition to a new lifestyle is a very significant opportunity for growth, and the pain of your current circumstances may well provide the very incentive you'll need as you struggle to achieve that growth. And don't forget that in your pain and struggling, God is on your side, His Spirit is working for you! One of our Compass Scriptures reminds us that God "heals the brokenhearted and binds up their wounds" (Psalm 147:3). With God's help, there's always hope for the broken-hearted, so let's get down to work on turning things around.

No-Man's Land

After a divorce, transitioning from being married to being single involves significant changes that are fraught with unknowns. If you were in an unhealthy relationship, some of the changes may actually be welcome, but inevitably, some of the other changes will be unexpected, unwanted, and unprepared for. Here's a simple diagram of the path forward.

Married → → → → → No-Man's-Land → → → → → Single

As this diagram shows, and as you've probably guessed, there's no direct path from a married lifestyle to a lifestyle of being single again. The No-Man's-Land along the way is characterized by the first four stages of the Crisis Cycle that we described in Chapter 2: denial, anger, bargaining, and depression. Now, if you don't remember anything else from this diagram, remember this maxim: *All of us have to go through No-Man's-Land, but getting bogged down there is optional.*

Refusing to come to terms with the finality of a divorce or not taking the steps necessary to move through it, will prolong the healing process and the journey through No-Man's-Land. Transitioning to a new lifestyle begins with facing and embracing the status of being *single again*. While it may be hard to accept, resisting this transition means that problems will persist and unnecessarily extend your stay in No-Man's-Land. At Divorce & Beyond, we've encountered people who've remained stuck there for as many as twenty years. Please don't procrastinate.

A common reason for people staying stuck in No-Man's-Land is the "Why me?" syndrome in which they paint themselves as powerless victims. "Why?" is a valid question, and we've addressed it in Chapter 1. But the question "Why me?" forestalls any progress.

For example, if your car were to get stuck on train tracks with a train coming, how much good would it do to sit there and ponder, "Why me?" The sooner you quit asking, "Why me?" and get out of the car, the sooner you'll be safe. If you stay in the car, even if you survive, that choice to sit and ruminate over an unanswerable question only will make things worse. Was it fair that your car got stuck on the train tracks? No, but dwelling on the unfairness and staying in the car won't change anything and will only intensify your pain. After the initial hurt and shock of divorce, there'll come a time when you'll have a choice to stay in the "Why me? car" or get out. Take control of your life, and don't allow yourself to become a victim.

Here's a story of one woman's very purposeful transition from a married mother to a single parent.

Divorce changes everything: day-to-day activities, roles and responsibilities, birthdays and holidays, goals and dreams. The task of sifting through all that your life was and figuring out what you want it to look like moving forward can be daunting and fearful.

My children ranged from pre-school to high school at the beginning of our transition. Divorce impacted them too, and, just like me, they were also adjusting to a new lifestyle. I wanted them to feel safe to share their fears, needs, and whatever else was on their hearts during this difficult time. We took one step, one decision at a time. Changes in day-to-day activities, roles, and responsibilities formed a new normal. I strived to make the best decisions for myself and my children, and I sought counsel when it was needed. Each step forward helped me gain confidence and a clearer picture of what it meant to be a single parent.

The kids and I dealt with the reality that birthdays and holidays would have to look different. We talked about the traditions we liked, and what new traditions they would like to begin. Their opinions were invaluable. We found healing in keeping what could remain the same and in choosing to change what couldn't. That required forgiving others and trusting Jesus to heal, guide, and restore us. When I did that, I was able to slowly release the weight of fear and pain. I began to look to the future again, setting new goals and dreams of what could be.

I participated in counseling and in Divorce & Beyond. Once I completed that program's 13-week support group and saw the growth I was achieving, I went through the whole seminar and its follow-up group again. Being able to see where healing had occurred was encouraging, and it offered me hope. It also revealed where more healing was needed.

When it's summarized in those four short paragraphs, this transition story may sound like it was easy, but there's no denying that it's an immense challenge to pick up the remnants and rebuild our lives. (Note the crucial role of forgiveness. Perhaps it would be valuable to reread Chapter 6.) For me, the transitional period was very demanding. I suddenly became a single parent with no family close by to lean on. As I've said before, my ex-spouse's priority was his career, not the rearing of our children. In fact, when our son became a teenager, my ex chose an international work assignment, so he was largely out of the picture. This left me with the titles of full-time wage-earner, lone chef, solitary homemaker, solo chauffeur, and… you can finish the list. I distinctly recall getting a speeding ticket once when I was rushing from one school to another, dropping off the children. That period of adjustment was a hard, fearful season!

Understanding Fear

In those stressful times, I also found that understanding my fears could be very helpful in dealing with them. Dr. Zachary Sikora, a psychologist at Northwestern Medicine, has written about the various aspects of fear.[43] I'll summarize what he's said about three of those aspects, and after each one, I'll explain how it applies to the divorce experience.

Fear Is Physical

Fear originates in the brain, and it triggers a strong reaction in the body. As soon as you perceive something that you fear, your amygdala goes to work. (the ah-MIG-dah-la is a small organ in the middle of your brain.) The amygdala alerts the autonomic nervous system, which sets the body's fear response into motion. Stress hormones like cortisol and adrenaline are released. You start to breathe faster, and your blood pressure and heart rate increase.

Application: This explains why you experience a physical fight-or-flight reaction during an argument, or when you feel threatened or attacked emotionally or physically.

Fear Can Make You Foggy

During a fear reaction, some parts of your brain are revving up, while others are shutting down. When the amygdala triggers the fear reaction, the cerebral cortex (the area of the brain that handles reasoning and judgment) becomes impaired, and it can become difficult for you to make good decisions or think clearly.

Application: When you're fearful, you're prone to saying things that you'll later regret. You may scream and throw your hands up, along with exhibiting a range of other behaviors that might not make sense to you later. You might not even remember them; you might be running away, sheltering yourself or protecting others. It's not "wrong" to not remember.

Fear Can Keep You Safe

"Fear is a natural and biological condition that we all experience," says Dr. Sikora. "It's important that we experience fear because it keeps us safe." For example, a healthy fear of falling is what keeps us from trying to balance on the top rung of a step ladder.

Application: When fears are warranted, it's vital that you take steps to protect yourself and those you love. There's no shame in turning away from a raised fist or an irrational tirade. The classic bestselling book, Boundaries, *by Drs. Henry Cloud and John Townsend (Zondervan, 2017) details ways of establishing healthy limits on what you're willing to tolerate in a dysfunctional relationship.*

---

[43] Dr. Zachary Sikora, "5 Things You Never Knew About Fear," *Healthbeat*, October 2020, Northwestern Medicine Clinic.

Fears are a mixture of the rational and irrational. During the failure of a marriage, a rational fear of violence could help keep you safe, while an irrational fear of seeking support or talking to a counselor could be detrimental. Fears are mentally and chemically complex, and they can trigger a multitude of responses. Fear can energize, but fear can also neutralize, intimidate, and even paralyze. Most fear tends to arise from the prospect of unwanted circumstances or outcomes. Fear can be positive and healthy, but it can also have negative and unwelcome consequences to your physical, emotional, and spiritual life.

Before we go on, let me go down a short sidetrack and mention that one common side effect of fear is *anxiety*. Garden variety worry is temporary, and it can prod you to use your problem-solving skills to resolve your challenges. In contrast, anxiety is a more persistent sense of apprehension about your problems and about the possibility that you won't be able to cope with them. Anxiety can keep you "keyed up" all day, and it can awaken you in the middle of the night, hounding you with dozens of thoughts and feelings that disrupt your sleep for hours. If that happens, and if there are legitimate concerns that need your attention, write them down (keep a notepad by your bed). Tell yourself that you'll think about those concerns in the morning and then entrust them to God's care until the alarm clock rings. And by all means, if anxiety persists, don't hesitate to get professional help. There aren't any rewards for unnecessarily enduring anxiety.

Now, returning to our main topic of the fears that surround the process of establishing a new lifestyle, be aware that there are all kinds of fears that you might encounter along the way. Some of these fears include:

- Fear of being alone
- Fear of raising children on your own, or not having the chance to have children
- Fear of financial change
- Fear of career failure or beginning a new career
- Fear of rejection
- Fear of dating
- Fear of making decisions
- Fear of the unknown (fear of change itself)

Pause for a moment and do a little self-evaluation: Take a few minutes to jot down those fears you struggle with and why. How are fears compromising you? How are you handling them? What are your coping strategies, and are they effective? If this little exercise has left you feeling uneasy, please trust that I do have some concrete suggestions to offer on how to deal with unresolved fears. But first, let me share some of my own struggles.

During my own divorce recovery, some of my greatest fears were about raising my children on my own. Previously I've shared that as an African American female, I dreaded being viewed as just another statistic: a single Black woman with two children. I dreaded the preconceived ideas that led to "the looks" and gossip of others. I retained my married last name for that very reason, thinking it would protect our family from being identified as a single parent household. Plus, my children wanted me to keep the same last name as theirs. I desperately wanted to shield my kids from the stigma of not having a father in our home and the false narratives that I believed that stigma would lead to. I thrust all of my energy into my children's activities, attending every school and extracurricular event. Several times, the kids and I had honest conversations about our new family structure. Before long, I found that becoming a single parent was actually easier to navigate than I had feared.

I also struggled with financial fears. My ex-spouse had provided a higher income than I did. How was I going to be able to support the rest of us with just one income? Child support did come many months later, and it did provide a needed additional resource, but then my ex-spouse started telling the children that since he was paying for child support, I should give the money to them. Meanwhile, my children were accustomed to a certain standard of living. For example, we'd always enjoyed traveling as a family, but after our divorce, I knew we wouldn't be able to travel as much, if at all. Along the same lines, we immediately had to move because I was no longer able to afford the house we lived in. That resulted in my children having to transfer to different schools and facing the loss of friends and the challenge of making new ones. I tackled the financial fear by continuing to work full-time and doing the very best I could to budget my income. Yes, we missed out on some extras, but I taught my children the fundamentals of money management and how to be frugal with what they had. I also explained the importance of doing well in school so they could apply for college scholarships. I didn't want them to finish college weighed down with student loans. Thanks be to God, in due course, one of my children was able to get a full scholarship!

Of course, there's another side to this coin. Perhaps you're the one paying alimony and/or child support, and that monthly payment is now likely in addition to all your new expenses for setting up and sustaining an additional household. If so, you're probably facing a variation of this fear: "How do I stretch my income to pay for all of this? Will my children understand the needed changes?" You're probably agonizing over all kinds of decisions about where to live and how to provide the kind of space your children have been accustomed to. On top of that, it tugs at your heart to think about the reduced entertainment options that you can afford, and even the reduced appeal of the food you can supply. Children, almost regardless of age, don't understand the financial pressures you're facing, and you may even have to deal with their criticisms, especially if the kids are hearing criticisms of you from your ex-spouse.

Beyond the financial fears, I struggled with career fears. What if I were to lose my job? With no family nearby, would I have to seek public assistance? I was terrified! And to make things worse, my supervisor at the time wasn't very empathetic toward my situation. My performance rating took a dive, and that created even more fear. After several heated conversations with my supervisor, I decided to ask for a transfer to a different department where I would be accepted and rewarded for my contributions.

Thankfully, we don't need to be slaves to our fears. For one thing, if chemical imbalances become a factor in our fears, they can be treated medically. But in the long run, it's good mental and spiritual health that will pave the way for our fears to be quelled.

In terms of spiritual health, the apostles John and Paul both teach that we have spiritual resources available to us to deal with our fears. Our faith in Christ's love is the foundational antidote to fear's poisons. The Apostle John wrote, "There is no fear in love, but perfect love drives out fear" (1 John 4:18). In fact, the Holy Spirit provides power, love, and self-control to overcome the fear that plagues our minds. As the Apostle Paul wrote, "God did not give us a Spirit of fear but of power and love and self-control" (2 Timothy 1:7 NET). That's why Paul can admonish us to guard our thoughts: "Brothers and sisters, whatever is true, whatever is worthy of respect, whatever is just, whatever is pure, whatever is lovely, whatever is commendable, if something is excellent or praiseworthy, think about these things" Philippians 4:8 (NET).

Another scripture I learned to lean on constantly was Psalm 46:1: "God is our refuge and strength, an ever-present help in trouble." and I was in trouble, all the time! In my prayers, I continually reminded myself that in confessing my inadequacy, I was opening myself to experience God's provision and strength: "When I am weak, then I am strong" (2 Corinthians 12:10). These passages formed this often-repeated prayer, *When I feel alone with my fears, you, Lord, are my comforter and my strength. When I feel unable to carry on and move forward, you give me the strength I need to persevere. I trust you with my fearful thoughts and feelings.* Here then are some practical ways to employ these resources:

- Memorize one of these scriptures or another that specifically deals with fear (there are many). That'll ensure that you have those scriptures with you whenever you need them.

- Whenever you feel fearful, count to six as you breathe in slowly, then hold your breath, again counting to six. Then very slowly exhale and imagine yourself exhaling your fear. Repeat. That little exercise is simple and surprisingly effective.

- Utilize the "Five S Method" that was introduced in the previous chapter on Self-Image. Spot when fear begins. Choose to Stop it. Stand against it in the name of Jesus. Substitute. This fourth "S" is where a memorized scripture is valuable. Incorporate it into a prayer, something like, "God I affirm that there is no fear in love, and that Your perfect love drives out fear. I trust in Your perfect love for me, and I remind myself that *nothing* can separate me from Your love. Fill me with Your Spirit of power, love, and self-control to choose to think about that which is true, versus a lie. God, I am grateful for (make a list), and I choose to praise You for your trustworthiness. You are my refuge and fortress."

- After that fourth step, Seek the support of a trusted friend and ask them to regularly pray for and with you. Utilize music, studies, articles and books that can build your confidence.

- Finally go for a walk, preferably outside, but inside will work if the weather is bad. Talk to God or a friend while you walk.

In a conversation with one of my friends, he provided these words of wisdom for facing the fears that come with transitioning to a new lifestyle: "We are in a story of chaos and messiness. There might be one chapter left in the story, or there may be fifty. However unclear it might be to us, we can trust that God is using our choices in writing the story. Nothing irredeemable has happened or can happen to us if we pursue God's plan of redemption and recovery."

To summarize what I've written so far, some degree of fear is unavoidable when we're going through the lifestyle changes that follow divorce, but with the help of God and a healthy support system, we can defeat even our worst fears.

In my experience, our past influences us, and the costs of breaking free from the past may even offer some potent incentives for us to stay "stuck in a rut." But the past doesn't have to control our future, and if we're willing to pay the price, the cost of changing can ultimately be outweighed by the joy of being healed. God can create purpose from pain and give "beauty instead of ashes" (Isaiah 61:3).

Here's one example of what I've gained by accepting the cost of changing: As I write this chapter, there's a lot of buzz about Valentine's Day. This could be a "down" day for a woman with no man in her life. But you've probably heard of God being portrayed in Psalm 23 as the Good Shepherd who feeds, guides, and shields his sheep. In my singleness, this scripture is particularly comforting to me. I am seen, known, and loved by the Good Shepherd! No matter what I go through, nothing can separate me from His love!

> Who shall separate us from the love of Christ? Shall trouble or hardship or persecution or famine or nakedness or danger or sword? No, in all these things we are more than conquerors through him who loved us. For I am convinced that neither death nor life, neither angels or demons, neither the present or the future, nor any powers, neither height nor depth, nor anything else in all creation, will be able to separate us from the love of God that is in Christ Jesus our Lord (Romans 8:35,37-39).

By natural reflex, we all want to flee from the suffering in any of the first four stages of grief (denial, anger, bargaining, and depression). But our trials can actually become occasions for developing courage, love, and compassion. Surveys and articles show that people grow more as a result of suffering during seasons of loss, pain, and crisis than they do at any other time of their lives, as in the article written by Anuj Mahajan: "How Pain Serves as the Catalyst for Growth: Hard Times Make Strong People."[44] We discover the hidden value of suffering only by suffering—and by allowing God's redemptive transformation to take place in the midst of our trials. Growth through suffering is not

---

[44] Anuj Mahajan, "How Pain Serves as the Catalyst for Growth: Hard Times Make Strong People," *LinkedIn*, August 2023.

automatic. The default outcome of suffering is for old stories, bitterness, and cynical attitudes to rule. Growth is a choice, but a hard one. We can get overwhelmed thinking about how *things* will turn out; God seems more concerned with how *we* will turn out. Trust God with your future and with every step that you take.

As I've mentioned, I grew up on a Caribbean island where palm trees are the most prominent part of our landscape. I remember watching them during the fiercest storm I endured there, and wondering if they would survive. Picture with me a palm tree during such a storm. Gale-force winds are bending it, sometimes all the way to the ground. In the aftermath of the storm, though, the palm trees eventually, seemingly miraculously, bounce back. In the hurricane of divorce, through God's miraculous provision, you too can bounce back to a new life of health and peace as you establish a new lifestyle.

In conclusion, here's a portion of a song called *Greater Tomorrow*© by David Ekene Daniel.[45] The printed words don't pack as much a punch as listening to it on the music video, so find it on YouTube. It inspires me, and as you transition to your new lifestyle, I think this song will have you dancing:

My tomorrow must be greater than today

His hands are not short, that He cannot reach to you

His eyes are never blind, that He cannot see your tears

His ears are not deaf, that He cannot hear you cry

No matter what I see, no matter what comes my way

No matter how I cry, one thing I know, that is definitely in my heart

My tomorrow must be greater than today, my tomorrow must be greater than today

Weeping endures for the night; joy comes in the morning

Mama don't cry... you gonna sing in your tomorrow

Papa, my brother, sister don't cry... you gonna dance in your tomorrow

Wipe away your tears my brother, you gonna testify in your tomorrow

One thing I know that is definite in my heart

My tomorrow must be greater than today, my tomorrow must be greater than today

Check me out tomorrow

My tomorrow must be greater than today, my tomorrow must be greater than today

---

[45] David Ekene Daniel, *Greater Tomorrow* (Prophecy One, 2014).

Questions to Ponder:

1. Do you feel stuck in No-Man's-Land? If so, in what ways?

2. Write down the fears that you have made progress in overcoming. What strategies have worked for you?

3. Which fears continue to be the most challenging for you. Why do you think that is?

4. Would it be helpful to process those deep-seated fears with a professional?

5. What steps can you take to transition through the challenges of change?

6. As you consider the new lifestyle you'd like to transition to, what goals do you want to set? What steps can you begin to take toward them?

Concluding Thoughts from Bill

Now that you've reached the end of this book, I hope you can look back to when you started it and observe noticeable changes—emotionally, relationally, and spiritually.

As you know, Divorce & Beyond was born from the many challenges I faced while I was going through my own divorce. Although I've endured many difficult challenges since then, divorce was by far the most severe. I recall feeling for months like I was in a never-ending dark tunnel with no visible rays of light in sight.

There were lots of occasions I can recall that starkly depicted how I felt, but there's one that stands out more than any of the others. This next story is a re-telling and expansion of what I wrote in the second part of the chapter, The Crisis Cycle.

A friend of mine owned a 48-foot motor-powered sailing boat, and he invited two other friends and me on a four-day trip in the Gulf of America. On the last day of our trip, we were returning to our dock in gusty winds that were generating 6- to 8-foot waves. That evening, I ventured out onto the boat's pulpit. (You know, like in the movie *Titanic*©: "I'm the king of the world!") At the time, I'd been feeling like I was stuck on an emotional rollercoaster with no exit. And right then, on that skinny plank extending off the front of our boat, surrounded by darkness, unable to see where we were going, and hearing and feeling the relentless ocean crashing against our cruiser, I felt like I was in a movie clip of my life.

I had a sense of God offering me an emotional lifejacket. My response was anger, and I remember yelling out, "I don't want your damn life jacket! I want out of this storm!" as I defiantly shook my fist at the waves.

Later that night, during the 3-6am shift, I was monitoring the autopilot that was steering the boat. Since we were beyond any sight of the mainland and in the midst of rough weather, the night was pitch black. The scene again eerily matched my life. But then the lyrics of a song came to my mind: "The darkest hour is just before dawn." And as dawn broke over the horizon, I wondered, "Will that ever occur in my life?"

You might be wondering right now if dawn will ever break for you, but hopefully you're seeing some rays of light. My desire for you is that, sooner rather than later, like me, you'll look back and remember the pain of this season, but the calamitous feelings will be largely gone.

Also, if you're "seeing the first rays of light," I'd encourage you to follow those rays back to their source and consider whether you're facing a new decision about your relationship with God. Maybe before you picked up this book, you would have described yourself as a person who hadn't really experienced a "relationship with God," or maybe that relationship seemed merely conceptual or abstract. Now that you've studied this book, I sincerely pray that you've recognized and even had moments when you've tasted that a relationship with God can be much more personal than that, and recognize God is the one who created you, loves you, deeply cares about you, and can bring forgiveness, hope, and healing to you. He very much wants to redeem you from your past failures, and to restore you to a life full of grace and truth.

If this readiness to know God better describes you, then you have an opportunity at this point in time to respond to Him by simply saying something like the following:

God, I've begun to recognize the wonder of who You are, and in contrast, I also acknowledge the fallenness and brokenness of my life. I now believe that through Jesus Christ, You are the one who can forgive me, cleanse me, and make me a new creation. So, I ask You to do that: forgive me, cleanse me, and make me new. I commit my life totally to You. Fill me with Your Spirit, and I will endeavor to follow You, through Your Word and Your leading all the days of my life.

If you've made that prayer yours, then welcome to the family of God, people who've tasted and experienced the vast love of the Father, and who, while still quite imperfect, are being restored to who He created them to be! The most important next step you can make is to find others in this family who can encourage and guide you as you begin to develop your relationship with God.

In addition, the steps I've outlined below are designed to further assist you.

1. Connect with God in ever more meaningful ways. There are three main ways that your relationship with God can grow:

    a. Invest time in reading the Bible. The YouVersion app at youversion.com/the-bible-app is a good resource for that.

    b. Invest time in praying with God. A simple outline for that is the acronym PACT.

        i. Praise God for who he is.

        ii. Ask—then listen.

        iii. Confess—then listen.

        iv. Thank—then listen.

(Did you notice that there's a lot of listening going on here?)

    c. Invest time in gathering with others who are in relationship with God.

2. Connect with DivorceCare© at divorcecare.org. It's an international ministry that has produced small-group resources for churches to use in assisting people who are recovering from a divorce. By visiting their website, you may find a group near you. Generally, these groups last 13 weeks, and they can provide an opportunity to experience ongoing teaching and relational support from other people who are also on the recovery journey.

3. Connect with a church in your area that can support your growth. If you're not an active part of a church, or if for whatever reason you think you need to find a new church, then exploring and identifying a supportive church home is crucial for sustaining and encouraging your growth.

4. Furthermore, connect with a ministry that helps people with something other than divorce recovery. When you're struggling, serving others not only encourages their growth, but helps your personal growth as well.

5. Connect with our online host, the Relational Peace organization at relationalpeace.org. That platform is rich with classes on developing your interpersonal skills.

6. Connect with us by visiting our website, divorceandbeyond.org. If you'd like to join us in the mission of promoting and facilitating recovery and healing for those going through divorce, please contact us at info@divorceandbeyond.org. There are a number of ways that people can assist. We can also keep you informed about upcoming seminars and other pertinent events.

Regardless of whether your relationship with God is new, or long-standing, or not quite yet established, we hope that this book has launched you into recovery from divorce. Our goal for each reader is that this journey will be transformational. That's why we encourage you to also enroll in our online companion course at: relationalpeace.org/courses/the-divorce-beyond-journey. Remember to use the 50% discount code, **dbjourney50.**

About
Kharis Publishing:

Kharis Publishing, an imprint of Kharis Media LLC, is a leading Christian and inspirational book publisher based in Aurora, Chicago metropolitan area, Illinois. Kharis' dual mission is to give voice to under-represented writers (including women and first-time authors) and equip orphans in developing countries with literacy tools. That is why, for each book sold, the publisher channels some of the proceeds into providing books and computers for orphanages in developing countries so that these kids may learn to read, dream, and grow. For a limited time, Kharis Publishing is accepting unsolicited queries for nonfiction (Christian, self-help, memoirs, business, health and wellness) from qualified leaders, professionals, pastors, and ministers. Learn more at: https://kharispublishing.com/

www.ingramcontent.com/pod-product-compliance
Lightning Source LLC
Chambersburg PA
CBHW052130270326
41930CB00012B/2827